E. W. BULLINGER
A Biography

E. W. BULLINGER
A Biography

REVISED AND EXPANDED EDITION

JUANITA S. CAREY

kregel
PUBLICATIONS

Grand Rapids, MI 49501

E. W. Bullinger: A Biography

Revised and expanded edition

© 2000 by Juanita S. Carey

Published in 2000 by Kregel Publications, a division of Kregel, Inc., P.O. Box 2607, Grand Rapids, MI 49501. Kregel Publications provides trusted, biblical publications for Christian growth and service. Your comments and suggestions are valued.

Unless otherwise indicated, Scripture quotations are taken from the King James Version of the Bible.

Frontispiece and page 73 portrait courtesy of the Trinitarian Bible Society, London.

For more information about Kregel Publications, visit our web site: www.kregel.com

ISBN 0-8254-2372-4

Printed in the United States of America

1 2 3 4 5 / 04 03 02 01 00

For
Dave and Margot
Steve and Carol
Kathleen and Reinoud
Chris and Lani
Mike and Miriam . . .
with love

Contents

Preface to the Second Edition

In the autumn of 1983, I traveled to Great Britain to find out more about the life of Ethelbert William Bullinger—a student of the Bible whom time seemed to have forgotten.

I had become acquainted with his work a number of years earlier when I began to study the Bible. Dr. Bullinger's *Critical Lexicon and Concordance to the English and Greek New Testament* was among the first volumes I acquired for my Bible study library. Later, I read and enjoyed many of his other works: *How to Enjoy the Bible, Number in Scripture,* and *The Witness of the Stars,* to name a few. The minute detail with which Dr. Bullinger handled God's Word, and his reverence and love for it, greatly impressed me.

Curious to learn more about the man, I looked for his biography. To my surprise, I discovered that none had ever been written.

The challenge proved irresistible. I decided to go to Great Britain and see what I could find for myself. The end result you see before you.

During my three-year stay in Great Britain, I was aided by many individuals. Notable among them was Mrs. Dorothy Bullinger Fielder, Dr. Bullinger's granddaughter. Mrs. Fielder graciously opened her home and her family papers to me, and I spent many pleasant hours listening to her reminisce about her grandfather and Elizabeth Dodson. To Mrs. Fielder's generosity I owe all personal accounts, letters, documents, and photographs.

The Trinitarian Bible Society made available material pertaining to Dr. Bullinger's term as secretary. Mrs. Winifred Carpenter gave me information and papers pertaining to her father, Mr. Charles Welch.

This work was first published in Great Britain in 1988 and could not have been produced without the encouragement, expertise, and hospitality of Rev. Chris Geer and his wife, Barbara. They, together with their staff, not only gave me a temporary home but also edited, proofread, and consulted on the manuscript as well as helped me through the difficult times in the closing phases of this long project. My sincere thanks to them.

Authors are always delighted to hear from readers who like their work. The first edition of this book elicited many letters from admirers of Bullinger's work all over the world. Several of these responses added to my store of knowledge of Dr. Bullinger's life and work; one even gave valuable new information about the completion of *The Companion Bible.*

In September 1997, I returned to Europe to continue my research. When I arrived in London, I was deeply saddened by the news of Mrs. Fielder's death. She passed away early in 1997.

Once more, I received a warm welcome and research assistance at the Trinitarian Bible Society. I was also happy to speak again with Mrs. Winifred Carpenter and to meet with Mr. and Mrs. Alan Schofield of the Berean Forward Movement. They have been unfailingly generous with their time and information.

As before, many people have helped to produce this enhanced second edition, and I am deeply indebted to all of them. In particular, I would like to thank Rev. Chris Kent and his wife, Nancy, and Rev. Robert Wilkinson and his wife, Barbara. Through the years, they have remained warm and supportive friends, often hosting me during my trips to Great Britain as well as faithfully and kindly responding to my frantic trans-Atlantic calls for added information.

When it came time to take up the work again after so many years, Elena Whiteside, my dear friend and editor, came to my rescue, as did my daughter, Kathleen Carey Brandt. They went over the now-familiar manuscript and helped to give it more clarity and simplicity. It seems that there can never be too many revisions. Thank you. Thank you.

I wish I could say that my recent research has unearthed new details about Dr. Bullinger's life, but such is not the case. With the added personal letters, official records, and firsthand accounts, however, as well as more thorough editing of the original work, I believe this second edition is yet another step toward understanding the life and commitment of this singular man.

JUANITA S. CAREY

Introduction

BORN IN CANTERBURY, England, in 1837, the year that Victoria came to the throne, Ethelbert Bullinger lived out his life within the Victorian Era. That time of transition from the England of yesteryear to the England of modern times was the context of his life.

It is common for us to interpret the lives of others (both those we see around us and those we see from afar by way of books or film) in terms of our own experience—in terms of the context of our own lives. This tendency can lead to misunderstanding, especially when the person in question is of an era or culture other than our own. Only knowledge of that time or culture, of the events, ideas, and people that characterized it, can help us to view that person within his or her proper context.

For this reason, I believe that the reader who first takes the time to learn about the Victorian Era will better profit from Ethelbert Bullinger's life story. That reader will not only more easily comprehend the characters and events that figured in Bullinger's life but also will gain a better appreciation of the man himself. Ethelbert Bullinger was, first and foremost, a man of the Bible; but he was also a man of Victorian England and a man of the Anglican Church. This necessarily brief introduction will deal with both the general conditions of Victorian England and the conditions of the Victorian church—for Bullinger's involvement with the religious community of his day formed much of the fabric of his life.[1]

An authoritative portrait of the Victorian Era is difficult to sketch. It resists easy catchwords; the facts often seem contradictory. It is fairly clear, however, that when Victoria ascended the throne on June 20, 1837, the prestige of the British monarchy was at a very low ebb. It was freely predicted that she would be the last British sovereign.[2] The two previous kings, Victoria's "wicked uncles," George IV and William IV, had been so personally corrupt that the Duke of Wellington had called them "the damnest [sic] millstone about the necks of any government that can be imagined. They have insulted two-thirds of the gentlemen of England."[3] Yet, despite their offenses, they wielded great power, as did the nobles surrounding them.

English society at the beginning of the Victorian Era consisted almost exclusively of rigidly fixed upper and lower classes, in which one's station was determined by birth, not by financial status. The middle class, to which the Bullinger family belonged, was small and politically powerless. The economy was, for the most part, still based on agriculture. The Industrial Revolution, with its accompanying growth of cities, had appeared over the horizon late in the previous century but was only beginning to have an impact on the economic and social life of the country.[4]

The challenges facing the eighteen-year-old who ascended the throne were great, but historians generally agree that Victoria proved more than equal to the task. Together with Prince Albert, whom she married in 1840, Victoria reconstructed the moral tone of the monarchy and gave such an example of "a dutiful, godly, and serious life" that she won for the British crown a respect that lasted far beyond her lifetime.[5] The following entry in her journal, penned hours after she became queen, proved to be a telling comment on her character:

> I am very young and perhaps in many, though not in all things, inexperienced, but I am sure, that very few have more real good will and more real desire to do what is fit and right than I have.[6]

As her reign progressed, Victoria's emphasis on "what is fit and right" showed itself not only in the royal family's lifestyle but also in the prevailing values of English society. Along with heightened national pride, an emphasis on home, family, respectability, and hard work became the mode. Left a widow in 1861, Victoria retreated into a seclusion that lasted many years. Even out of the public eye, however, she exerted a firm hand over her family, her government, and her nation. The term *Victorian* has come to signify not only the era of Victoria's reign but also the morality of that time—a morality known for its narrow-mindedness and prudishness. Perhaps more than any other characteristic, this strict moral code has become the hallmark of the Victorian Age. It was a code

> based on duty and self-restraint shared by most groups in society, including scientists, creative artists, and intellectuals. Institutions like the school, the voluntary organization, the trade-union, and, above all, the family emphasized the maintenance of those values which held society together.[7]

The position of women was difficult in this rigid society and much in need of reform. Both the law of the land and the expectations of society conspired to limit, in the extreme, the options—and freedoms—open to women.

Repressive and judgmental as it may seem to us now (and its very rigidity may well have opened the door for much hypocrisy), this code nonetheless enjoyed widespread acceptance. In fact, the rigid Victorian moral code is said to have contributed to England's rise to world eminence by the middle of the nineteenth century. The increases in England's economic prosperity and national security, resulting in stable social institutions, also factored in this rise.

The economy is often a barometer of public opinion, and in the early years of Victoria's reign, the spread of prosperity to wider sections of the population boosted her popularity. It is true that many people remained in poverty, but as the century progressed, significant numbers of people had more food on their tables and more money in their pockets. Wages and conditions slowly improved and, despite some setbacks, the economy stabilized. It has been said of this period that, "Britain was the world's workshop, the world's shipbuilder, the world's carrier, the world's banker, and the world's clearinghouse."[8]

If the average Victorian had cause to be satisfied with the nation's economy, he or she also had cause to feel secure and defended, for England had stronger armed forces and more internal police protection than ever before. Britannia ruled the waves, and her island kingdom was safe no matter how many storms raged throughout the rest of Europe and the world. Lord Palmerston, one of Victoria's prime ministers, boasted in 1850, "As the Roman, in days of old, held himself free from indignity, when he could say *Civis Romanus sum* [I am a Roman citizen], so also a British subject, in whatever land he may be, shall feel confident that the watchful eye and the strong arm of England will protect him against injustice and wrong."[9]

The growth of prosperity and security continued steadily throughout the latter half of the nineteenth century, as did advances in industry and the sciences. By the sixtieth anniversary of Queen Victoria's coronation in 1897, England's prestige was at its peak.[10] As England celebrated this auspicious occasion, a young man who watched the great Jubilee procession in London described the national mood:

> Seated at a first-floor window halfway up Ludgate Hill I watched the little old Queen driving to the service of thanksgiving at St. Paul's escorted by troops drawn from every quarter of the globe. The blaze of their uniforms has not yet quite died from my eyes. I awoke with quickly beating heart to some conception of the Empire over which she ruled, some realization of the gigantic growth in our wealth and power during the two generations that she had sat on the throne. Then followed the Naval Review. It was as though we flung a mailed gauntlet in the face of anyone who should venture to doubt our supremacy.[11]

This contemporary account aptly describes the optimism and the pride (many have called it arrogance) so characteristic of the Victorians. Yet beneath this confident surface there were darker factors frequently overlooked by twentieth-century observers. Notable among these was a widespread sense of unrest and worry caused by the rapid changes in society. Author and philosopher John Stuart Mill phrased it thus: "Mankind have outgrown old institutions and old doctrines, and have not yet acquired new ones."[12]

In 1860, William Thackeray wrote the following concerning the contrast between the Victorian Era and the years preceding it:

> It was only yesterday; but what a gulf between now and then! *Then* was the old world. Stage-coaches, more or less swift, riding-horses, pack-horses, highway-men, knights in armour, Norman invaders, Roman legions, Druids, Ancient Britons painted blue, and so forth—all these belong to the old period. I will concede a halt in the midst of it, and allow that gunpowder and printing tended to modernize the world. But your railroad starts the new era, and we of a certain age belong to the new time and the old one. We are of the time of chivalry. . . . We are of the age of steam.[13]

Of course, there was also much enthusiasm for the developing industries and sciences and the advantages they brought with them. Thomas Macaulay, one of the most eloquent of Victorian writers, summarized this enthusiasm:

> It [science] has lengthened life; it has mitigated pain; it has extinguished diseases; it has increased the fertility of the soil; it has given new securities to the mariner; it has furnished new arms to the warrior; it has spanned great rivers and estuaries with bridges of form unknown to our fathers; it has guided the thunderbolt innocuously from heaven to earth; it has lighted up the night with the splendour of the day; it has extended the range of human vision; it has facilitated intercourse, correspondence, all friendly offices, all despatch of business; it has enabled man to descend to the depths of the sea, to soar into the air, to penetrate securely into the noxious recesses of the earth, to traverse the land in cars which whirl along without horses, to cross the ocean in ships which run ten knots an hour against the wind. These

are but a part of its fruits, and of its first-fruits; for it is a philosophy which never rests, which has never attained, which is never perfect. Its law is progress.[14]

Transitional periods in history are often times of progress tempered by turmoil and doubt. Victorian England was no exception. As early as 1838, Thomas Arnold, one of the most famous educators of the Victorian Age, remarked that he had noticed a new "atmosphere of unrest and paradox hanging around many of our ablest young men of the present day."[15] And the statesman John Morley echoed these sentiments a number of years later when he wrote, "It was the age of science, new knowledge, searching criticism, followed by multiplied doubts and shaken beliefs."[16]

The same uneasy combination of progress and doubt that characterized other Victorian social institutions was present in the church as well. Referred to as the Anglican Church, this institution had been England's official church ever since Henry VIII broke with Roman Catholicism in 1532. Historians have noted that by the beginning of the Victorian Era the Anglican Church as an institution had become stagnant, materialistic, and isolated from the life of the people. If the character of William Howley, Archbishop of Canterbury and head of the Church of England, is any indication of the institution he headed, then it was certainly in need of revitalization:

> [William Howley] . . . was typical of the prelates of the earlier Victorian Age. Throughout his life he carefully avoided any action that might annoy the comfortable, and he never expressed any opinions that might disturb the indifferent. . . .[17]

Sir Walter Besant, looking back in 1887, made a comment on the services, preachers, and doctrine of the Anglican Church of the 1830s.

> The musical part of the service was, to begin with, taken slow—incredibly slow; no one now would believe, who is not old enough to remember, how slow it was. The vol-

untary at the beginning was a slow rumble; the Psalms were read by the clergyman and the clerk alternately, the Gloria alone being sung also to a slow rumble. . . . Two hymns were sung; they were always of the kind which expressed either the despair of the sinner or the doubtful joy of the believer. I say doubtful because he was constantly being warned not to be too confident, not to mistake a vague hope for the assurance of election, and because, with the rest of the congregation, he was always being told how few in number were those elect, and how extremely unlikely that there could be many of those few in one flock. . . . There were many kinds of preachers, just as at present—the eloquent, the high and dry, the low and threatening, the forcible-feeble, the florid, the prosy, the scholarly—but they all seemed to preach the same doctrine of hopelessness, the Gospel of Despair, the same Father of all Cruelty, the same Son who could help only a few. . . . Wretched, miserable creed![18]

By the late 1830s, reform—in the guise of two fiercely competitive groups, both bent on revitalizing the Church in their own way—began to make itself felt. The first of these two groups was called the Evangelical, or Low Church, Party. The second, known as the Oxford Movement, or High Church Party, was at times also referred to as Tractarianism. Because the drawn-out, bitter controversy that raged between these groups played a significant role in the religious atmosphere of Bullinger's day, and indeed in his career in the Church, it is worthwhile examining both of them in turn.

To understand the Evangelical, or Low Church, Party of Victorian times, one must first make a detour back in time to look at the life of the man from whose ministry it originated: the great English reformer John Wesley. This detour is of double interest in the life story of Ethelbert Bullinger, for from Wesley's ministry also originated the Methodist Church, of which the Bullinger family were members. Ethelbert Bullinger's early Methodist training was to leave a significant mark on his later ministry and writings.

John Wesley was born in 1703, fifteenth of the nineteen children of Rev. Samuel Wesley and his wife, Susannah. As a young
divinity student at Oxford University, Wesley observed with dis-
may the apathy and moral decay of the Anglican Church. In
response, he and his brother Charles founded a small society of
undergraduates, young men who endeavored "to observe the
prayer book more closely, to keep its appointed fasts, to attend
Holy Communion regularly, and to apportion their time me-
thodically."[19] This lifestyle was in such contrast to the surrounding undergraduate society that the small band of devout young
men soon became an object of ridicule for fellow students, and
they were contemptuously labeled the *Methodists*. Nevertheless,
the movement persevered and grew.

> His gospel . . . won small welcome with the ecclesiastical
> powers . . . and he soon found the churches closed to
> him. He cheerfully moved his meetings to the town green
> or to a nearby field, and more than one English village
> church stood empty while the crowds flocked to hear
> John Wesley or one of his Methodist preachers and to
> be moved by the sweet, simple message. "Dear friends,
> brothers and sisters, whom I love as those for whom my
> Lord has died, I know what this great blessedness is;
> and because I know it, I want you to have it too. I am
> poor like you: I have to get my living with my hands; but
> no lord nor lady can be so happy as me, if they haven't
> got the love of God in their souls."[20]

In popularity or persecution, Wesley remained faithful to his
goal of bringing Christ to all who would hear. Toward this end
he traveled on horseback several thousand miles a year (it was
once reckoned that he covered a quarter of a million miles) up
and down the British Isles, often preaching four or five times a
day, for a remarkable fifty-two years.[21]

> The central theme of Wesley's preaching was justification
> by faith. . . . It involved the sinner's acceptance by God and
> the annulment of his guilt through the work of Christ
> consummated in His sacrifice. Justification was appropriated

by faith, and its consequence and demonstration were good works. Clear and logical preaching together with a dominating presence—though he was small of stature—and an intense conviction that he was working the work of God, were Wesley's strengths.[22]

Throughout his lifetime, Wesley considered himself a member of the Church of England whose mission was that of reform from within. He had been ordained in the Church and never sought separation from it; yet he was aptly likened by one of his followers to "an oarsman who faced the Church of England while he rowed steadily away."[23]

Even before Wesley's death, his followers had begun to align themselves into two separate camps. One identified with Wesley's traveling ministry of open-air meetings and small local societies; the other remained loyal to the Church of England and its fixed, centrally controlled parochial system. After Wesley's death in 1791, the former group further evolved into what is now known as the Methodist Church. The latter was the beginning of the Low Church, or Evangelical, Party of the Church of England.[24]

The warm response of some Anglican clergy to the work of Wesley and Whitefield eventually produced within the Church an Evangelical movement, which . . . put the Bible, held to be verbally inspired, above tradition. . . . They recoiled from a "churchy" piety, in particular taking a "low" view of the Sacraments, rejecting baptismal regeneration and the Eucharist as a sacrifice; and, while taking the authority of bishops for granted, they had little or no desire to sanctify it by claiming it to be apostolic. The pulpit counted more than the altar, which, following the Prayer Book, they preferred to call "the Lord's Table," and they regarded the Church not as a repository of grace mediated through priests but as a fellowship of ministers and laity, and a voice calling on individuals to come face to face with God.[25]

In sharp contrast to this approach was that of the opposing group, the High Church Party. This group, also called the Oxford Movement, had its beginnings at Oxford University, where its founder, John Henry Newman, was able to gain much attention and support from the student body with his eloquent teachings and dynamic leadership. Newman and his colleagues advocated that the Church of England shift from its primarily Protestant orientation to become more like the Roman Catholic Church; in fact, they advocated an Anglo-Catholic Church, which would be a "middle way" between the Anglican Church and Catholicism. This church, they proposed, would draw its inspiration from the early Roman Catholic Church and would include such practices as the ritual of the Mass, the use of vestments by the clergy, the belief in purgatory, confession to a priest, and prayer to saints.[26]

The contrasts, and the fuel for controversy, between these two opposing parties are evident. The High Church Party followers looked to the fourth-century apostolic fathers for inspiration, whereas those of the Low Church looked to the men of the Reformation. Roman Catholicism was, for the High Church, an important source of guidance and doctrine (in later years, in fact, John Henry Newman converted to Catholicism and eventually became a cardinal), whereas the Low Church considered it the Antichrist. The followers of the High Church Party urged people to attend church services, into which they sought to incorporate more and more ritual; the advocates of the Low Church Party emphasized good works out in the communities and a return to the Bible.

The advent of a common enemy often makes warring factions join ranks out of self-defense. But the rise of spiritualism, widespread skepticism, and new scientific theories in late-Victorian England does not seem to have quelled the dissension within the Anglican Church. In the case of science, at least, the Church as a whole had been slow to sense the coming threat.

> To the Early Victorian, whether Evangelical or "High Church," Science raised no difficulties and caused no qualms. Indeed, he regarded it as part of the general

advance of knowledge, promoting the prosperity of the country, and in no way threatening the established order.[27]

Not until the 1860s did the true nature and significance of the conflict between religion and science become apparent. During this turbulent decade, the infallibility of the Bible (a point previously taken for granted by both High Church and Low) was first called openly into question.[28] New discoveries in geology initiated arguments about the age of the earth. The traditional understanding of the opening chapters of Genesis was disputed. Charles Darwin also challenged the biblical record of Creation with the publication, in 1859, of his controversial *On the Origin of Species*. He introduced the theory that animals had not been separately created "after their own kind," as stated in Genesis, but rather had originated and survived by processes he called "natural selection" and "evolution." His book *The Descent of Man,* published in 1871, was a further challenge to traditional belief. It refuted the key doctrine that humankind had been specially created by God, claiming instead that humans were only a highly developed species of the anthropoid apes.[29]

These arguments generated new interest in biblical criticism. If science could prove that the record in Genesis was incorrect, scholars reasoned, then what other inaccuracies did the Bible contain? The field of "higher criticism"—meaning the examination, often from a starting point of skepticism about the authorship, date, place of origin, and composition of the books of the Bible—gained great influence during this time. The field of "lower criticism," which examined the internal evidence of the Bible and concentrated on unraveling translational difficulties, was more compatible with a standpoint of belief in the Bible's accuracy. But the prevailing atmosphere of skepticism ensured that lower criticism was pushed into the background. Higher criticism, with its accompanying doubts and challenges to the traditional faith of the church, became the norm in many universities.

This same atmosphere of skepticism facilitated the rise of another competitor for the allegiance of the Victorian churchgoer. Spiritualism, a movement based on the belief that the spirits of the dead can communicate with the living, originated in New

York State in 1848 and rose to immense popularity on both sides of the Atlantic. In 1873, the British National Association of Spiritualists was formed; in 1882, the Society of Psychical Research was founded in London; and in 1891, the Spiritualists National Union was established.[30] Many people viewed spiritualism as a newly developing science, and as such it was granted the credibility accorded to all other sciences.[31] The church, however, viewed the rise of spiritualism with great alarm.

It is, perhaps, difficult for modern-day readers—to whom the concepts of evolution, higher criticism, and spiritualism (regardless of whether or not one agrees with them) are no longer revolutionary—to appreciate the impact these movements had upon Victorian society. These schools of thought presented radical departures from the long-settled systems of belief embraced by the Victorians; the effect was profound and unsettling. It is hardly surprising that historians have said of the Victorians that "the religious question of the last forty years of the century is the appearance of unbelief," for unbelief in many guises came to permeate the religious community. It became important to say "the Word of God is *in* the Bible" instead of "the Word of God *is* the Bible"; and for the first time in English history, agnosticism (the belief that no knowledge of God or spiritual matters can be certain) became accepted as an alternative to belief in God.[32]

Even during this intellectually turbulent time, many people simply continued on the familiar paths of their religious practice, as the following assessment of the late Victorian period suggests:

It is commonly supposed that the Victorian age was an age of religious faith, and at first sight it is a supposition that has much to support it. Churches and chapels were crowded with worshippers. In the middle classes and upwards you were not quite respectable if you did not go regularly to church. It was an age of much church building and restoration. The Evangelical and Tractarian movements had many adherents and nonconformity [any organized religion other than the Church of England] was thriving. There was a tremendous output of religious and theological literature in the form of books, pamphlets, tracts, sermons, periodicals, and newspapers.

It was a time of notable missionary zeal and expansion. Certainly, there were multitudes of people who had a simple and unshaken confidence in the faith of their fathers, and who were devoted to its practice and propagation. Surely these are all evidences of an age of faith.

But on a more discriminating view there is reason to question this characterization of the Victorian era. Beneath the surface of respectable religious conformity there was a turmoil of doubt and uncertainty. Nearly all the representatives of Victorian thought, nearly all the intellectuals, had to struggle with the problem of belief. Most of the influential teachers of the age were either unbelievers or professed a faith more or less far removed from conventional Christian orthodoxy. Thomas Carlyle, John Stuart Mill, George Eliot, James Anthony Froude, Francis Newman, John Morley, Matthew Arnold, Leslie Stephen, Thomas Hill Green, George Meredith—the teaching of all these was calculated to unsettle, if not to destroy, traditional Christian belief. Moreover, those teachers who did not themselves renounce Christian belief bore witness to the insistent pressure of doubt.[33]

There can be little doubt that Ethelbert Bullinger knew of the restlessness that permeated the society in which he lived. His location in London, the center of religious and scholarly circles; his wide-ranging interests and voluminous reading; his friendship with many in positions of influence—all suggest his inevitable awareness of controversial issues. In many ways, these social and religious influences around him can also be traced in his writings. Bullinger's staunch, lifelong defense of the principles of lower criticism and his, at times, quite fierce rejection of higher criticism become more understandable when seen in the light of the intellectual atmosphere of his day, as do his relentless campaign against Roman Catholicism, his frequent warnings about the dangers of spiritualism, and his cautions against the random adoption of untried scientific theories.

All of these matters interested him; all of them gave him food for thought and fuel for sermons and articles. Yet his greatest love and abiding passion was the study of the Scriptures.

Ethelbert Bullinger was a man of the Bible. As a close friend once said, "To him it was the Word of God, the revelation to men of the mind and Will of God; he was a convinced upholder of its inspiration and a stout defender of its verbal accuracy, apart from defective translation weaknesses."[34] As a dedicated upholder of the Bible's inspiration and accuracy, Bullinger walked a lonely path. The following quotation shows Bullinger's attitude toward the Bible in comparison to the mainstream of biblical study:

> By 1900 all serious scholars had accepted without hesitation the main conclusions of [higher] biblical criticism. Fundamentalism was now confined to a group of extreme Evangelicals and nonconformists, who clung to the Bible in its literal sense as the final authority which could not be touched. . . .[35]

But Bullinger never was a man of the mainstream. He was one of those rare individuals who lived his life influenced by neither the praise nor the fear of other people. As he himself once wrote, "Popularity is not to be our aim; success is not to be our object; results are not to be our guide; we are called to be faithful in our testimony."[36]

I invite you to open these pages and to meet this unique individual. May you enjoy becoming acquainted with him as I have, and may his faithful witness be as much an inspiration to you as it has been to me.

CHAPTER ONE

Childhood

A<small>T HALF PAST FIVE</small> on the morning of Friday, December 15, 1837, Ethelbert William Bullinger was born in Canterbury, Kent.

One of the oldest cities in England, Canterbury has often been referred to as "the Mother city of England." Daniel Defoe wrote the following of Canterbury in the eighteenth century:

> . . . its antiquity seems to be its greatest beauty; the houses are truly ancient, and the many ruins of churches, chapels, oratories, and smaller cells of religious people, make the place look like a general ruin a little recovered.[1]

It is true that Canterbury was old, even in Defoe's day. It was already a settlement when Rome was founded in the eighth century before Christ.[2] When Julius Caesar brought his invading army into Britain in 55 B.C., he found an already well-established tribal capital in Canterbury. In the four hundred years that Rome occupied Britain, the city grew and flourished as an important road junction, connecting the coastal towns with London and beyond.[3]

Canterbury has also been called the "Cradle of Christianity" in Great Britain.[4] It was to Canterbury that Augustine came in 597, bringing forty monks sent by Pope Gregory I to bring Christianity to the Saxon tribes. Ethelbert, King of Kent, welcomed Augustine and invited him to speak, the only requirement being that they meet in the open air so that the Christians could not practice magical arts on their hosts.[5]

By 601, King Ethelbert and many of his people were converted to the new faith. Augustine died within a few years of
coming to England, but the foothold that he had gained for
Christianity there remained and grew stronger. Before
Augustine's death, King Ethelbert gave him the plot of land on
which, centuries later, magnificent Canterbury Cathedral would
be built.[6]

The seat of ecclesiastical power in Great Britain, Canterbury
Cathedral has undergone many alternations since Augustine's
day. But it has always dominated Canterbury, towering over the
roofs of the city—first thatched, later red-tiled—with quiet dig-
nity. Countless people have come to see it: invaders, then pil-
grims, and later, tourists.

Canterbury at the time of Ethelbert Bullinger's birth looked
with promise to the future. *The Topographical History and
Directory of Canterbury,* published in 1838, heralded this new
optimism:

> Great improvements have been made in the general
> appearance of the city within the last few years; it is now
> well paved, furnished with a good supply of water from
> the river Stour, and an efficient police has been
> established.[7]

The Bullingers lived on Westgate Without, a street that even
in their day was old and full of history. Rising up a gentle hill
away from the magnificent Roman west gate of the city, the
road branched off higher up to meet the London road. It was a
street of little houses with gabled roofs, whose most striking
feature was the view:

> The traveller coming down the hill towards the city has
> before him Yevele's masterpiece, [the Cathedral] . . .
> above the huddled roofs of the city, the cathedral rises
> in all its stateliness. This is a panorama that any other
> city of the land would find it hard to equal.[8]

The Bullinger family had lived in Canterbury for more than
250 years and traced its ancestry proudly back to Heinrich

Bullinger (1504–1575), the distinguished Swiss pastor of the Reformation. William Bullinger owned a successful grocery business and lived above the shop with his wife, Mary (Bent) Bullinger, and their five children. James, the eldest son, was born on November 2, 1828; Hester Ann on April 15, 1831; Eliza on May 25, 1834; Zillah Jane on March 16, 1836; and Ethelbert William, the youngest child, on December 15, 1837.[9]

The Bullingers were members of the Methodist Church; in fact, in later life, William Bullinger would refer to himself as a "Wesleyan Preacher" as well as a grocer.[10]

There had been a flourishing Methodist congregation in Canterbury since 1750, when John Wesley first visited the city. St. Peter's Street Methodist Chapel had been built in 1811 for £8,287, an enormous sum in those days. The debt incurred by the congregation in building this chapel marked a distinct departure from the teachings of John Wesley, who "would not let a chapel be built unless two-thirds of the money was subscribed before a stone was laid."[11] It continued to be a burden on the congregation until the 1880s.

Each of the Bullinger children was baptized in St. Peter's Chapel. Ethelbert's baptism, performed by Rev. Samuel Webb, took place on March 11, 1838. The text chosen for the occasion was Malachi 3:16:

> Then they that feared the LORD spake often one to another: and the LORD hearkened, and heard *it,* and a book of remembrance was written before him for them that feared the LORD, and that thought upon his name.[12]

The fact that the Bullinger family was Methodist tells much about the tenor of Ethelbert's childhood. The following account gives a glimpse into Methodism in early Victorian days, the time of Ethelbert's childhood:

> The call of the Methodists of this period was for disciplined, simple, pious lives removed from worldly pleasures and centered on home, chapel and business. The duty of hard work, the evils of luxury and extravagance, the virtues of foresight and thrift, moderation and

> self-discipline, were instilled into ordinary church mem-
> bers and provided an undergirding to the moral ear-
> nestness characteristic of Victorian England. And the
> key here is undoubtedly the home. . . . Family prayers
> were assumed to be the norm in Methodist homes. . . .[13]

At a time when the general standard of education was extremely poor, the Methodists put great emphasis on reading.
John Wesley had maintained that "the work of grace would die
out in one generation if the Methodists were not a reading
people."[14] Each church had its own magazine, for preachers were
expected to be disseminators of Methodist literature as well as
preachers of the gospel.[15]

Historians of the period have claimed that it was the Methodists who first introduced the practice of "hymnody," the writing and singing of hymns.[16] Charles Wesley, John Wesley's brother
and coworker, wrote hundreds of hymns, and all Methodist services included congregational singing.

Music was, in fact, to play a major role in Ethelbert Bullinger's
life. He had a fine singing voice and had displayed musical talent while still quite young. His father had great ambitions for
the boy and wanted him to become a church organist. Anxious
to further Ethelbert's musical studies, William obtained a position for his son in the Canterbury Cathedral choir. Ethelbert,
for his part, wanted to become a clergyman. A compromise
between father and son resulted in Ethelbert's promise that he
would not neglect his music while serving in the ministry.[17] This
was a promise he was to keep all of his life.

On January 6, 1848, ten-year-old Ethelbert Bullinger was admitted as a chorister to the Canterbury Cathedral choir, an event
that would shape his future.[18]

Canterbury Cathedral was more than just a church. To young
Ethelbert, brought up in the simplicity of Methodism, it must
have been a profound change to don a purple cassock with
white surplice and stiff ruff around the neck and to become a
part of High Church tradition. The stately nave of the cathedral, the Gothic choir, the intricately vaulted roof high above,
the stained-glass windows that rivaled any in Europe, the tombs,
the memorials, and the inscriptions—all of these signified cen-

turies of English Christendom. Ethelbert truly had come to the Mother Church of England.

Ethelbert derived great benefits from being in the choir. He was given the musical instruction and individual voice training that all of the boys received and that made the Canterbury Cathedral choir one of the finest in the land.[19] An even greater benefit, however, especially in light of the general lack of schooling available at the time, was the opportunity to attend the choir school. There Ethelbert made connections with men who would help him further his education while receiving training that would otherwise have been out of reach for the son of a grocer.

The following is an account of the choir school at that time:

> The Choristers are taught singing three times a week in the Church, where there is a musical schoolroom; and learn Reading, Writing, and Arithmetic at private schools, at the expense of the Church.[20]

Ethelbert's extraordinary talents, both musical and intellectual, brought him to the attention of his teachers. Joshua Stratton, the overseer of the musical services and the choir, wrote later of his former chorister:

> I have known him from his, I believe seventh year when he was admitted a Chorister of Canterbury Cathedral.[21] He remained in this situation eight years, during the whole of which time his conduct was most exemplary and secured for him the esteem of all the Members of our Chapter.
>
> Feeling myself a great interest in his welfare and knowing his anxious desire to get to College and become a Clergyman, I commenced a course of study with him upon his leaving the Chapter School and this progress was so satisfactory and his diligent application such as to lead me to entertain great hopes of him. His principles are sound. His manners gentle, and pleasing, and his disposition most amiable. . . . He has been well grounded in music, has been accustomed to devote his Sundays and much of his time on weekdays to the parochial schools. . . .[22]

Joshua Stratton and Ethelbert Bullinger were to remain great friends. Many years later, Ethelbert named his second son, Bernard Stratton Bullinger, in honor of his old mentor.

The following appraisal of Ethelbert's musical talents is found in a letter to him from W. H. Longhurst, the assistant organist of Canterbury Cathedral and the singing master of the choristers:

> I have known you and tried your musical capabilities in a variety of ways for twelve or fourteen years and have ever found you attentive to your Musical Studies as a boy and certainly containing promise of great future excellence as a man. Your voice *at present* is not strong, but your reading is good, and your judgement and good taste in singing will soon bring about all the other requisites. . . .[23]

Many years later, while he was vicar of Walthamstow, Bullinger was invited to submit a short autobiographical sketch for a "Register of Past Choristers" being compiled by Dr. Longhurst. He wrote the following on his years in the choir school:

> Ethelbert William Bullinger entered as a chorister January 6th 1848 at the age of 9 years, and left January 6th 1855. He desires to place on record his gratitude to Dr. Longhurst for the many extra lessons given beyond the general routine of instruction; and also to the late Rev. Joshua Stratton, then Precentor, who both before he left the school and for nearly five years after gave him stated daily reading in Latin and Greek.[24]

CHAPTER TWO

King's College

WHEN HIS ASSOCIATION with the Canterbury Cathedral choir ended in January 1855, Ethelbert, then seventeen, began to prepare himself for his theological training. He received daily lessons in Latin and Greek from Canon Stratton and regularly attended services at St. Stephen's in Hackington, a small village adjacent to Canterbury on the River Stour. The vicar, John White, later described the young man as "a sincere, and conscientiously attached, member of the Church of England."[1] It is not certain if Ethelbert was then living at the family home on Westgate Street.

In 1858, Canon Stratton recommended that Ethelbert go to the tiny village of Berden, about fifty miles northwest of Canterbury, to assist the pastor, Rev. Frederick G. Nash. In May 1859, Rev. Nash wrote the following regarding his aide:

> I can bear testimony, and have much pleasure in doing so, to his excellent moral character, his sound principles as a young member of our Church and his consistent conduct.[2]

On January 4, 1859, Ethelbert's mother, Mary Bullinger, died in Canterbury. By this time there had been other changes in the family as well. Ethelbert's brother, James, had emigrated to America sometime during the 1850s and had married there. In 1856, their sister, Zillah Jane, had married John Sanders, a missionary, and had gone with him to the West Indies, where in

1858 their daughter, Eveline Viola, was born. In 1859, Mr. Sanders died, and Zillah returned to Canterbury with her daughter to become her father's housekeeper.[3]

In May of that same year, Ethelbert, now twenty-one, applied for admittance to New College in Oxford University. Among the oldest of the colleges of Oxford, New College was aptly described at that time as a society "at once contracted, indolent, orthodox and obscure."[4] Founded in 1375, New College during its long history had admitted only a handful of commoners.[5] In an attempt to introduce new blood into the New College choir, the director of music, a former Canterbury Cathedral chorister, made a number of choral scholarships available for incoming students.[6] Ethelbert's application for one of these scholarships was turned down. His subsequent application to King's College, London, however, met with more success.

A significant contrast to the inbred traditionalism of New College, King's College was modern and progressive. It stood at the forefront of the nineteenth-century movement to make higher education available to the middle class. The curriculum included religious instruction and classical learning as well as history, modern languages, mathematics, natural philosophy, medicine and surgery, chemistry, and jurisprudence.[7] The college was located on the Strand in central London in a handsome building that had been especially erected in the 1830s to house it.

The Theological Department of King's College, to which Ethelbert applied, had been instituted in 1847 in order to accommodate the needs of the many young men who were "debarred from taking holy orders simply because they could not afford the expense of going to the older universities [Oxford and Cambridge]."[8] The Theological Department also accepted men without degrees who were recommended by their bishop and accepted by the principal.[9]

Ethelbert took the entrance exam on October 5, 1859. It required a knowledge of the following:

1. The four Gospels in Greek
2. The historical books of the Old Testament
3. The Church Catechism with Scripture proofs

4. One Greek and one Latin book to be selected by the candidate (authors included Homer, Herodotus, Thucydides, Cicero, Caesar, Livy, Tacitus, Virgil, and Horace)
5. Latin and Greek grammar
6. One standard book in English literature (*viz.*, Bacon's *Essays*)
7. A small pamphlet on the Hebrew alphabet by Rev. A. McCaul, D.D.[10]

Ethelbert was admitted to King's College for the Lenten term beginning January 24, 1860. He was placed in the third class, which was made up of those who had ranked lowest in the entrance examination.[11]

In the Theological Department of King's College Ethelbert began a course of study that was as strenuous as it was exacting. The following subjects were required for all students:

1. Dogmatic Theology—The Thirty-nine Articles
2. Ecclesiastical History
3. Exegesis of the Old Testament
4. Hebrew and Rabbinical Literature
5. Exegesis of the New Testament
6. Pastoral and Liturgical Theology
7. Evidences of Christianity
8. Latin
9. Theory and Practise of Vocal Church Music
10. Public Reading
11. Laws of Health and Disease in Their Relation to the Ministerial Office[12]

Daily morning service in the chapel, attendance at all lectures, precise note-taking, and voluminous outside reading were expected from all theological students. Periodic oral examinations were mandatory and had to be passed satisfactorily before final examinations could be taken.[13]

In spite of the strenuous schedule, Ethelbert did not neglect his music while at King's College. In the words of a fellow student and friend:

His musical attainments I can answer for myself. He is
one of the most accomplished amateur musicians that I
have ever had the good fortune to meet. With an
agreeable tenor voice he unites a great knowledge of
Church music, a correct ear, and a simple unaffected
manner. His excellence in these respects is, I believe,
due to the musical education which he enjoyed when a
boy at Canterbury.[14]

King's College had excellent professors during Ethelbert's
student years, men whose great learning could not help but
inspire and guide the students. Four among them stand out in
particular:

Dr. Alexander McCaul (1799–1863), a distinguished Hebraist,
was Ethelbert's professor of Hebrew and Rabbinical Literature
and Ecclesiastical History. He had spent many years in Poland,
Russia, and Germany and was vitally interested in Jewish issues.[15]
He was the author of several well-known works, including *Testimonies to the Divine Authority of the Holy Scriptures,* a notable defense of the integrity of the Bible, published in 1862.[16]

Dr. Charles John Ellicott (1819–1905) occupied the chair of
New Testament studies during Ethelbert's student days. In 1854,
Ellicott published the first of a series of commentaries on the
Pauline epistles, which were widely read and recognized as "the
best in the English language for scholarship and breadth of
view."[17] Ellicott left King's College to become the Bishop of
Gloucester, a position he held for forty-two years. During that
time he was actively involved in a great work of biblical scholarship undertaken by the Church of England in the latter half of
the nineteenth century—the preparation and publication of the
Revised Version of 1881.

James Stewart Perowne (1823–1904) was another of Ethelbert's
instructors who actively participated in the preparation of the
Revised Version of 1881. He was an eminent scholar and the
professor of Old Testament studies at King's College. In 1864
Perowne published his best-known work: a translation and commentary of the book of Psalms. He was also general editor of
The Cambridge Bible for Schools and College.[18]

Finally, Dr. Edward Hayes Plumtre (1821–1891) was professor of Pastoral Theology and the chaplain of King's College. His friendship with Ethelbert was to continue long after King's College. Plumtre was known as a "most sympathetic teacher, [who] took a genuine interest in the future welfare of his pupils."[19] He was also a prolific author on biblical subjects and he encouraged Ethelbert's early literary endeavors.

Regarding Ethelbert's King's College days, Plumtre wrote the following:

> I can truly say that we have never had a student whose life and conversation, soundness in the faith, and loyalty to the Church of England we could look back on with more thorough satisfaction.[20]

That Ethelbert made a great impression on his professors can also be seen by the following recommendation written by Dr. Perowne:

> Mr. Bullinger was for two years my pupil at King's College London, and during that time his character and conduct were in all respects exemplary; and such as to gain him the esteem and regard of the Professors of the College, as well as of his fellow-students.[21]

Ethelbert completed the required six terms, for which two years were normally allotted, in a year and a half. On June 22, 1861, he received the degree of Associate of King's College, which also admitted him as a candidate for holy orders. The excellent instruction and Ethelbert's own diligence had paid off; he was placed in the first class, the section for those with the highest grades.[22] More importantly, he left King's College "a sound Greek scholar, with a mastery of Hebrew which few could boast."[23]

On July 7, 1861, in the Chapel within Farnham Castle, the Bishop of Winchester admitted "Ethelbert William Bullinger Theological Associate of King's College London (of whose virtuous and pious life and conversation, and competent Learning and Knowledge in the Holy Scriptures, We were well assured) into the Holy Order of Deacons according to the manner and form prescribed and used by the Church of England."[24] This brought Ethelbert one step closer to his goal: to be an ordained clergyman in the Church of England.

On July 8, came warm congratulations from the old friend and mentor of Ethelbert's Canterbury choir days, Joshua Stratton:

My dear Bullinger,

I forgot when I saw you that we should be leaving home this week. I shall not have the pleasure of seeing you. I must therefore congratulate you by letter on being admitted to the sacred office of the ministry. I hope you may be enabled to discharge the high important duties that will now devolve upon you to God's glory, and the good of those over whom you will be appointed.

I told Mrs. Harrison last evening that you would call upon her and I beg you to do so, and also on the dean; the archdeacon will be glad to see you. If you have a Sunday . . . be sure you offer your services to your kind friend the vicar of St. Stephens. I dare say he will be glad of your help.

I wish you to have some books from my library. Call at my house and tell my cook you have my permission to go to my library. On one of the lower shelves, I think the last but one on the left hand side you'll find four interleaved volumes. The Greek text with notes by Trollope, if you think they will be useful to you. And you should like them. Write your name in them as a small gift from me in remembrance of the many happy hours we have spent together. . . .

With my best wishes and earnest prayers that God's blessing may always attend you. Believe me, your sincere and affectionate friend.

Joshua Stratton

Let me have a letter soon.[25]

CHAPTER THREE

The Early Parishes

ON TUESDAY, OCTOBER 15, 1861, Ethelbert Bullinger married Miss Emma Dodson. Ethelbert was twenty-three years of age, and Emma, daughter of John and Mary (Miller) Dodson of Epping, Essex, was thirty-five. When they met is unknown, but the fact that both bride and groom gave the same address on their marriage certificate indicates how they may have become acquainted. The house, a few doors away from King's College, was owned by Robert Dodson, very likely a relative of Emma's.[1]

The wedding took place in St. Mary-le-Strand Church in London, across the street from King's College and their residence. The newly married couple settled in St. James Place, a cul-de-sac of small, newly built houses off Upper Grange Road in Bermondsey, southeast London. There, Ethelbert had his first assignment in the Church of England. He was to be an assistant curate in the parish of St. Mary Magdalene, Bermondsey.

Close to the Thames, Bermondsey had originally been a stretch of marshland cut through by tidal streams. Its name is thought to be derived from the Saxon chief, Lord Boermund, who chose this pleasant and strategic location for his settlement. It thus became known as Boermund's "eye," or island.[2] Once a beautiful and favored rural spot, Bermondsey had, by the beginning of the nineteenth century, evolved into one of the great manufacturing hubs of London. It was a major trade center with huge wharves and warehouses for storing goods from all over the world. The many small rivers and creeks that

39

intersected the area had become nothing more than industrial dumping grounds and open sewers. The following description is quite apt:

> It is no good pretending that coal wharves, guano facto-
> ries and Bathing Creek, though socially necessary, are
> commonly edifying. They are glum, and if the wind is in
> the wrong quarter you wish you were not there.[3]

The presence of industry with its accompanying offenses
had long since driven the wealthier classes out of Bermondsey.
In their place came the teeming poor; people from the de-
pressed rural counties and immigrants from Ireland made up
the majority of Bermondsey's population during the nineteenth
century.[4] Living conditions were wretched. Overcrowding and
poor housing were everyday facts of life, while epidemics of
tuberculosis, dysentery, diphtheria, and cholera raged un-
checked throughout the population, particularly among the
young. One out of every three children born in Bermondsey
in the early part of the nineteenth century died by the age of
five.[5]

It was in large part the local churches that attempted, by car-
ing for the poor, to fill the huge gaps in the Victorian social
structure. In a parish such as St. Magdalene's, this was a constant
struggle, and as one of two assistant curates, Ethelbert immediately set to work. His greatest personal concern was to help young
people, a priority he was to keep in every parish that he served.
He was a member of the Board of the Bermondsey United Charity Schools, founded by the Tanner's Company almost a century
before to give schooling to local children. He also instituted a
special Friday evening fellowship for the children in the school.[6]

On Sunday, July 6, 1862, in the Chapel within Farnham Castle,
Ethelbert William Bullinger was ordained into the Holy Order
of Priesthood of the Church of England by the Bishop of
Winchester.[7]

A crucial event in Rev. Bullinger's spiritual growth took place
during this time. Many years later, the story was retold by a
close friend:

At the time of his ordination as a Church of England clergyman in 1861, Dr. Bullinger was still a stranger to that vital experience which is known as conversion. This took place during his first curacy. There was, among those attending the church, a godly lady who was in the habit of expressing her opinion on the sermons preached. Feeling interested in knowing what she had said after a week night sermon which he delivered in the absence of the Vicar, he was surprised to learn that her only comment had been "Poor blind young man." These words led subsequently to his conversion, for they set him thinking, and he went on his knees to ask God to show him if he was indeed blind. One of his regrets in after life was that this lady died without ever knowing the result of her words.

His ministry thenceforth bore abundant evidence of his faith in the Gospel as "the power of God unto salvation to everyone that believeth." With this new experience came also that profound and abiding reverence for the Word of God which so notably characterized all his sermons and writings. For him the Book became the supreme authority. He was often heard to advise his audience not to believe anything simply because he said it, but to search the Bible for themselves.[8]

On Friday, July 18, 1862, at four in the afternoon, a son was born to Ethelbert and Emma Bullinger. They named him Ethelbert Augustine, two distinguished names from the history of Ethelbert's birthplace, Canterbury. And it was in Canterbury, in St. Martin's Church, that the baby was baptized on the first anniversary of his parents' wedding. Rev. Bullinger himself performed the ceremony.[9]

Despite his ordination, Ethelbert still found himself in one of the lowest paying positions available in middle-class nineteenth-century English society, that of an Anglican curate. Until a clergyman could secure his own parish as a vicar, he was forced to accept not only a meager salary but also uncertain working conditions and low social status. Many curates moved from parish to parish contending for the few available choice situations, always with the hope of some day acquiring their own vicarage.[10]

Now with increased family responsibilities, Rev. Bullinger looked for a better position, calling upon his friends and former teachers for advice and recommendations. In May 1863, Dr. Alexander McCaul, lecturer in Hebrew at King's College and a good friend of Ethelbert's, wrote on his behalf for a position in Tittleshall, Norfolk:

> I have great pleasure in stating that Mr. E. W. Bullinger is one of the most satisfactory students, that we have ever had at King's College. From all that I have seen of him, since he has been engaged in the work of the Ministry, I believe him to be a faithful and devoted Minister of Christ, a gentleman in manner and feeling, and possessing tact, temper and judgement. He is moreover a man of ability, diligence, and more than ordinary acquirements.[11]

The vicar of St. Mary's Church in Tittleshall was Rev. Kenelm Henry Digby, who had labored in that tiny parish and at the neighboring parish of St. Andrew's, Wellingham, for twenty-eight years. Digby was looking for a curate who could assist him in the care of these two churches and also teach the youngsters in two schools he had just opened. Rev. Bullinger applied for the position and, in late summer of 1863, was accepted.

On August 24, a congratulatory letter came from Dr. Perowne, his former professor at King's College and now the Bishop of Worcester:

> It gave me much pleasure to hear from you and I was truly glad to find you were going into the diocese of Norwich. Your course at King's College was in every respect most satisfactory, and I can bear testimony and do so most willingly to the diligence and success with which you pursued your studies.
>
> My personal intercourse with you led me to believe that you were actuated by the highest motives in taking the Ministry and I pray that God will abundantly bless you in all your labours as His servant to the promotion of His glory and the salvation of immortal souls.

I rejoice to hear that you are to be with Mr. Digby. I think you could be very well qualified to teach young pupils and you are perfectly at liberty to make use of my name or to refer to me if you like.

You can if you like take this letter to the Bishop as an introduction or make any use of it you please.[12]

The place to which Rev. Bullinger took his family in Norfolk stood in sharp contrast to their former home in Bermondsey. An area of broad, green plains and shallow lakes, Tittleshall was in the middle of one of the most picturesque sections of England and had a population of about five hundred people.[13] St. Mary's Church, serenely situated by a quiet pond, had been built in 1320.[14]

Ethelbert began his curacy in Tittleshall on September 8, 1863, and remained there until October 25, 1866, the longest tenure he was to have as curate. During that time, he was described as:

A pious, diligent hard working clergyman, with a very good knowledge of music. He has taken great pains and much interest in training a village choir, and gained for himself the respect and love of [the] parishioners.[15]

The amicable relationship that had developed between Rev. Digby and his assistant during those years can be seen in Rev. Digby's letter dated July 26, 1866, after Rev. Bullinger had told him of his decision to return to London. And, with careful Victorian propriety, Rev. Digby hinted at the probable reason for the move:

Dear Mr. Bullinger,

I confess that I read your letter with deep feelings of regret to find our connection as Rector and Curate will have to terminate. Though I rejoice in anything that may tend to your increased usefulness, and lead I hope to preferment; you may be assured that regret for ourselves and the Parishes are the predominant feelings. Your letter came when I am a little low in spirit and a little uncomfortable in health, and it has not helped you may be sure to raise them. . . . I know not whether I ought to congratulate you or not *now* on one bit of news in your letter remembering John XVI:21[16] but I feel sure and I speak as the father of 9 children that it will be with God's blessings and subject for future congratulations.[17]

Rev. Digby's allusion to childbirth proved to be correct. Emma Bullinger was pregnant and due early in December 1866. Looking for a better situation for his family, Rev. Bullinger had traveled to London in July to investigate an available curacy in St. Peter's Church, Notting Hill. While there, he was asked to deliver a sermon to the congregation. The response from the parishioners was favorable, as the following letter from J. Lark, Esq., church warden of St. Peter's Church, attests:

After our conversation of Sunday week I think it due to you to say that I was *very much pleased* with your sermon on *Sunday evening.* With a little *more vigour* in the *delivery* and a store of subjects equally well digested I have every hope that your ministrations will prove useful.

Nothing tends more to this than the impression on the mind of the hearer that the preacher *feels what he says.* It is the strongest proof of the *heart* being in the work as well as the head.[18]

By August 23, the matter of Rev. Bullinger's new employment was settled, and Mr. Lark hastened to send his best wishes:

It affords me much gratification to think that I in any way contributed to make your visit to our neighbourhood agreeable. It is not often that I feel any interest in the movements of those who happen to be utter strangers, but in your case I did so; and with regard to your ministrations in our Parish Church I believe I may say that the impressions made on those who heard you were of the most favourable kind.[19]

The Bullingers' new home proved once again quite a change from their former one. The Notting Hill area, west of the city, was a welter of little houses that had mushroomed in this previously rural spot to keep up with the growth of London.[20] The Bullinger family moved into a small house at 24 Horbury Crescent, close to St. Peter's Church.

On Sunday, December 2, 1866, at 4:15 A.M., Emma Bullinger gave birth to a second son.[21] He was named Bernard Stratton Bullinger, the middle name being for Ethelbert's great friend and mentor, Joshua Stratton, who had died in Canterbury two years earlier.

Emma's older unmarried sister, Sophia, now made her home with the Bullinger family, as did their widowed mother, Mary Dodson, who remained in the Bullinger household until her death on May 10, 1869.

At about that time, a tragedy in Emma's family resulted in consequences that were to prove very significant in Ethelbert's life. Emma's brother, Henry Dodson, had died in 1864, leaving his wife Hannah and three very young children. When Hannah herself died of tuberculosis in 1868, the three children—Harry, George, and Elizabeth—remained with those members of the family who could care for them. The Bullingers adopted Elizabeth a few years later. As the years passed, she would become an increasingly important person in her uncle's life.

On August 9, 1867, within a year of Rev. Bullinger's move to St. Peter's, Notting Hill, he was reassigned to the neighboring church of St. John's, Notting Hill. As always, Rev. Bullinger performed his parish duties with care and diligence. Already recognized as a notable preacher of the Word, he now began to help people study the Bible for themselves.

Bullinger's first major literary work, *A Critical Lexicon and Concordance to the English and Greek New Testament,* was started during these years in Notting Hill. Word studies that Bullinger had undertaken for himself and that he later shared with friends were the seeds of this project. In the book's preface, he explained its beginnings, the magnitude it took on, and finally the perseverance needed to complete it:

> "Not unto us, O Lord, not unto us; but unto thy name give glory." Such were the words that filled the author's heart on bringing to a close the labours of nine years,

begun amidst the duties of a London parish and continued in various parts of the Master's vineyard; it is the
fruit of time redeemed from less noble recreations, and
devoted to the Master's service.

The need of such a work arose from the study of certain words of more or less importance, for his own edification and that of certain friends; when the thought
occurred that it might be useful to himself and to many
others if the work were made complete and rendered
accessible to all students of God's Word.

With this view a certain portion was done and submitted to the judgement of some who are renowned for
their biblical knowledge and criticism. Their kind expressions of opinion encouraged the author in the pros-
ecution of his design.

It is obvious that such a work could not be designed
in a day, and the consequence was, that as it grew, the
earlier portions (A, B, and C) were written and rewrit-
ten, until the design became complete.

There are but few who will really appreciate the nature and character of the labour demanded by the work,
and consequently, the daily need of strength, health, courage, and prayer, to persevere unto the end: "thy God
hath commanded thy strength" has indeed been verified by experience, and so has the prayer, "Strengthen,
O God, that which thou hast wrought for us."[22]

One year after Bullinger began his curacy at St. John's, Notting
Hill, he received the following letter from his vicar, John Philip
Gell, dated August 1868:

> I cannot and ought not to hope to retain you continu-
> ally at Notting Hill, but it will be a day of sincere regret
> when the time comes for you to move upwards, so far as
> I am myself concerned at least.[23]

The time did come, however. On October 26, 1869, Ethelbert
began his new duties as curate in St. John the Baptist Church in
Leytonstone, northeast of London. Like Notting Hill,

Leytonstone was a former rural area, struggling with a surging population. So great was this boom that St. John's Church did not have room to accommodate all its members, particularly the poorer ones. Soon after his arrival, Rev. Bullinger helped to establish a street mission where open-air services could be held. Called the Harrow Green Mission, it was located at a site on the High Road in front of the Great Eastern Railway lines.[24]

On December 8, 1870, after only fourteen months at St. John's, Rev. Bullinger resigned his curacy. On December 10, the parishioners presented him with a silver tea and coffee service, a silver pocket communion service, and a purse containing thirty-five sovereigns.[25] The accompanying expression of appreciation says much about the impact of Rev. Bullinger's care for his people, even during such a short time of service:

> Presented to the Reverend Ethelbert William Bullinger on his leaving the curacy of Leytonstone, December 10, 1870. As a proof of our affection and appreciation of the sterling earnestness and unflinching sincerity with which he has fulfilled his ministry amongst us. For his labours in our Church (which speak for themselves); for his training of the choir (which under his unwearied attention has been brought to great excellence); for his kindness to our poorer neighbours and his efforts in establishing the Mission at Harrow Green (in which he has been so ably assisted by his noble wife). He must look for his reward from a Higher Source than from his fellow man.
>
> We present the accompanying gifts as a tribute of our affectionate sympathy and our kind regards. With our sincere good wishes for the future happiness of himself and those dear to him.[26]

CHAPTER FOUR

The Bethnal Green
Workhouse School

LIKE MANY OTHERS, Ethelbert Bullinger was deeply concerned about the plight of Victorian England's disadvantaged children. Homeless children roamed the streets of every city in the land, eking out an existence by begging or by crime. Children, even young ones, worked long hours in factories, mines, and workshops; others, described as "orphans, deserted children, or children of idiots, invalids or felons" were confined in workhouses and lived under deplorable conditions. Originally designed to house the poor and to teach them how to work, these workhouses of Victorian England had long since deteriorated into dens of corruption and violence.[1]

This shameful situation was not new. In 1835, two years before Victoria became queen, an estimated forty to fifty thousand children had been living in workhouses throughout England.[2]

In 1836, George Müller had opened the first of several orphanages in Bristol, England, to provide shelter for homeless children.[3] Then, in 1837, Charles Dickens had published his famous novel *Oliver Twist*, which brought the plight of unfortunate youngsters, both on the streets and in the workhouses, to public attention.[4] With public opinion aroused, church and government were now forced to initiate social reform, a process that would take decades.

Thus it was that during the 1860s the parish of St. Matthew's,

Bethnal Green, London, undertook the construction of what was intended to be a model facility for the housing and education of workhouse children. The chosen site was outside of the parish in the more rural area of Leytonstone. The school opened in 1868 in temporary buildings with 118 children.[5]

Two years later, in October 1870, Rev. Bullinger, then curate at St. John's in Leytonstone, applied to fill the vacancy as chaplain for this institution. It was a part-time position that had traditionally been held by curates from nearby churches. The Local Government Board of St. Matthew's Parish hired him at a salary of £40 per year.[6]

During Bullinger's first year at the Bethnal Green Workhouse School, many changes and challenges occurred in his own life. In December of 1870 he resigned from St. John's, Leytonstone for reasons that are not fully known. Early in 1871, he lived by himself in Cambridge Park, Leytonstone. His wife, Emma, along with their two sons, eight-year-old Ethelbert Augustine and four-year-old Bernard Stratton and Emma's sister, Sophia Dodson, lived on Holly Road, Leytonstone, together with two young servants.[7] What occasioned the separation is not clear. In August, Rev. Bullinger moved to the neighboring village of Walthamstow, about two and a half miles away, having been asked by the vicar of St. Mary's Church in Walthamstow to serve as curate. Sometime after his move to Walthamstow, the Bullinger family was reunited. During all of this time, Rev. Bullinger continued his research for the *Lexicon and Concordance*.

Rev. Bullinger's tenure as chaplain of the Workhouse School seems to have begun uneventfully. In October 1871, after he had held the position for about a year, he asked the Board of Governors of the school for funds to provide a library for the children. His request was referred to committee. He also asked for an increase of salary and was given £10 more per year.[8]

The early 1870s was a time of great upheaval in the English educational system. The Education Bill of 1870 dictated that education for every child, funded by the government and outside of religious control, was to be made available.[9] Many religious institutions, as they saw their power over educational policies waning, reacted quickly to reinvigorate their existing schools. One result was that on May 23, 1872, the Local

Government Board of St. Matthew's Parish instituted sweeping changes in the Bethnal Green Workhouse School. Regarding the duties of the chaplain of the Workhouse School, the following rules were published, with the title "Article 64 of the Government of the School":

1. To read prayers according to the Liturgy of the Church of England, and preach a sermon to the children and other inmates of the School on every Sunday, and on Good Friday and Christmas Day, unless the Guardians, with the consent of the Local Government Board, shall otherwise direct.
2. To attend in the school daily for the purpose of imparting religious instruction to the children, and to ascertain, by frequent examination of classes, their general intellectual and moral progress.
3. To make record of every such examination, as also of the general progress and condition of the children, in the book to be kept for that purpose, to be laid before the Guardians at their next ordinary meeting, to be termed "The Chaplain's Report Book."
4. To visit and minister to the sick children according to their several necessities and capacities.[10]

These new regulations changed the position of chaplain into a full-time responsibility, one that required a great deal more work than had been proposed originally. Rev. Bullinger wrote to the Board of Governors of the school requesting changes in their agreement, including a higher salary. The request was denied, the Board insisting that he carry out his duties according to the new regulations.[11]

This conflict simmered for a number of months. Then, in October 1873, a report appeared in the daily papers alleging that "hundreds of children entered the workhouse schools and came out again without receiving any religious instruction whatever." The Board of Governors of the school, incensed by the accusations, wrote to the papers, demanding to know, "Did these remarks apply to the Bethnal Green Workhouse School?"[12]

This public focus put pressure on both sides: on the School

to keep up standards set by others and on Rev. Bullinger to work under conditions to which he had never agreed. In December 1873, the Board of Governors of the School fired the first salvo in what was to become an intense battle of politics and principles by issuing the following abrupt resolution at their regular meeting:

> Clerk was instructed to write to Chaplain requesting him to carry out his duties in accordance with Clause 2, Article 64 of the School Order.[13]

In January, Rev. Bullinger answered the School Board, making plain his grievances with that institution and referring the matter to the higher authority of the governing board of the entire parish. He wrote:

> As the Guardians [of the Workhouse School] had called upon him [Rev. Bullinger] to do six times the amount of work than he was engaged to do and had declined to increase his salary he had submitted the whole matter to the consideration of the Local Government Board [of St. Matthew's Parish].[14]

In response, the governing board of the school appointed a committee to deal with the matter. On March 17, the dispute intensified when the committee issued the following recommendation to the School Board:

> As the Chaplain still neglects to carry out the duties mentioned in Clause 2, Article 64 of the School Order, your committee recommends the Board to call upon him to resign.[15]

The committee recommended that, should the chaplain not comply, they write to the governing board of the parish requesting that they remove Rev. Bullinger from his office. Furthermore, the school board accused the chaplain of failing to carry out his duties and cited Rev. Bullinger's move from Leytonstone to Walthamstow as reason for "his reduced performance." The new regulations, to which he had never agreed, were not mentioned. The School Board stated:

> Guardians are not so limited in choice of chaplain as Mr.
> Bullinger says (Mr. Bullinger having been himself appointed when he was curate of Leytonstone) . . . either of
> the parochial clergy would be glad to hold the chaplaincy
> at the present salary together with his other duty. . . .[16]

They resolved not to increase the chaplain's pay and requested his immediate resignation. On May 9, Rev. Bullinger sent the following letter to the Local Government Board of St. Matthew's Parish:

To the Guardians of St. Matthew, Bethnal Green

Gentlemen:

> As I must decline to have six times the amount of
> work imposed on me, with no increase of salary, I beg to
> inform you that you are at liberty to appoint "either of
> the Parochial Clergy" who you assert in your letter of
> the 16th will be "glad to hold the Chaplaincy at the
> present salary."
> If either of the "Parochial Clergy" have made this offer to you, I beg to enter my strong protest against such
> a conspiracy.
> If they have not I shall indeed be surprised if you find
> a clergyman able and "glad" to superintend *daily* the
> educational work of the schools in addition to the visitation of the Infirmaries and the service on Sundays for
> 19/2 ½ [19 shillings, 2 ½ pence] a week.
> I for one repudiate the offer and shall terminate my
> engagement with you one month from the date of this
> notice.[17]

His resignation was accepted immediately, and the School Board set about to find a replacement. They sent a letter to Mr. Waller, the vicar of Leytonstone, to know if he would undertake the duties of chaplain in the school.

On May 26, Mr. Waller replied, addressing the clerk:

> May I ask you to be so kind as to convey to the Board of Guardians thanks for the honour they have done me in placing the post of Chaplain at my disposal.
>
> Please inform the Board, that although I am desirous to fill the position, I do not find it possible without alteration made in remuneration.
>
> The duties require the Chaplain to attend 365 days a year at the School, during 6 days in one week he has to instruct the children, on Sunday to conduct Divine Service and of course he would answer for any other duties he might as clergy be required to attend in a large establishment of this nature. . . .
>
> Will you submit to them the above facts and add that if they will very kindly reconsider the question of the Chaplain's remuneration and substitute annual payment of £100 in place of £50 proposed, I shall be happy to do the best in my power to meet their requirements.[18]

Upon receipt of Mr. Waller's letter, the Board elected him chaplain and immediately moved to increase his salary from £50 to £100 per year.

Thus, with or without regret, Rev. Bullinger and the Bethnal Green Workhouse School Board went their separate ways. The Board did not see fit to send the customary letter of thanks to the resigning chaplain.

No more is known about this painful incident in Bullinger's life. All that has been recorded comes to us from the minutes of the meetings of the Board of the Workhouse School. Bullinger, for his part, was silent. The success of his work with young people in each of his past (and future) parishes and the testimonies of many of the young people themselves speak to his love for and ability with the youth. That he left his other parish work to devote himself entirely to teaching underprivileged children certainly would indicate high ideals and aspirations. At Bethnal Green, however, both his aspirations and his capabilities seem to have been dashed against the rocks of politics and bureaucracy.

CHAPTER FIVE

The Walthamstow Years

THE LOCAL GOVERNMENT BOARD of St. Matthew's Parish was correct about one thing: Rev. Bullinger's move to Walthamstow had brought about new demands upon his time. In 1871, while he was serving as curate in St. Mary's, his name had been proposed as vicar for a parish that would soon be established in the rapidly developing area of Walthamstow. The new parish was to be called St. Stephen's.[1]

After thirteen years of curacies and assistant curacies, this would at last be a vicarage of his own. In the autumn of 1874, with the unpleasantness at Bethnal Green now behind him, Rev. Bullinger directed his energies to the challenges of organizing a new parish. The opening service was planned for November 21, 1874, but an explosion and fire on that very day did extensive damage to the temporary church building and forced the fledgling congregation into borrowed quarters.[2]

The new parish was finally inaugurated in its repaired temporary church on January 12, 1875, with a congregation of four hundred people. The *Walthamstow Chronicle* reported on the "air of earnestness about the crowded congregation which told of a quiet rejoicing that yet another House of God was founded in this place." As befitting the convictions of its new vicar, the church was to be evangelical in outlook.[3]

Rev. Bullinger's new community had been aptly named. In the *Domesday Book,* William the Conqueror's survey of England, completed about 1087, the area was called "Wilcumestou," the

Saxon word for "the welcome place." Charmingly situated between the River Lea on the south and forest lands to the north,
Walthamstow deserved its reputation as "the prettiest place
within a horse-ride from London."[4] In 1871 Walthamstow boasted
a population of 11,072; after the arrival of the railroad in 1870
this figure was to double each decade until 1901.[5]

During the years that the Bullingers lived there, however,
Walthamstow was still a choice spot. They lived in a gracious
home with a large, walled garden on the corner of Orford Road.
Gone were the insecurities of a curate's life and the frustration
at the Workhouse School. As vicar, Rev. Bullinger moved with
his family into a more comfortable position and made friends
with many of the affluent families in Walthamstow. William
McCall, part-owner of a successful provisions business in London, and Alfred Janson, a wealthy and influential underwriter,
became close friends of the Bullingers. Mr. Janson's two sisters,
Caroline and Eliza Janson, lived in Walthamstow in a beautiful
home called "The Chestnuts" where Rev. Bullinger became a
regular visitor. He found the two sisters "learned students of
the Bible and ready helpers in all good work."[6]

The congregation of St. Stephen's was diverse. A member
described it thus:

> Throughout his ministry at St. Stephen's, Dr. Bullinger
> held together a large congregation, many members be-
> ing of marked individuality, strong convictions and di-
> verse views on religious and other issues of the day. The
> bond of union was a spiritual bond. Certainly Dr.
> Bullinger was an attractive personality, a man of many
> gifts, but his people knew that with him everything was
> subordinated to the one great spiritual aim of his minis-
> try—and they responded in a wonderful way.[7]

Rev. Bullinger's ministry flourished in this atmosphere of
mutual care and genuine enthusiasm for the work of the Lord.
Years later, many members of his congregation were to remember with great pleasure the special comradeship that from the
beginning developed between the vicar and his people.[8]

The first order of business was to build a permanent church.

A contract was signed on October 20, 1876, and the first stone was laid on April 14, 1877. Although the wealthier patrons of St. Stephen's were very generous, a fund drive was immediately implemented to augment their donations. Besides a house-to-house collection throughout the parish, the children in the Sunday school were asked to give one penny weekly until they had each paid for at least one brick. Altogether, the cost of building the church was £6,581, quite a bargain even in those days.[9]

The consecration of St. Stephen's Church took place on April 6, 1878, with the Bishop of St. Albans officiating and a large congregation in attendance. Mr. W. H. Monk, the organist and choir director of King's College and a friend of Rev. Bullinger's, presided at the organ.[10]

Even before the move to the new church, Rev. Bullinger had begun the organization and implementation of many parish activities. His administrative talents were formidable, but even more important was his ability to work with people. As one member of the congregation fondly recalled:

> The Vicar was a very genial, tactful man and had the faculty of setting people to work, whilst his organising powers were remarkable.[11]

This large, eclectic congregation provided many avenues for service, and Rev. Bullinger seems to have taken an active part in all of them. As always, the music ministry remained close to his heart. He organized and trained the choir and was involved in the selection of hymns used at services. He highly valued simplicity, reverence, and suitability for congregational singing.[12]

Rev. Bullinger's work with young people in St. Stephen's was successful from the beginning. The Sunday schools that he started shortly after moving into the temporary church were so popular that they had a long waiting list. The vicar wrote five series of *Sunday School Lessons*, which were printed so they would be available for those children who could not attend the regular classes.[13]

Moreover, his program for teenagers, called "The Institute for Young People," was well ahead of its time. Rev. Bullinger treated his young adults to a lecture series that was both diversified and current, and all for a few pennies per class. The speakers were chosen from many fields and nationalities; authorities on current affairs, poets, historians, and experts in all phases of biblical scholarship were among those who addressed the young people.

The following schedule for the winter season of 1885 is an example:

> Rev. Frank White, "The Tabernacle of Moses."
> (With limelight lantern illustrations).
> Rev. Dr. Ginsburg, LL.D., "The Bible."
> (Illustrated by ancient MS. and earliest editions).
> Rev. E. P. Cachemaille, "The Human Foot."
> (Illustrated by diagrams).
> Dr. Albert Wilson, "Germs and Ferments, their relation to disease."
> Mr. Eliot Howard, J.P., "The Steam Engine."
> (Illustrated by experiments, models and diagrams).
> Dr. Bullinger, "The Outlines of Botany."
> (Illustrated).[14]

But of all Rev. Bullinger's many contributions during his fourteen years of service at St. Stephen's, he was most remembered and honored for his great knowledge of the Bible and his powerful manner of teaching it. A friend later wrote of him:

> Dr. Bullinger was also a great teacher. He was a Hebrew and Greek scholar, and had a marvellous knowledge of the Bible, with the gift of interesting his hearers in the exposition of its innermost truths. To him it was the Word of God, the revelation to men of the mind and Will of God; he was a convinced upholder of its inspiration and a stout defender of its verbal accuracy, apart from defective translation weaknesses, as his numerous works clearly demonstrate. None who were privileged to attend his Teacher's meetings for the exposition of the Sunday School Lessons he prepared are likely to forget those remarkable gatherings. There was nothing sensational in Dr. Bullinger's methods—his fine presence

and quiet, easy delivery in the resonant voice that charmed all hearers, are still remembered by those who knew him in his prime.[15]

In 1877, nine years after its beginning in Notting Hill, Rev. Bullinger completed his first major publication, *A Critical Lexicon and Concordance to the English and Greek New Testament*. The first edition was published by Longmans, Green & Co., in London. The dedication page of this first edition read as follows:

This work is dedicated to, and designed for, ALL ENGLISH BIBLE STUDENTS, and is so arranged as to be understood also by those who are unacquainted with Greek.[16]

In compiling this great work, Bullinger did not rely solely upon the Stephen's Greek text of 1550, used in the translation of the King James, or Authorized Version, of 1611. The following excerpt taken from the book's preface explains:

In saying that a certain English word is the translation of a certain Greek word, was only saying that that Greek word had the authority of Robert Stephens. It appeared therefore to be a matter of the first necessity to add the results of biblical research in this department since 1624, and to give every variation from Stephen's Text which modern editors have for various reasons thought to be necessary.

But in order that the student may be able to come to some conclusion in the matter for himself, when he sees that certain editors prefer a certain word, and that others do not, it is necessary to give here a brief account of those editors and the principles on which they formed their various Texts.[17]

The publication of the *Lexicon and Concordance,* a landmark achievement in its own right, also marked the commencement of the work for which Bullinger would be best remembered in years to come. Thereafter, and with increasing frequency, he wrote small works and large—books, pamphlets, poetry, and hymns—until his death thirty-six years later. The underlying principle of his later works was the same as that stated in the preface of the *Lexicon and Concordance:* to open the Bible so that all could study it for themselves.

It did not take long after the publication of the *Lexicon and Concordance* in 1877, for recognition of its great value to pour in from all sides. One of its earliest admirers was Dr. Plumtre, Bullinger's professor of Pastoral Theology from King's College days. Speaking before the Croydon Church Congress on October 12, 1877, on the subject of "The best methods of diffusing Biblical and Theological Knowledge," he publicly recommended it:

> Such a book as . . . that very admirable and elaborate English Greek Concordance to the New Testament just published by Mr. Bullinger . . . honestly studied and used, will lead the student of the Word of God to a more enlarged apprehension of its meaning. . . .[18]

The British Quarterly Review, in its October 1877 issue, also praised the new work and noted Bullinger's unique approach:

> The first impression on turning over the pages of this work is a feeling of wonder at the vast amount of literary labour which it represents. The author tells us in his preface that it is a labour which has extended over nine years; and we are sure the labour must have been both hard and continuous to achieve such a result. The plan of the work is new; its aim is to combine a Greek and English vocabulary, lexicon, an outline of grammar, Greek index, textual criticism, and even etymology, in one volume. And we unhesitatingly express our opinion that these departments have been well, carefully, and conscientiously carried out. The Greek scholarship seems generally sound and accurate, and the greatest pains appear to have been taken to ensure correctness, both in the printing and editing.[19]

The Record, another publication of the time, commented:

This is a work of great industry, and of great usefulness.
. . . We heartily commend it as a valuable help to New
Testament study." [20]

From 10 Downing Street, on September 20, came thanks from
Lord Beaconsfield, the prime minister, for the receipt of a copy
of the *Lexicon and Concordance,* stating his "great pleasure in
accepting this elaborate and useful work."[21]

On October 3, the Dean of Canterbury Cathedral sent congratulations to the former chorister:

Nothing but absence from home has prevented me from
acknowledging before your kind present of the copy of
your Lexicon and Concordance to the English and Greek
New Testament. It is a most valuable work very carefully
executed and must have cost you an infinite amount of
labour and careful study. I congratulate you on having
completed so great a labour and one so useful to all
students of God's Holy Word and wish that it may meet
as it deserves with general acceptance.

Believe me, ever
C. Payne Smith,
Deanery, Canterbury

I think it is a great honour to our Cathedral that one of
our choristers should have produced such a work.[22]

Archibald Campbell Tait, Archbishop of Canterbury and Head
of the Church of England, wrote to thank and congratulate
Rev. Bullinger, noting Ethelbert's well-known ancestor, Heinrich
Bullinger:

I trust that it will be found useful by the persons to
whom it is designed and that it may tend to a better
knowledge of the New Testament, a knowledge with
which the name of Bullinger is already appreciated.[23]

On August 17, 1881, four years after the publication of the
Lexicon and Concordance, the Archbishop issued the following
ecclesiastical order to his representative:

> Having thought fit upon the recommendation of the Bishop
> of St. Albans to confer the Degree of Doctor of Divinity on
> The Reverend Ethelbert William Bullinger (clerk), Vicar of
> St. Stephen's Walthamstow in the County of Essex (and
> Diocese of St. Albans) in recognition of his eminent ser-
> vice in the Church in the department of Biblical criticism.
>
> These are to Order and require that you issue forth
> Letters Testimonial of his creation in that Faculty under
> your Seal of Office according to the usual and accus-
> tomed form in the like cases observed and for your so
> doing this shall be your warrant.
>
> Given at Lambeth Palace this 17th day of August in
> the year of our Lord One thousand eight hundred and
> eighty-one.[24]

The Lambeth Degrees, initiated in 1534, were for the most
part theological; degrees in law, medicine, and music were
granted only in very rare cases. The following guidelines were
in effect for conferring the Lambeth Degree in theology:

1. To men who have attained eminence in the Foreign and
   Missionary Work of the Church by some special service,
   generally of a literary character; e.g. translating the Scriptures into a new language; and,
2. In some cases *dignitalis causa* to enable an eminent man
   to hold some office for which the Degree in question is
   technically required.[25]

The Degree of Doctor of Divinity was conferred upon the
Reverend Mr. Ethelbert William Bullinger on August 31, 1881,
after he had signed the Book of Degrees and taken the required
oath of allegiance to the Monarch and the Thirty-nine Articles
of the Church of England. As was the custom, the candidate
wore the academic dress of the university of his own bishop, in
this case the Bishop of St. Albans.[26]

On September 9, 1881, from Westminster Palace, Queen Victoria issued the following proclamation in the official language of the day:

> Victoria by the Grace of God of the United Kingdom of Great Britain and Ireland, Queen, Defender of the Faith. To all to whom these Presents shall come, Greeting! We have seen certain Letters of Creation to those presents annexed which and everything therein contained according to a certain Act in that behalf made in the Parliament of Henry the Eighth heretofore King of England Our predecessor. We have ratified approved and confirmed and for Us Our heirs and successors. We do ratify approve and confirm by these presents so that The Reverend Ethelbert William Bullinger Clerk, Vicar of St. Stephens Walthamstow in the County of Essex and Diocese of St. Albans in the Letters aforesaid named may use have and enjoy freely and quietly with impunity and lawfully all and singular the things in the same specified according to the form force and effect of the same without any impediment whatsoever although express mention of the certainty of the promises or of any gifts or grants by Us are heretofore made to the said Ethelbert William Bullinger by Us made in those presents or any other thing cause or matter whatsoever in anywise notwithstanding. In Testimony whereof We have caused these Our Letters to be made patent. Witness Ourself at Our Palace at Westminster the Ninth day of September in the forty fifth year of Our Reign.[27]

Although the language to modern readers seems woefully obscure, this document put the official Royal seal to the Archbishop's order.

Letters of congratulation to the new Dr. Bullinger poured in. W. H. Longhurst, the Canterbury choir director; Rev. John Philip Gell, the former vicar of St. John's, Notting Hill; and Rev. Kenelm Digby of Tittleshall were among the many who hastened to send their best wishes. Dr. Edward Hayes Plumtre, Bullinger's friend and mentor, wrote the following:

I now have the pleasure of offering you my best congratulations. The honour is one which your labours have well deserved, and I trust that the publicity which in the natural course of things will be given to it will help to call attention to the Concordance and promote its sale. It is a great satisfaction to me to have been in any way instrumental in bringing about this result.[28]

Dr. Bullinger's many friends among his congregation at St. Stephen's expressed their great pleasure in the honor conferred on him. They also gave him a black silk gown with the proper hood, and covered all of the expenses of his degree.[29]

Elizabeth Dodson, the Bullinger's orphaned niece, then seventeen and away at school, wrote to her beloved uncle immediately upon hearing the news:

My dear Uncle,

No words will express my delight when I got Auntie's letter this morning telling me of this grand degree. I am sure even Crusoe must have or ought to have jumped for joy. Fancy Dr. Bullinger, I can scarcely realise it is true. I am so delighted and quite frightened Miss Adcock with my shouts. She wishes me to congratulate you for her. What a stir it will make in Walthamstow. I wonder what Mr. Parry will say? No thoughts will come to me except "Dr. Bullinger."

With oceans of love and congratulations.

Believe me, your ever loving niece, Lizzie[30]

It is difficult to assess the relationship between Ethelbert and his wife, Emma, during this time. While there is evidence to show that sometimes they lived apart during the years in Leytonstone, in Walthamstow Emma's contributions in St. Stephen's parish alongside her husband seem to have been substantial. When William Exton, Weslyan pastor in Brixton, London, and old friend of the family, wrote to Ethelbert congratulating him on the acquisition of the doctor's degree, he hinted that the added workload of the *Lexicon and Concordance* may have been a source of irritation to Emma. He wrote:

> Please give my kind regards to Mrs. Bullinger, and say that I hope that henceforth she will *banish* for ever those predictions she has heretofore uttered concerning you, should you ever attempt another "Book," and try rather to find her own way to future fame by *help-meeting* you all she can, should you deem any improvements essential in any new edition of that already out.[31]

Of course, the age difference between Ethelbert and Emma (she was eleven years his senior) could have become more marked with the increasing years. Emma's health deteriorated as the years passed, and as she grew older, she spent increasing amounts of time "taking cures." She was described by a member of the family as someone "who enjoyed ill health" and each year she resorted to the spas in Bath, a popular spot in the south of England.[32]

It could partially have been Emma's health, and it certainly was his own, that compelled Dr. Bullinger to retire from the heavy burdens of St. Stephen's. On October 19, 1888, as vicar in Walthamstow, he sent the following letter to his congregation:

> To the Congregation of St. Stephen's, Walthamstow.
>
> My dear Friends,
>
> For some time past I have experienced very painfully the great pressure of my work. This pressure is much increased by the feeling that the work is never finished, and that I cannot overtake it.
>
> Two years since, more than one high medical authority warned me very seriously, and gave me three years as the utmost limit at which this high-pressure could be maintained. At first I thought lightly of it, and heeded it not, but since the last winter my own feelings have compelled me to listen, and I began to wonder whether I

was to go on (as so many do) till I broke down permanently, or whether the pressure could in any way be lightened.

In this state of feeling I began, early in this year, to pray that in *some* way I might be relieved of a portion of my work, but in what way this was to be I could not possibly foresee. Could I have curtailed some of my other labours the solution would have been more simple, but whichever way I looked the difficulties were quite beyond my own powers, so that I could only commit my way unto the Lord, and continue in prayer.

At length light seemed to dawn, but it shone in a totally different quarter from that in which I had been looking for it. Without wearying you with each step, it became gradually clearer that the Lord was opening a door, and it was evident that He had other work for me to do. Having enabled me to give the best seventeen [three years curacy in St. Mary's, Walthamstow and fourteen years in St. Stephen's] years of my life to Walthamstow, He would remove me to a sphere, very much less arduous, but not less important.

At first I could not endure the thought of separation, but I became more reconciled to it, when I felt that it was not to be a removal merely to another church and parish, for no church could ever be to me what St. Stephen's has been. In my new sphere I shall have no parochial duties, but shall be engaged chiefly, in directing the Biblical studies of Ladies preparing for Missionary work, while I shall have sufficient opportunities for preaching at the Chapel of the Princess Mary's Village Homes, at Addlestone. I shall thus have less work for my voice, be relieved of all parish details, and have more leisure for important literary work which God in His providence has prepared for me.

The place of our future residence is not yet fixed, for it is not compulsory within certain limits. It will, however, probably be some 20 miles S.W. of London.

I cannot but believe that the Chief Shepherd will provide you with a Pastor who will carry on the work on the same lines; and who will, with more energy and strength, fulfil the work of a Teacher and Pastor amongst you.

I have much comfort in feeling that I have been permitted to see the commencement of the New Building, which with the Church, School, and Vicarage, will complete the necessary organisation of St. Stephen's. I am glad also, that I have been able to take part in making the Parochial Arrangements, etc., for the ensuing winter.

I fear that my labours amongst you must close with the present year. But as I write these words I begin to feel what it will be to leave so large a circle of friends, whose kindness I never before so fully realised. For all this kindness I sincerely thank you; for all the harmony and peace which we have enjoyed, I praise God; and for all the prosperity which He has given to our work, I bless His name.

Separation cannot be otherwise than painful at any time. I feel it to be specially painful in my own case, as I had never suffered myself to contemplate it. Nevertheless, it may be a needful discipline for us all, whereby our loving, ever faithful, and unchanging Saviour is leading us to a more entire reliance on Himself. May He cause much fruit to be borne for His glory by this painful separation.

It may be, also, that this is God's way of causing all things to work together for our good. He may see that the work of "Sowing" has been finished, and that the work of "Reaping" is necessary, so that we may be made to understand the words of Jesus in John IV, 37, "Herein is that saying true, one soweth and another reapeth."

I ask your very earnest prayers for myself, that I may be blessed in the work to which I believe God has called me, and that He may send you a successor who shall labour amongst you for His glory and your good.

Believe me, Your faithful friend and Pastor,

Ethelbert W. Bullinger[33]

The following week, Dr. Bullinger received a letter from the Bishop of St. Albans, who had recommended him for the Lambeth Degree.

> My dear Bullinger,
>
> I have read your most touching address to those to whom you have ministered so faithfully and so happily. I can only say that your words have gone to my heart. May the Lord bless and prosper you in the work to which He has called you—and raise up another in your stead to feed the flock you have tended with all a loving Pastor's care. I did not think we were to lose you![34]

In the final days before his departure, the congregation gave a gift of money and the following declaration, embossed on parchment and decorated with gilt lettering, to their beloved pastor:

> To The Reverend Ethelbert William Bullinger, DD
>
> From the Congregation of St. Stephen's, Walthamstow and other Friends:
>
> Reverend and Dear Friend and Pastor:
>
> With mingled feelings of joy and sorrow we meet you on the eve of your departure from our midst to give expression to our esteem and affectionate regard and to offer you our heartfelt gratitude for the lasting and priceless benefits which you have conferred upon us during the period of 17 years, perhaps the best part of your life, by the faithful proclamation of the Gospel of Our Lord Jesus Christ and the declaration of His Word in all its fullness and the abounding grace of God.
>
> That Word by the divine power of the Holy Spirit has reached our hearts and we record with deep thankfulness to God that He has enabled you to speak as the ambassador of Him, "To preach deliverance to the captives, and

recovering of sight to the blind, to set at liberty them that are bruised, to preach the acceptable year of the Lord."

We unite in accompanying our words with a token of gratitude and praise to the Author of all our blessings and beg you His servant accept it for your own use. We beg to express to Mrs. Bullinger our love and esteem for the efficient way in which she has seconded your efforts for our welfare, according to the measure of her strength and we heartily wish that health and happiness may be bestowed upon yourself and those belonging to you and we pray that your career of usefulness to the Church of Christ may be prolonged.

We hope we shall frequently see you amongst us and we are joyful in the anticipation of meeting you again when Christ shall gather His elect in one communion and fellowship and present them faultless before the presence of His glory with exceeding joy.

The Lord bless thee and keep thee. The Lord make His face shine upon thee and be gracious unto thee. The Lord light up His countenance upon thee and give thee peace.

Signed on behalf of the congregation and friends,

H. W. Carter
Edward Tomlinson Church Wardens[35]

Dr. Bullinger's final teaching to his congregation at St. Stephen's took place on New Year's Day, 1889. It was a time of sorrow for both vicar and congregation, but the vicar expressed his desire to dwell on the truth of God's Word rather than on the sad facts of human parting. Psalm 107:7—"He led them forth by THE RIGHT WAY"—was his text, and his message was one of trust in God's ability to lead His people:

"The right way" is a way of love and grace and mercy, whether we see it, understand it, believe it, or not. . . .

Let these thoughts, dear friends, not only comfort us, but let them really enable us to rejoice. Let them fill us with holy confidence that God will guide and provide.[36]

The Trinitarian Bible Society

IN THE SPRING OF 1867, Rev. Bullinger, then twenty-nine and assistant curate in St. Peter's, Notting Hill, was accepted for the office of clerical secretary to the Trinitarian Bible Society. Ethelbert Bullinger's affiliation with this society was to be long and fruitful, lasting the rest of his life and deeply influencing both parties.

The Trinitarian Bible Society came into being on December 7, 1831. It was an institution born of protest. A look at the history of its parent institution, the British and Foreign Bible Society, will explain what occurred.

The British and Foreign Bible Society was established in 1804, during a time of great upsurge in foreign missionary work. It had been conceived as a worldwide, interdenominational effort to bring the Bible to all peoples in their own languages and, as such, had flourished from its inception. Yet it wasn't long before the very diversity of the membership began to cause difficulties.[1]

The first difficulty seriously to trouble the ranks was the question of which version of the Bible should be distributed under the name of the British and Foreign Bible Society. The King James, or Authorized Version had been used exclusively for the first ten years; in any case, there is no record of the "versions question" coming up during that time.[2]

By 1814, however, the Society's branches in predominantly Roman Catholic and Lutheran countries had greatly increased in number. To accommodate them, the original regulations were relaxed to include the sending of Apocryphal versions that had been in use in those denominations. When this practice came to light among the members of the Society, much disagreement ensued. British members, in particular some of the Scottish Presbyterians, objected on the grounds that the Apocrypha was not inspired. Its inclusion, they maintained, would contaminate the true Word of God and "perpetuate the error of those who vested the Apocrypha with a false authority."[3] Was it morally right to send Bibles containing the Apocryphal books to Lutherans and Roman Catholics outside of England because they would accept them more readily than the Authorized Version? Was it worth compromising on doctrine for the sake of numbers?

The controversy was never really resolved. On paper, the British members were placated and their patronage assured, but in reality many Apocryphal Bibles were still distributed on the Continent under the auspices of the Society.

The second major difficulty arose several years later when it became apparent that the membership of the Society now included large numbers of Unitarians. Unitarianism, which denies the deity of Christ, had spread rapidly in Europe in the early part of the nineteenth century. Before long, many of the Society's branches (or auxiliaries, as they were called), especially those on the Continent, consisted almost exclusively of Unitarians. The more conservative members of the Society, who believed in the deity of Christ, found this situation unacceptable.[4] Complaints escalated when other Christian societies began to close their memberships to Unitarians, declaring that only "persons professing a belief in the Holy Trinity could be members or governors."[5]

At the same time, it became quite popular in Christian circles to open meetings with prayer. When this question came up within the British and Foreign Bible Society, the leadership refused to commit itself. Certain members, convinced that this was due to fear of offending the Unitarians by public prayer "in the name of Jesus Christ," pressed the question, but to no avail.

Still not quite satisfied with the way in which the "versions question" had been handled, these members now felt doubly determined to make themselves heard. After a fruitless attempt to voice their opinions in committee, they decided that they

DR. ETHELBERT WILLIAM BULLINGER, SECRETARY 1867–1913

had no recourse but to force the issues of opening prayer and
Unitarian membership at the Annual Meeting in May 1831. The
gathering erupted into chaos. Old resentments, doctrinal differences, and religious prejudices all finally surfaced. At the
end of a stormy five-and-a-half-hour session, the membership
voted, by a majority of six to one, to retain the *status quo*.[6]

On May 20, 1831, the following resolution was passed by a
committee formed from those who had been in the minority:

1. That the persons now present do form a Provisional Com-
    mittee, with power to add to their number, for the pur-
    pose of uniting in such measures as may induce the British
    and Foreign Bible Society to reconsider the decision of
    the late Anniversary General Meeting of that Institution,
    and to bring about a separation in point of Membership
    from those who do not acknowledge the doctrine of the
    Holy Trinity.
2. That a Society whose exclusive object is to circulate the
    pure Word of God, containing that Gospel which is the
    power of God unto Salvation to everyone that believeth,
    must be considered decidedly a Religious Society.
3. That considering the British and Foreign Bible Society to
    be a Society of the character above described, it is the
    opinion of this Meeting that the deniers of the doctrine
    of the Holy Trinity cannot consistently be admitted as
    Members of it.[7]

For a number of months, the members of the Provisional
Committee attempted to persuade the parent Society to recon-
sider its policies. By November 1831, however, it was decided
that there were no grounds for reconciliation. A resolution was
passed to form a new Bible Society.[8] And so it was that on December 7, 1831, more than two thousand people gathered at
Exeter Hall in London to found a new Society and very explic-
itly to affirm its basic beliefs.

That it is the opinion of this Meeting that a Society engaged in circulating the pure word of God, and upon
which devolves the responsibility of preparing and issu-

ing new translations of the Holy Scriptures, must be considered decidedly a religious Society, and one that should be conducted on scriptural principles; and that those only who are Protestants and acknowledge the scriptural doctrine of the Holy Trinity, can consistently be admitted Members of such a Society, or be fit agents to conduct or carry on such a work.[9]

The following excerpts are from the laws and regulations also adopted at that meeting:

I.   That this Society be designated the TRINITARIAN BIBLE SOCIETY.
II.   The object of this Society is to promote the Glory of God and the salvation of men, by circulating, both at home and abroad, in dependence on the Divine Blessing, the HOLY SCRIPTURES, which are given by inspiration of God, and are able to make men wise unto salvation, through faith which is in Christ Jesus.
III. This Society shall circulate the HOLY SCRIPTURES, as comprised in the Canonical Books of the Old and New Testaments, WITHOUT NOTE OR COMMENT, to the exclusion of the Apocrypha; the copies in the English Language shall be those of the authorised version. . . .
IV.   The MEMBERS of this Society shall consist of PROTES-TANTS, who acknowledge their belief in the GODHEAD OF THE FATHER, OF THE SON, AND OF THE HOLY GHOST, THREE CO-EQUAL AND CO-ETERNAL PER-SONS IN ONE LIVING AND TRUE GOD. . . .
XII. [Now XIII]. This Society, acknowledging the ignorance and helplessness of man, deems it a bounden duty to express its entire dependence upon the Blessing of JEHOVAH, the FATHER, the SON, and the HOLY GHOST, in its "work of faith, and labour of love, and patience of hope," by offering up Prayer and Praise at all its Meetings.[10]

In the years following its birth, the Trinitarian Bible Society struggled with insufficient funds but continued to print and distribute Bibles both in England and abroad. It also became involved in Bible translations, the initial undertaking being the first-ever Protestant translation of the Bible into Portuguese. Rev. Thomas Boys, M.A., of Trinity College, Cambridge, was put in charge of the project. A pioneer in the field of biblical structure, Rev. Boys was the author of *Key to the Book of Psalms,* later edited and further developed by Ethelbert Bullinger. Bullinger also edited and added references to Boys's Portuguese translation of the Scriptures in 1872, producing the first-ever Portuguese Reference Bible.[11]

This first step was followed by translation work in Spanish. In both of these endeavors, the Trinitarian Bible Society held fast to its rule of not translating or circulating any version other than the Authorized Version. This, of course, led to frequent skirmishes with the British and Foreign Bible Society, which continued to circulate only the Authorized Version in England but on the Continent any version "that the people would accept."[12]

The greatest battle facing the young organization, however, proved to be its depleted treasury. By the 1850s and early 1860s, the financial situation had deteriorated so badly that the Society was frequently without staff because they were unable to pay them. In the ten years before 1867, three "clerical," or executive, secretaries had come and gone with little being accomplished. In that year, because of pressing financial problems and the death of many of the original founders, the Society seemed at the brink of dissolution.[13]

At this desperate juncture, Ethelbert Bullinger applied for the position of clerical secretary. Rev. John Robbins, vicar of St. Peter's, Notting Hill, and Bullinger's employer, wrote to the committee of the Trinitarian Bible Society on behalf of his young assistant:

Gentlemen:

I understand that the Reverend E. W. Bullinger at present serving with me as assistant curate is a candidate for the post of secretary to your society which is about to become vacant by the resignation of my friend the Rev. H. B. Clissold. I beg to state that Rev. Bullinger takes this step with my full concurrence. I have now known him several years and am well assured that such is his character that neither the interests of your society nor of my parish would suffer by his undertaking both. . . . I consider Mr. Bullinger to be a sincere earnest and sound Christian man, businesslike, methodical and accurate. He is a good composer and a preacher far above the average and from what I can see of his manner of addressing a large and highly educated congregation I should say he would make a good and weighty public speaker.[14]

The appointment of Ethelbert Bullinger to this position marked the beginning of a new era in the history of the Trinitarian Bible Society. In Bullinger the Society had at last found a man whose intelligence, energy, and resourcefulness could put it above water financially and, more importantly, whose adherence to principle matched their own. Ethelbert Bullinger was willing to fight for principle if a fight was necessary. "If a matter is *personal,* do not strive about it," he would say, "but, if it is a matter of *principle,* then strive for it, and, if need be, die for it."[15]

This conviction was made evident again and again during his tenure as clerical secretary for the Society, a post he held until his death forty-six years later. Despite his heavy parish duties and increasing literary output, Bullinger was tireless in his efforts on behalf of the Society. He traveled all over Europe, organizing auxiliaries, addressing meetings, and publicizing the work of the Society. He spoke up again and again on the vital question of the circulation of Roman Catholic versions on the Continent, usually inviting public comment, frequently bringing criticism upon himself, and sometimes incurring harsh accusations. The "versions question" was debated with members of the British and Foreign Bible Society in pamphlets, the religious press, and newspaper columns. Controversy had never been a thing from which Bullinger shrank, certainly not for a cause he espoused so completely. During one heated exchange regarding the Roman Catholic Vulgate version of the Bible, he wrote:

Surely, sir, the duty of a *Bible* Society is to circulate the
revelation God has vouchsafed to give us, in the purest
possible translation "whether they will hear or whether
they will forbear," mindful of God's denunciations against
those who "add to" or "diminish from" that "pure Word."
But what is the duty of the British and Foreign Bible
Society, as set forth by themselves in their own printed
documents? "The work of the Bible Society is to circulate the best translation that people will take" and "are
willing to accept." To an unprejudiced reader the simple
statement of this will carry with it its own refutation.[16]

Bullinger's opposition to the British and Foreign Bible
Society's open policy of accepting versions other than the Authorized Version was often quite forceful. In reply to a demand
from a Mr. Knapp for an apology during a correspondence later
printed in the *Portsmouth Times,* Bullinger wrote:

If in my zeal and jealousy for that Word I have said anything that may wound Mr. Knapp, I beg him to pardon
me. They are the wounds of a friend. I love *the Bible*
better than a Bible *Society*. I prefer to put my confidence
in God rather than in noblemen or committeemen, however eminent, but I am not become their *enemy* because
I tell them the truth.[17]

One verse Bullinger frequently cited as being a "doctrinal
corruption" in the Vulgate Bible was Exodus 20:5,[18] where
changes in the wording enlarged the meaning so as to justify
the Roman Catholic tradition of the veneration of images.

Exodus 20:5:
(Vulgate Version)

Thou shalt not adore them, nor serve them: I am the
Lord thy God, mighty, jealous, visiting the iniquity of
the fathers upon the children, unto the third and fourth
generation of them that hate me.

(Authorized Version)

Thou shalt not bow down thyself to them, nor serve them: for I the Lord thy God *am* a jealous God, visiting the iniquity of the fathers upon the children unto the third and fourth *generation* of them that hate me.

Likewise, he cited Matthew 3:2,[19] where the word *repent* had been changed to *do penance*, thereby supporting the Roman Catholic practice of auricular confession, penance, and priestly absolution.

Matthew 3:2:
(Vulgate Version)

And saying: Do penance: for the kingdom of heaven is at hand.

(Authorized Version)

And saying, Repent ye: for the kingdom of heaven is at hand.

Yet, the most frequent target of his criticism was the translation of Genesis 3:15,[20] which, according to Roman Catholic interpretation, referred to Mary—rather than Christ—as the bruiser of the serpent's head.

Genesis 3:15:
(Vulgate Version)

I will put enmities between thee and the woman, and thy seed and her seed: she shall crush thy head, and thou shalt lie in wait for her heel.

(Authorized Version)

And I will put enmity between thee and the woman, and between thy seed and her seed; it shall bruise thy head, and thou shalt bruise his heel.

Bullinger wrote,

> I can produce evidence from Pope, Archbishop, Bishop, Abbot, and Priest, besides a number of Romish books, to show that this text, thus corrupted, is universally referred to the Virgin Mary, and made the ground of transferring to the creature the glory belonging to the Creator.[21]

In July 1875, under the direction of Rev. Bullinger, the Trinitarian Bible Society announced an essay contest. Prizes amounting to £375 would be awarded for the "four best Essays on the origin, growth, and effects of the circulation of Romish and other corrupted Versions of the Holy Scriptures in Foreign Countries by a large section of Protestant Christians; and on the best means of putting an end to this pernicious practice."[22] Despite protests from the British and Foreign Bible Society that this contest was nothing more than a "systematic attack which is being made throughout the country," 101 competitors submitted entries. The winning essay was printed and distributed free to every clergyman in England.[23]

Yet, debate and controversy, though seemingly ever present, were not the only matters that took up Dr. Bullinger's time on behalf of the Society. From the very start of his tenure, he made outreach a high priority, particularly among the auxiliaries or branches.

The Trinitarian Bible Society's method of operation was similar to that of the British and Foreign Bible Society in that any group of interested people could form a local Society auxiliary, hold meetings, promote the distribution of Bibles, and collect funds.[24] Bullinger's many travels and speaking engagements among the auxiliaries yielded more interest, more members, and, of course, increased funding. New life was breathed into the Society.

One area of renewed activity was Spain. The printing of the Protestant New Testament in Spanish had been undertaken as early as 1845; yet, financial difficulties had caused the distribution of it to be delayed until 1858. Even then, the work proceeded slowly because of governmental restrictions placed on any religious activity besides that of the official (Roman Catholic) Church. In 1868, the year after Bullinger assumed the secretariat of the Society, the time finally seemed right. The Spanish Revolution of 1868 had ushered in an era of relative religious tolerance, and the Society, now with fresh funds and greater vigor, decided to renew its efforts.

The first Bible Depot was opened on Calle de San Geronimo, one of the principal streets in Madrid, and proved a great success. Along with the depot, a horse-driven "Bible-coach" to take the Bible to outlying areas was partially funded by the Society.[25] All in all, so many Bibles were distributed that the Society decided to start printing them in Spain itself rather than sending them from England. In 1875, the Society purchased printing equipment and sent it to Spain for this purpose. Rev. Bullinger took a personal interest in this work, making several trips there during his frequent visits to the Continent.

During one journey in 1883, Dr. Bullinger took his first trip to the Breton Mission in Tremel, France, in the province of Brittany. The Trinitarian Bible Society had been approached about underwriting the cost of translating the Bible into Breton, one of the Celtic languages. Dr. Bullinger went to Tremel on behalf of the Society to investigate the possibility of work in this new area.

Brittany, situated in northwestern France, was inhabited by people of Celtic origin, a heritage they shared with many who had settled in Scotland, Ireland, Wales, and Cornwall. Brittany had lost its political sovereignty to France in 1495, but it had always retained a fierce cultural independence, using its own language and following its own customs. Religion had evolved into a mixture of ancient druidical superstitions intertwined with strict Roman Catholicism.

To introduce the Bible into this area would take a unique person. Such a one was Pasteur Guillaume LeCoat, born in 1845 in Cotes-du-Nord in Brittany, the grandson of a well-known Breton fabulist, or storyteller, and national poet.[26]

LeCoat had first became acquainted with the Bible as a young man. He had embraced it wholeheartedly and immediately began a course of study. The only available Bible teacher lived in the neighboring village of Morlaix, about thirteen miles away.

In the beginning, LeCoat made the trek on foot once a week, but soon he was going three times weekly. His diligence was rewarded when, after three years of study, Pasteur William Monod of Paris decided to sponsor him at the College of the Reformed Church in Paris. Three years later, LeCoat success-fully passed examinations at the Sorbonne and took degrees in letters and law. In 1866, he returned to Tremel to preach the gospel in a small mission under the auspices of the Baptist Mis-sionary Society.[27] It was there that LeCoat realized the impor-tance of having the Bible translated into Breton, a language still spoken by about two million people.

The following incident illustrates something of Pasteur LeCoat's rare commitment:

> At a reception given to the members of the *Société des Savants* in Paris in 1881, Monsieur Ferry, the Minister of Public Instruction, said to him:
> "I have heard, M. LeCoat, that you are going to trans-late the Bible into the Breton language?"
> "Yes," was his answer.
> "Well," said M. Ferry, "you are going to do a useless work. This Breton language is coming to an end, and in fifty years French will be spoken everywhere in France."
> "Well, sir," said M. LeCoat, "in fifty years, if God will spare us, we can do something."
> M. Ferry, putting his hand on M. LeCoat's shoulders, said:
> "There is a Celtic head on these shoulders."
> LeCoat's translation was to lead to a revival of the Breton language.[28]

When Ethelbert Bullinger came to Tremel, he met in LeCoat a man whose drive and conviction matched his own. They be-came fast friends and remained so for the rest of their lives. As Dr. Bullinger himself stated, "From my first visit in 1883 I have seldom let a year go by without going to see our friends and their work."[29]

With the support of the Trinitarian Bible Society, Pasteur LeCoat began that same year to translate the New Testament.

In 1884, the Old Testament was begun while sections of the Gospels, already completed, were printed and distributed. The entire Bible was published in 1889 and received gratefully by many Breton believers.

In writing the story of the Breton Mission many years later, Dr. Bullinger described how one man received it:

> On the morning of the arrival of the Bibles an aged man was at LeCoat's door at 5 o'clock, with the money he had saved up, a sou at a time. He thought the Pasteur was late in getting up; and that Christians were later still in letting the poor Bretons have the Bread of Life. He asked "Why are we the last of the nations to have the Bible put into our hands?" Alas, they are not the last; but it was something accomplished when, at length, the time arrived for the Bretons to have the first Bible in their own language.[30]

During this time, developments in a distant part of the world were to prove fateful to the Breton Mission. Henry M. Stanley's discoveries in Central Africa had drawn the attention of the great missionary societies away from their smaller existing works toward the exciting goal of opening the "Dark Continent." The Baptist Missionary Society was no exception to this trend. Because of its increased interest in Africa, it withdrew its support of Pasteur LeCoat's work, thus leaving the young mission suddenly bereft of funds. Pasteur LeCoat sent a desperate plea for help to his friend Dr. Bullinger.

With the aid of Bullinger and others in the Trinitarian Bible Society, a new organization was formed: the Breton Evangelical Mission. Day-to-day operations were left entirely in Pasteur LeCoat's hands, but funds were provided by the Breton Evangelical Mission Society, based in London. This Society, made up predominately of Trinitarian Bible Society members, "helped and sustained" the Breton mission with fund-raising and by arranging speaking tours for Pasteur and Madame LeCoat. Dr. Bullinger was the new society's first honorary secretary.[31]

On that first visit to Tremel in 1883, the following incident occurred, as described later by Dr. Bullinger:

GROUP AT TREMEL, FRANCE. CENTER SEATED ARE PASTEUR AND MME. LECOAT TO BULLINGER'S RIGHT, ELIZABETH DODSON IN BACK ROW, BEHIND MME. LECOAT.

On the occasion of my first visit I went to the Sunday worship in Tremel, and I was surprised not to hear any Breton Tunes.

I asked the Pasteur afterwards how it was; and why they had French and American music? He replied that they could not have Breton Tunes when they had the Harmonium. I asked whether they were so difficult that they could not be played?

No, he said, we do not have the music of them from which to play, so we sing them without accompaniment.

Are you so poor then (I replied) that you cannot afford to buy the music. No, he said we cannot buy it, because it does not exist. It has been handed down from generation to generation and has never been written down.

Well then, I replied, it shall be written down; and at once.

So, on the same afternoon, several people were brought in to sing to us. As they sang I wrote down the music (for as John Hullah once said, "a musician is one who can see music with his ears and hear it with his eyes.")

That afternoon, I wrote down 19 tunes, and, having harmonized them, I left them in MS. for the use of the congregations.[32]

In 1888, Dr. Bullinger completed this work with the help of a grant from the Society of Religious Treatises of London. Pasteur LeCoat described the method:

Several people, one of whom was aged 79 years, came and sang before him; and from their lips, after an assiduous piece of work lasting several days, he collected the means to enrich his former collection and crown his work with success. Dr. Bullinger collected 66 of these airs, which he harmonized in such a way that they could be sung by four voices and played on the organ, the harmonium and on the pianoforte, or accompanied by these instruments. . . .

Nothing of this kind has appeared up to the present in our Breton language.[33]

Two allied achievements that distinguished the Trinitarian Bible Society during Dr. Bullinger's secretariat were the publishing of the Old and the New Testaments in Hebrew. The Society had long been interested in the distribution of the Scriptures among European Jews and had given grants to various organizations active in missionary work with them. One such organization was the Mildmay Mission to the Jews, founded in 1876 by a close friend of Dr. Bullinger, Rev. John Wilkinson. Reverend Wilkinson introduced Dr. Bullinger to Isaac Salkinson, a man who had been described as "by far the finest writer of Hebrew that Europe in this century has produced."[34]

The meeting was recounted by John Wilkinson in his autobiography:

> After a while I thought of the Trinitarian Bible Society, the secretary of which Society, the Rev. Dr. Bullinger, I knew well, though of the Society itself I knew little or nothing. I wrote to Dr. Bullinger at Walthamstow, and requested an interview.
>
> Through an oversight I received no reply to this request, though other matters were answered. The matter stood over til the 26th of December 1882. This being a holiday, I walked over for a constitutional, and laid the whole matter before Dr. Bullinger. His reply was, "It seems quite providential, for we have just had a legacy, and have been praying for guidance as to its use; lay the matter in writing before our committee, and they will probably take it up." This was done. Mr. Salkinson and the committee came to terms. Shortly after, however, and before the translation was finished, dear Salkinson was called to rest.[35]

Convinced of the importance of the task, the Trinitarian Bible Society now began to search for a Hebrew scholar to continue the work on the New Testament. The man whom they engaged was Dr. Christian David Ginsburg, a friend of Salkinson and a Hebrew scholar of outstanding capabilities and commitment.

Born in Warsaw in 1831, Ginsburg had studied at the rabbinic college in that city, but he was converted to Christianity in 1846. He came to England and for a time was connected with the Liverpool Branch of the London Society for Promoting Christianity Among the Jews. Soon, however, he gave up this work to devote himself almost exclusively to literary endeavors. In 1855, he embarked on the great work of his life—the publication, with explanation, of the Massorah, the unique Hebrew system of notation used by ancient scribes to ensure accuracy in the text of the Old Testament.

When the Trinitarian Bible Society contacted him, Ginsburg temporarily set aside his work on the Massorah and took over the New Testament project, which he saw to its completion. In 1885, a first edition of two thousand copies of the Hebrew New Testament was published. It sold out within a month. The second revised edition of 110,000 copies was published in 1886 and sold out within three years. It circulated as far as North Africa, Hungary, Poland, Rumania, Germany, and Russia.[36]

Both Rev. Wilkinson and Dr. Bullinger were instrumental in opening up the Russian Empire to the distribution of the Hebrew New Testament early in 1887. Rev. Wilkinson described how it occurred:

> While all this was going on abroad, and our hands pretty full with the growing work at home, we were earnestly praying that the Lord would open Russia, where nearly 4,000,000 Jews are located, or about 1/3 of the Jewish population of the world. Mr. Mathieson [superintendent of the Mildmay Mission] and I had a very friendly interview with the Russian Ambassador, His Excellency Count Staal, who advised us to put ourselves in communication with our own Ambassador in St. Petersburg. The Reverend Dr. Bullinger in the meantime sent copies of the New Testament to all the leading Censorships in the Russian Empire, and obtained permission to send them into the country.[37]

That opened the doors that led to the distribution of more than 100,000 Hebrew New Testaments all over the Russian Empire.

After completing his friend Salkinson's work on the Hebrew New Testament, Dr. Ginsburg returned to his own life's work. His connection with the Trinitarian Bible Society had not ended, however. When one phase of his monumental research project, a new edition of the Hebrew text of the Old Testament, was finally ready in 1894, the Trinitarian Bible Society published it. As the Society's account explains:

> All the best Hebrew manuscripts contain a mass of information written by the scribe in the upper and lower margins of each page, and also frequently between the columns.
>
> This information is called the Massorah, which means tradition. It contains nothing in the way of comment or interpretation of the sense of the text, but only that which relates to the words, their structure, form, and place, with the object of preserving and transmitting the text in its purity and integrity; for which reason it is often called "a fence to the Scriptures."[38]

Dr. Bullinger had made the offices of the Trinitarian Bible Society available to Dr. Ginsburg. In his own pamphlet on the Massorah, Bullinger described in detail how this prodigious task had been completed. He praised not only Dr. Ginsburg for his massive effort but also the British government for its support of the project:

> . . . the Massorah, as it gradually increased, far outgrew the small compass afforded by the margins of the mss.; and even when it extended in some cases to separate treatises at the end of the books of the Bible, no one ms. could contain the whole. Hence it became dispersed and spread over all the mss., some having parts of it common to many other mss., others having portions almost, and in some cases quite, unique. It became necessary, therefore, to examine every accessible ms. and collect and transcribe the whole so far as this could be done. For the accomplishment of this task Dr. Ginsburg spent more than thirty years of his life in collating mss.

in Europe and Asia, devoting his own private resources
in no unstinted measure, aided by grants of public money
made by both political parties. The Massorah which has
been thus collected has been published in four large
folio volumes. It may be called in some sense a national
work; at any rate, it is a work of which the English nation may be proud; a work which does honor to his own
indomitable patience and perseverance, and a work
which was the issue of labors fraught with such important results to all who are interested in Biblical studies.[39]

In 1897, Ginsburg's *Introduction to the Massoretico-Critical Edition
of the Hebrew Bible* was published by the Trinitarian Bible Society.
In the preface, Dr. Ginsburg noted his friend's assistance:

To my friend the Rev. Dr. Bullinger, the learned secretary of the Trinitarian Bible Society I am entirely indebted for the elaborate Indices as well as for his help in
reading the proofs.[40]

With the passing years, Bullinger continued to pour time and
energy into the work of the Society and was intimately concerned with every phase of its operations. "He carried the affairs of the Trinitarian Bible Society at his fingers' ends,"
someone commented of him after his death.[41] Indeed, Bullinger's
lifelong contribution to the Trinitarian Bible Society should not
be underestimated—nor should the Society's influence on his
life.

CHAPTER SEVEN

The Last Parishes

WHEN THE BULLINGERS left Walthamstow in early 1889, they moved to the little village of Woking in Surrey, southwest of London. A quiet and beautiful rural spot, Woking was, in the words of a contemporary sales catalogue:

> . . . in the heart of one of the loveliest parts of the coun-
> try, and from its commanding position all the beauties
> of the neighborhood are open to it . . . its surroundings
> of large heath covered Commons constitute it one of
> the healthiest spots in the Country, a fact well known to
> the leading physicians who strongly recommend it to
> their patients.[1]

The Bullingers' home, which they named Bremgarten after the small Swiss community where Heinrich Bullinger had been born, was situated in the Mount Hermon area. A large tract "of superior character," this area featured spacious plots along gently curving roads with comfortable Victorian homes.[2]

Dr. Bullinger became the chaplain for two allied institutions, the Princess Mary Village Homes and Byfleet Hall, in the neighboring villages of Addlestone and Byfleet. Both were establishments for the education of young women. Their founder and directress, Susanna Meredith, was Bullinger's new employer. He soon found that her energy, conviction, and love of the Bible were similar to his own.

Born in Ireland in 1823, Susanna at a young age had exhibited unusual intelligence and love of learning. She studied French, German, Latin, and later Hebrew. She was also a skilled biblical scholar. Often, early in the morning, she would trace the roots of Hebrew words in the text, claiming that this gave rest to her mind. She was passionately fond of music, played the piano well, and had a fine contralto voice.[3]

Left a childless widow after only a few years of marriage, Mrs. Meredith moved to London in 1860. Once there, she became interested in the problems of women of the lower classes. One day a friend said to her, "Why do you not do something for the most helpless class of women in the world, those discharged from prison, who drift out of it without friends, home, or character? What can they do but return to its shelter? Do go and see Brixton Prison."[4]

A visit to the prison, during which she talked to many of the inmates, convinced Susanna to help these women. In 1864, she rented a small house opposite Tothill Fields Prison, and there she opened a mission house. Every morning, she and her helpers provided breakfast for the women who were leaving prison. They proclaimed the love of God to them and gave encouragement and practical advice. The Prison Mission enjoyed immediate success. Many of Susanna's friends came to help, and soon the work included sewing classes for those women looking for a means of employment.[5]

In 1865, Susanna rented a house near her own in Bayswater, London, and outfitted it as a laundry as a further avenue of employment for the women. Those who wanted to work had to arrive at 8:00 A.M. in time for prayers. This endeavor, called Nine Elms Mission, was also quite successful. Lord Shaftesbury, famous lay leader of the Evangelical Party of the Church of England, became its first president, and Queen Victoria was numbered among its benefactors.[6]

Much of the success of Susanna's efforts to help these women must be attributed to her own determination and personality. The following description, given by her sister, Mary Anne Lloyd, indicates some of the qualities that made Susanna unique:

> Mrs. Meredith had an uncommon personality. To her friends she was often very amusing, her fund of humor,

pathos, and power of adaptability to her audience being
remarkable. She was distinctly "human," and had an intense sympathy with the circumstances and conditions of
all who applied to her for help or counsel; and this formed
one of her greatest attractions. She was a great lover of
young people, and inspired many to be useful in their
day and generation; idle people she could not bear, and
she often said that constantly going to religious meetings
might degenerate into a feeble Christian life. "Be in earnest," she frequently said to the young, "anything is better than being neither hot nor cold; even the Lord Himself
could not make use of that service. . . ."[7]

Her influence on the women of the Mission was a
strongly personal one, and her love and interest in them
and their children, and even in their relations, was in-
tensely real. She remembered everything about them,
even after long lapses of time; her memory for faces was
wonderful. She rarely "sermonized," but gave them
wholesome, practical advice.[8]

Susanna's deep involvement led to the founding of the Princess
Mary Homes in the early 1870s. Concerned about the plight of
the children of these women, Mrs. Meredith prevailed upon
some of the mothers to allow her to place their children in safe,
healthy environments outside of London. The powerful support
and generous financial contribution of Princess Mary Adelaide,
Duchess of Teck, got the building program under way and by
March 1872, children had moved into the first cottages.[9]

Like many other programs that Susanna Meredith established,
the Princess Mary Homes were ahead of their time and eventually became the model for similar institutions to follow. The
complex consisted of a "number of brick cottages, the central
building forming a school house, having a small tower containing a clock, striking the hours."[10] A quiet green and gardens
surrounded the buildings, each of which was designed for small,
family-like groups of about ten children with a housemother to
care for them.

Nearby Byfleet Hall housed older girls and gave them sound
religious and practical training. This program included prepa-

ration "for the Oxford and Cambridge local examinations and for all higher branches of women's education,"[11] thereby ignoring the conventions of the day that kept women out of these institutions.

A major portion of Dr. Bullinger's duties as chaplain of Princess Mary Village Homes and Byfleet Hall was conducting divine services in the chapel on Sunday mornings and evenings. Other duties included the monthly celebration of the Lord's Supper and the overseeing of the religious education of the students according to the following guidelines:

> The children shall be religiously brought up in the knowledge of the Holy Scriptures, and shall be brought up as members of the Protestant Episcopal Church, now by law established in England, and known as "Evangelical." There shall be daily family worship, morning and evening, in each dwelling, and the daily reading and explanation of Scripture shall form a part of the course of instruction in the Schools.[12]

The following comment was written years later by a young woman who had been a student at the school:

> As chaplain to a girls' boarding school in the country, he fathered and taught a number of girls and my sister and I were among a few who got to know him and value his friendship. His scholarship, his student mind, his kindliness and his sense of humor endeared him to us all and I have always reckoned it as one of the privileges of my life that I was allowed to know him.[13]

Dr. Bullinger obviously had not lost that love and concern for individuals that had so endeared him to previous congregations. His personal touch was a habit too deeply ingrained ever to be abandoned; it remained, indeed, a hallmark of his life until the very end.

Yet, the truth is that the Woking years would mark a most significant change in Bullinger's career: a move away from one-to-one work with people toward literary endeavors that would, in future years, touch the lives of so many all over the world. He was now finally free from the demands of pastoring a large congregation, with its endless committees, constant need for diplomacy and, as he himself had said, "the work [which] is never finished and that I cannot overtake. . . ."[14]

This period saw no extensive literary output, although several small works were published, including *The Name of Jehovah in the Book of Esther* and *The Spirits in Prison*. The importance of these years lay rather in the fact that the research work, which had of necessity been kept in the background, now came to the forefront. The foundation of biblical knowledge that had been laid many years before with the preparation of the *Lexicon and Concordance* was now built upon and expanded. And more and more frequently, Bullinger was called upon to speak at Evangelical conferences and congresses.

Called "Missions to the Converted," these gatherings were aimed toward spiritual revitalization and reaffirmation. Notable among these gatherings were the Mildmay Conferences organized by William Pennefather, vicar of St. Jude's Church, Mildmay Park, London. In 1869, Rev. Pennefather established the Mildmay Conference Hall, which seated twenty-five hundred people. It was the site of frequent evangelical gatherings during his life and for many years following his death in 1873.[15]

Pennefather's goal in these conferences was to draw "into closer sympathy and brotherly love those whom ecclesiastical divisions and party differences tend to estrange from each other, and who yet are one in spiritual life and true love for the Lord Jesus."[16]

Bullinger's first known lectures outside of his parish, a series of ten sermons on the "Second Advent of the Lord Jesus Christ," were given at St. Ebbe's Church, Oxford, in November 1887, the year before he left Walthamstow. These sermons became the foundation for his tenets not only on the Second Coming but also on the identification of the three groups of people named in the Bible—the Jews, the Gentiles, and the church of God—and the differentiation between the "kingdom" and the "church."

In the sermons, Bullinger allied himself with a small number of other people who were also studying Bible prophecy. These same teachings, however, set him apart from most Bible scholars of his day and would become the cause of much comment and criticism in the years to come.

In the first sermon of this series, titled "The Importance of Prophetic Study," Bullinger stated:

> However unimportant the Study of Prophecy may be in the judgement of men, we learn from our text that it is a subject of the greatest importance in the sight of God.
>
> It is true that the great majority of professing Christians dismiss prophecy as being at once unimportant and uninteresting. This may be because instead of allowing God to mean what He says, each interpreter declares that He means something very different, and thus the ordinary Bible reader is bewildered with the Babel around him: or it may be that the belief that Christ will not come till at least a thousand years, makes it useless to look for Him or to study the Scriptures which speak of His return: or it may be that the belief that, practically, Christ comes at the death of each believer, renders it a matter of little consequence whether He will return before or after the Millennium. . . .
>
> As to ourselves, all our hopes are built on prophecy. The promise of future victory, the pledge of Resurrection, the joys of Heaven, the hope of glory and all that we know about them is nothing but prophecy.
>
> Surely, if we may judge of the importance of a doctrine by the prominence given to it in the word of God, then we may say that we have in prophecy a subject "whereunto ye do well that ye take heed in your hearts." . . .
>
> Surely we should not lightly esteem that part of God's word to which we are specially exhorted to "take heed in our hearts"; and on which He has thus specially set His seal. Nor can it be right to speak of those who "love His appearing" as eccentric! Alas, that they are eccentric is only too true, but this only shows how far the bulk of professing Christians have drifted from the Divine order and the Divine importance of God's Word.
>
> If this doctrine which holds so large a place in the

Bible is neglected, and unheeded by the majority of professing Christians, we need no other evidence that the Church is departing from the faith, and has entered on the "down-grade."

If we were asked to name the subjects which are put forward to-day with the greatest frequency and urgency, we should say, they are *Baptism* and the *Lord's Supper*. But note the place which these occupy, and the position given to them in the Epistles, which were written specially for the instruction of the Church. Baptism is mentioned only 19 times in 7 Epistles (the noun 5 and the verb 14), and it is not once named in 14 out of the 21 Epistles; and as for the Lord's Supper there are not more than three or four references to it in the whole of the New Testament. In 20 (out of 21) of the Epistles it is never once alluded to! From the prominence given to it by man, one would imagine the New Testament to be filled with it. It is not a question of one subject being important, and another not; but it is a question of *proportion* and relation; and certainly if the Scriptures contain *twenty* references to the one subject of the Lord's Coming, to *one* reference concerning another, we may say that God has settled for us what He deems profitable for us, and important.[17]

Sentiments like this were certainly controversial, but Dr. Bullinger was never one to fear controversy. Despite his religious background and education, he never allowed himself to be limited by ingrained habits of religious tradition. The testimony of the Bible was most important to him. Time and time again he endeavored to bring people back to the Bible even if this defied their religious traditions. "Tradition is like the tether," he would say, "which prevents an animal from getting a blade of grass beyond the length of that tether."[18]

The series, *Ten Sermons on the Second Advent*, was published the year following its delivery and occasioned much comment. A fragment of a letter dated May 17, 1888, gives one reader's reactions:

I am longing to tell you my beloved friend, with what deep interest and I trust instruction I have been carefully reading Dr. B's sermons, they seem to me most precious and valuable, so clear that no intelligent reader could misunderstand, so strictly scriptural that every statement is based upon the imperishable truth of God. Some of his statements were new to me but very striking, the very prominent place given to the second coming in N.T. even compared to other solemn declarations and injunctions.

I think the style very attractive and the division of the chapters very effective. I am very thankful for such a man and such a teacher. How it proves that talent blessed by God is a great gift for the Church of God. May it be much owned to His praise in the establishing many in the faith as it is in Jesus.[19]

At the National Protestant Congress, held in London in 1890, Bullinger affirmed his stand on the inspiration and authority of Holy Scripture:

The Inspiration of Holy Scripture, and therefore its Divine authorship and authority, lies at the root and foundation of true Christianity—not only in its relation to infidelity, but also in its relation to the Romish controversy.

It was the one great question which underlay all others at the Reformation. For, what was the Reformation in its essence? Was it not just the abandonment of human authority for Divine authority? Was it not all contained in this—the giving up of the authority of the Church for the authority of the Word of God? . . .

What does God say about His own Book? What does God claim for His Word? What does that Word claim for itself?

Because, if those claims are not true, then the Book cannot possibly be a good Book! It cannot be worthy either of our consideration or our confidence. . . .

Protestants are *witnesses for* God and His Word. We

are not merely political partisans; we are God's witnesses. We must have infallibility somewhere. We must refuse to acknowledge an infallible Pope: we cannot believe in an infallible Church or discern its so-called "voice": we look in vain for infallibility in poor, fallen, human reason, or in the darkened understanding of mortal man, which needs to be illuminated with Divine Light. We must therefore hold fast the faithful Word, or we have nothing, absolutely nothing, to trust to. We must hold fast by the infallibility of the inspired Word, and ever maintain that "The Bible, and the Bible alone, is the Religion of Protestants."[20]

In April 1891, after two and a half years at Mrs. Meredith's schools, Dr. Bullinger resigned his position there and became the minister of Brunswick Chapel, in St. Marylebone, London. The family continued to live in Woking. The household at this time consisted of Dr. Bullinger, now fifty-three; his wife Emma, who was sixty-four; his sister-in-law, Sophia Dodson; his niece Elizabeth, now twenty-six; three young female boarders; and two servants.[21] The whereabouts of the Bullinger's two sons, Ethelbert Augustine, twenty-nine, and Bernard Stratton, twenty-five, is unknown.

The reasons for Bullinger's change of position are not clear. Certainly Brunswick Chapel was in a prestigious location and, as an increasingly prominent preacher, Dr. Bullinger could command a large congregation there. The fact that Brunswick was a "proprietary," or privately owned, chapel would make it possible for him to receive a greater income than the £45 per year he received from Mrs. Meredith.

Brunswick Chapel, located in the affluent area of St. Marylebone between Hyde Park and Regent's Park, had been purchased at auction in 1796 by Lord Portman as a chapel for his own use. At the time of the sale, it was described as a "spacious elegant chapel, built in an uncommon substantial Manner, and finished in a Stile [*sic*] of simple Elegance. The Situation surrounded by most respectable Inhabitants. . . ."[22]

After the chapel passed out of the hands of the Portman family little is known about it. Like so many other proprietary chapels all over England, once the patronage of its first owner was lost, it might have been leased to an individual who would sponsor a clergyman willing to make his living from it. Proprietary chapels were independent from local parish churches, and records show that they were often at odds with them. By the nineteenth century, the realities of church life were such that only chapels that employed superior preachers made any money. Most of them quietly closed their doors.[23]

Brunswick Chapel would seem to be no exception to this trend; Dr. Bullinger was the third minister in the four years immediately prior to 1891. His growing reputation as an excellent, if controversial, preacher of the Word was no doubt the incentive for offering him the position. Dr. Bullinger was to be the last minister of the chapel. In 1893 the lease on the building ran out, and the holders did not renew it. By February 15, 1894, the chapel was known as St. Mary's Mission Chapel and was run by the Salvation Army.[24] Sometime during these years, the Bullinger household moved to 39 Harewood Square, London. Later, they returned to the country again, this time to Bromley, Kent, about ten miles southeast of London.

Dr. Bullinger's three years at Brunswick Chapel were significant for his literary output. The third edition of the *Critical Lexicon and Concordance* was issued in 1892, followed closely by the publication of two major books: *The Witness of the Stars* in 1893 and *Number in Scripture* in 1894. Both of these volumes were results of Dr. Bullinger's reworking, refining, and restating of biblical research projects originated by others.

In *The Witness of the Stars,* Bullinger used material gathered by Miss Frances Rolleston and published posthumously in 1879 under the title *Mazzaroth,* or *The Constellations.* As he explained in the preface:

> Some years ago it was my privilege to enjoy the acquaintance of Miss Frances Rolleston, of Keswick, and to carry on a correspondence with her with respect to her work, *Mazzaroth:* or *The Constellations.* She was the first to create an interest in this important subject. Since then Dr. Seiss, of Philadelphia, has endeavoured to popularize her work on the other side of the Atlantic; and brief

references have been made to the subject in such books as *Moses and Geology,* by Dr. Kinns, and in *Primeval Man;* but it was felt, for many reasons, that it was desirable to make another effort to set forth, in a more complete form, the *witness of the stars to prophetic truth,* so necessary in these last days.

To the late Miss Rolleston, however, belongs the honour of collecting a mass of information bearing on this subject; but, published as it was, chiefly in the form of *notes,* unarranged and unindexed, it was suited only for, but was most valuable to, the student. She it was who performed the drudgery of collecting the facts presented by Albumazer, the Arab astronomer to the Caliphs of Grenada, 850 A.D.; and the Tables drawn up by Ulugh Beigh, the Tartar prince and astronomer, about 1450 A.D., who gives the Arabian Astronomy as it had come down from the earliest times.

Modern astronomers have preserved, and still have in common use, the ancient names of over a hundred of the principal stars which have been handed down; but now these names are used merely as a convenience, and without any reference to their significance.

This work is an attempt to popularize this ancient information, and to use it in the interests of truth.

For the ancient astronomical facts and the names, with their signification, I am, from the very nature of the case, indebted, of course, to all who have preserved, collected, and handed them down; but for their interpretation I am alone responsible.

It is for the readers to judge how far my conclusions are borne out by the evidence; and how far the foundation of our hopes of coming glory are strengthened by the prophecies which have been written in the stars of heaven, as well as in the Scriptures of truth.

For the illustrations I am greatly indebted to Jamieson's *Celestial Atlas,* 1820; Flammarion's *L'Etoiles;* Sir John W. Lubbock's *Stars in Six Maps,* 1883; and to the late Mr. Edward J. Cooper's *Egyptian Scenery,* 1820. For the general presentation and arrangement of the Constellations

I am responsible, while for the drawings my thanks are due to my friend Miss Amy Manson.

It is the possession of "that blessed hope" of Christ's speedy return from Heaven which will give true interest in the great subject of this book. . . .

May the God of all grace accept and bless this effort to show forth His glory, and use it to strengthen His people in waiting for His Son from Heaven, even Jesus which delivered us from the wrath to come.[25]

Was there a witness during the years before the Bible was written down? In the written Word itself, Bullinger declared, God states that His purposes were revealed in the heavens, that the stars were set by God "for signs and seasons." What could these signs signify if not the coming of the Messiah and the nature of his great work?

For more than two thousand five hundred years the world was without a written revelation from God. The question is, Did God leave Himself without a witness? The question is answered very positively by the written Word that He did not.[26]

For the most part, *The Witness of the Stars* was received with high interest and good reviews. "Well worthy of careful study" and "has a most fascinating influence upon its readers" were quotes from ecclesiastical journals.[27]

Others took exception to Bullinger's conclusions. Indeed, with every new publication the number of his critics seemed to multiply. Although he took notice of what was being said against him, he continued, unperturbed, to share his findings with those who wanted them.

"It is good of you to take so much trouble to defend a poor worm like myself," he wrote to a friend, Mr. Roth, in 1892, "and sad indeed that any such defence should be needed. I shall be glad to hear from you again when you have read the little books, [1.] "The Kingdom" and [2.] "The Church" which were written for you. Please

give our Christian love to your dear wife and believe me,
yours affectionately. E. W. Bullinger."[28]

In 1894, a year after the publication of *The Witness of the Stars,*
Robert Brown, himself an author on biblical subjects, wrote a
booklet titled *A Reply to Dr. Bullinger's So-Called 'Witness of the
Stars.'* He opened with some of the major criticisms being leveled
against Bullinger before taking up his own case against the book:

> Dr. Bullinger has lately published several small works, in
> which he has set forth doctrines which are opposed to
> the teaching of the Divine Word; —as for instance, that
> "the kingdom" and "the Church of God" are *"totally and
> altogether distinct";* and that they *"can never be identified*
> without serious loss of sense and truth." . . .
>
> Again, he has taught . . . very erroneous doctrines as
> to the second coming of the Lord, with reference to the
> Church of Christ—dividing the second coming of Christ
> in effect into *two* comings, the one *for* His Church *previ-
> ous* to "the great tribulation," and the other to the earth
> in judgement upon His enemies *after* the tribulation—
> statements which are flatly contradicted by the Word
> itself. . . .
>
> In a later, and a larger, work, however, entitled, "The
> Witness of the Stars," I am sorry to say, that the Doctor
> has advanced views, which are not only equally unsound,
> but are far more dangerous than those I have already
> referred to: for in this Book he has taught doctrines which
> certainly savour of heresy; if indeed they be not in them-
> selves, as many even think, distinctly heretical. . . .[29]
>
> But the great evil of the Book lies . . . in its teaching
> *that we have* IN THE STARS, *another revelation from God,*
> which the Doctor asserts is as "pure and undefiled," and,
> therefore, as authoritative and true, as the revelation
> which we have in the Bible itself; and as the *so-called*
> science of *Astrology* is again rapidly coming to the front,
> and has many adherents, in these days, my solemn con-
> viction is that this work will greatly tend to foster and
> extend this abomination. . . .[30]

Seemingly unruffled by the barrage of criticism, Dr. Bullinger's only answer was to come out within the year with another major research work.

Number in Scripture: Its Supernatural Design and Spiritual Significance was the second of his books resulting from the study and reworking of previously published material. In a long-out-of-print work titled *Palmoni*, Dr. Milo Mahan of New York had compiled various existing studies on numerics in Scripture, some of them quite old and fragmentary. Dr. Bullinger reworked and expanded these in an attempt to explore the entire field, including the significance of numbers in the fields of botany, physiology, chemistry, sound, music, and color. He also affirmed his stand against the ever-increasing number of "scientific theories" so prevalent by the 1890s.

> Instead of making the Bible agree with science, science must agree with the Bible. If it does not, it is only because it is "science falsely so-called," and not real science. *Scientia* is the Latin word for *knowledge*. Whereas very much of what goes by the name of "science" today is not science at all. It is only *hypothesis!* Read man's books on this so-called science, and you will get tired of the never-ending repetition of such words as "hypothesis," "conjecture," "supposition," etc. This is the reason that such theories, which are falsely dignified by the name of *science,* are constantly changing. We talk of the "Science of Geology," or of "Medical Science"; but read books on geology or medicine, for example, written fifty years ago, and you will find that they are now quite "out of date." But *truth* cannot change. Truth will never be "out of date." What we *know* can never alter! This of itself proves that the word *science* is wrongly used when it is applied only to *hypotheses,* which are merely invented to explain certain phenomena.
>
> It is not for such *theories* that we are going to give up facts. It is not for *conjectures* that we are going to abandon truth. . . .[31]

As to God's design behind the use of numbers in the Bible, "the greatest and most important of His works," Bullinger stated:

> We can have neither words nor works without "number." The question which we have to answer is—Is number used with design or by chance? Surely if God uses it, it must be with infinite wisdom and with glorious perfection. And so it is. Each number has its own significance; and its meaning is found to be in moral harmony and relation to the subject matter in connection with which it stands. This harmony is always perfect. Every word of God's Book is in its right place. It may sometimes seem to us to be deranged. The lock may be in one place, and the key may sometimes be hidden away else where in some apparently inadvertent word or sentence.[32]

Dr. Bullinger then went on to explore the number of occurrences of specific words and phrases in the Bible, along with the significance of individual numbers, where they occur, and their meaning in context.

In *Number in Scripture*, Bullinger indirectly alluded to the work of a man who had died a few years before Bullinger was born but whose work in biblical studies was to influence him significantly. As he explained:

> The Church [in the first century] soon became corrupt, and before the Canon of Scripture was complete it had lost the true teaching concerning
>
> 1. The "Mystery" (or secret) concerning the Body of Christ, the Church of God;
> 2. Justification on the principle of faith alone; and
> 3. The work of the Holy Spirit.
>
> At the Reformation, the *second* of these was partially recovered. Some sixty years ago the *first* was recovered, but was speedily perverted; while the *third* has never been fully or properly recovered.[33]

In these cryptic remarks, Bullinger alluded to the work of Edward Irving, who had burst on the ecclesiastical scene about sixty years before like a blaze of light but whose short, controversial ministry was deemed a failure by contemporary opinion.

Edward Irving was a man of controversy. Some people called him a "brilliantly gifted man";[34] others said that he was a stubborn fanatic given to long-winded sermonizing.[35] Born in Annan, Scotland in 1792, Irving, at the age of twenty-seven, became the assistant to Dr. Thomas Chalmers, the famous Scottish minister of Glasgow. There, despite an uneasy relationship with Dr. Chalmers, he developed into a serious student of the Bible and a gifted preacher. A few years later, in July 1822, he was called to London to become the minister of the principal Scottish chapel in that city.

Irving's farewell sermon to the congregation in Glasgow was characteristic of this passionate, florid, and fiercely independent young man:

> There is a tide in public favour, which some ride on prosperously, which others work against and weather amain. Those who take it fair at the outset, and will have the patience to observe its veerings, and to shift and hold their course accordingly, shall fetch their port with prosperous and easy sail—those again, who are careless of ease, and court danger in a noble cause, confiding also in their patient endurance, and the protection of heaven, launch fearlessly into the wide and open deep, resolved to explore all they can reach, and to benefit all they explore, shall chance to have hard encounters, and reach safely through perils and dangers. But while they risk much, they discover much; they come to know the extremities of fate, and grow familiar with the gracious interpositions of heaven. So it is with the preachers of the Gospel. Some are traders from port to port, following the customary and approved course; others adventure over the whole ocean of human concerns; the former are hailed by the common voice of the multitude, whose course they hold; the latter blamed as idle, often suspected of hiding deep designs, always derided as having lost all guess of the proper course.

Yet of the latter class of preachers was Paul the Apostle
. . . of the same class was Luther the reformer . . . of the
same class was Calvin, the most lion-hearted of
churchmen . . . such adventurers, with the Bible as their
chart, and the necessities of their age as the ocean to be
explored, and brought under authority of Christ, are
not to be despised, because they are single-handed and
solitary. . . .[36]

With oratory such as this, Irving came to London in 1822
and took the city by storm. People of all classes and religious
backgrounds came to hear him, and soon the little Scottish chapel
in Hatton Gardens was filled to overflowing with a large and
loyal congregation. Irving also became active in the controver-
sies within the British and Foreign Bible Society as an outspo-
ken critic of the distribution of Apocryphal Bibles.[37]

During his years in London, Irving gave particular emphasis
to doctrines relating to the Second Coming of Christ. Together
with Henry Drummond, he organized a series of yearly conferences on the subject of biblical prophecy. These conferences
were attended by various members of Irving's congregation who
in later years would be numbered among the founders of the
Trinitarian Bible Society.[38]

During the summer of 1829, while convalescing from an illness, Irving translated *The Coming of Messiah in Glory and Maj-
esty* by Juan Josafat Ben Ezra (1747–1801), a Spanish Jesuit who
had been a convert from Judaism. Ben Ezra's only known work,
this book had been printed posthumously in Spain in 1812 and
subsequently translated into several European languages. From
these writings, Irving uncovered material that he then expounded in a series of five lectures delivered in Dublin in 1829.
In the final lecture, titled "The Second Advent of Our Lord,"
he stated:

The subjects, dearly beloved brethren, on which I dis-
coursed to you in the former Lectures, have been admitted by all; there is a ground for *them*, in the common
faith of the church, as well as for the *one* I am now about
to deliver, on the coming, and kingdom of our Lord; for

it [is] as constant an article of the church, that he should come again . . . as it is that he once came. . . . Yet, from the unwillingness of the mind of men to lay hold of the common hope of the coming of the Lord, it has come to pass, that it has almost escaped from the thoughts of the church: and instead of looking to that glorious event, and to all the circumstances connected therewith, the church has nearly forgotten it, and instead of it, to take up with miserable substitutes, such as that every man should think but of the day of his death; from which consideration there comes not joy nor strength, but weakness and oppression. . . .

But it is the duty of the church to look for the appearing of Christ, because it is the doctrine of the church; it is so expressed in all her creeds, confessions of faith, and articles; his coming is not a spiritual or providential coming, words which I re-assert were not heard of until within these fifty years; but a personal coming, a coming in person. . . .

The great end of the coming of the Lord, and which to us should be matter of joy, and not of alarm, will be to fulfill every jot and tittle of his book; to fulfil his own word, not to permit one jot or tittle of the law and the prophets to fail, but to fulfill all. . . .

Where now are the spirits of those who believed in him, while their bodies are in the grave? They are no doubt enjoying rest, and blessedness, and the vision of God; they are enjoying all which such souls can enjoy; but still they are not present with the Father as Christ is. The presentation to the Father is to be at the coming of the Lord, as is proved by the passages of Scripture to be found in 1 Thess. iii.13, and ii.19; Jude, 24 verse . . .

This then is the second thing which Christ has to perform, to raise his saints out of the grave, and to take them into his own glory, and there to present them to the Father.[39]

Edward Irving's adherence to this doctrine, that only at the return of Jesus Christ and not at the time of his or her own

death does the Christian appear before God, set him apart from
the mainstream of Christian teaching. His teachings on this subject were partially responsible for the resurgence of interest in
prophetic studies after centuries of neglect.

In 1892, E. W. Bullinger referred to Irving's work in "Christ's
Prophetic Teaching in Relation to the Divine Order of His Words
and Works":

> During the last sixty years [the Church's] testimony has
> been concerning Christ's Second Advent. Here, again,
> there is a slight overlapping, for all through the ages
> those have not been wanting who have expressed their
> belief in that article which is contained in all our creeds,
> and which testifies to the fact that "He shall come again
> with glory to judge both the quick and the dead"; just as
> ever since the Reformation, the truth as to the atone-
> ment, and justification only by faith through grace has
> been set forth more and more clearly. But none the less
> is it true, that during the last sixty years the Lord's re-
> turn from Heaven has become the great and blessed
> hope of the Church as it never has been before. When
> Edward Irving first translated the work of Ben Ezra, from
> the Spanish, he had reason to believe that there was at
> that time no other living testimony to that glorious truth.
> It is within our own knowledge how that testimony has
> spread, until now we have quite an extensive modern
> literature on all the departments of truth connected with
> the Second Advent, such as never existed before; and
> coming from all parts of the professing church, except
> Rome and the Romanizers.[40]

Nor was Irving the only scholar to bring to light views regarding prophecy that differed substantially from the religious *status quo*. During the 1820s, a group of men—among them
Benjamin Wills Newton, Percy Hall, J. G. Bellett, John Nelson
Darby, Henry Craik, and George Müller—formed a group that
became known as the Plymouth Brethren. They shared "a profound faith in the authority and adequacy of Holy Scripture
and the gospel contained therein" and were convinced that the

hope of the church, Christ's return, should be more widely studied and taught.[41] Distressed by the condition of the church, they decried what they felt was a too heavy emphasis on missionary work and a neglect of Christians' spiritual lives.[42]

Along with Edward Irving, the Brethren believed that Christ's second coming would be a personal return to gather His church, an event that would occur before the judgments recorded in the book of Revelation.[43] The Brethren defined the church as those believers who have lived or will live between the Day of Pentecost and the return of Christ, having Christ as their head, and the presence of the Holy Spirit as their distinctive characteristic.[44]

The Brethren also distinguished between the periods of the Old Testament law and the age of grace. It was Christ's perfect sacrifice, they claimed, that made possible an age of grace, which was not characterized by law but by believing in the risen Christ.[45]

E. W. Bullinger, in his work *"The Kingdom and The Church,"* written in 1892, also emphasized the differences between biblical classifications of people:

> A great principle was stated, and a solemn command was given, when the Lord Jesus said, "What therefore God hath joined together, let not man put asunder." (Matt. xix.6)
>
> But the converse must be equally true, and we may assert as a like divine principle—*What God hath put asunder, let no man join together!*
>
> It is scarcely too much to say that all the confusion that abounds in connection with God's Word, and especially with prophetic truth, arises from the violation of one or other of these two foundation principles. . . .
>
> Now this is the duty which we have to perform with regard to these two—"the Kingdom," and "the Church." Nowhere are they said to be the same; nowhere are the terms used synonymously: God has separated them. . . .
>
> "The Kingdom" is none other than that which forms the great subject of Old Testament promise and prophecy. The Kingdom which was offered and presented to Israel by the Lord Jesus in the Gospels is the same Kingdom

which we see set up with divine judgments and power in the prophecies and visions of the Apocalypse. . . .
[The Church consists] of those who have been born again by the Holy Spirit and made by Him new creations in Christ Jesus; who belong to God; whom the Father gave to the Son (John xvii), and whom the Son came to save, and did save with an everlasting salvation; who have eternal life, and shall therefore never perish. . . .[46]

Although the Brethren movement flourished at first, during the middle of the 1840s a severe split occurred between John Nelson Darby and Benjamin Wills Newton. Personality clashes and doctrinal disputes were blamed. The result was that Newton, Craik, Müller, and their adherents became known as the Open Brethren while Darby and his followers formed the Exclusive Brethren.

It was a sad and turbulent time, as can be seen by the following account, written by Mrs. Anne Evans, a member of the Bethesda Congregation, a branch of the Open Brethren:

[We were] for a time shattered from end to end. Friendships were broken up; families were divided—husband from wife, children from parents, business relations were dissolved, health and even reason wrecked. We sadly needed humbling. We had begun to think too much of ourselves. We had increased rapidly in numbers and even in worldly standing, for many had joined us from the upper classes. Our leading brethren, too, were without any check. . . . All this was more than flesh and blood could stand, so Satan was permitted to come down on us and humble our pride in the dust. . . .
At this time of sorrow Mr. George Müller was a grand stay to us; he did not lose his head; he held the reins with a steady hand; and when at last Bethesda emerged from the turmoil she was stronger, freer than ever before.[47]

While it is true that Bullinger and the Brethren shared many doctrinal positions in their study of Scripture, it is also true that, through the years, members of the Brethren became among his most persistent critics.

CHAPTER EIGHT

Things to Come

THE YEAR 1894 MARKED for Ethelbert Bullinger, then fifty-seven, both an end and a beginning. With the expiration of the lease on Brunswick Chapel, he ended his tenure as minister, and with his subsequent move to Bromley, Bullinger finally gave up formal church ministry. He had served in the Church of England for thirty-three years in various parishes and institutions, of which Brunswick Chapel was the last. From then on, he lived privately and devoted his time to his Bible study, writing, and work with the Trinitarian Bible Society.

During this same year, Dr. Bullinger began a project that was to involve him until the end of his life: the monthly publication of *Things to Come,* a scholarly journal of biblical studies. Bullinger was the very heart and soul of this publication, from its first issue in July 1894 until his death in June 1913. His own writings were printed in its pages before they were published elsewhere; many of his books appeared there in serialized form. The columns "Signs of the Times" and "The Editor's Table" became barometers of his concerns, prejudices, and views on current events. The twenty-one volumes (nineteen edited during his lifetime and two published posthumously) of *Things to Come* are today the richest source of information on Bullinger.

Things to Come was founded under a trust, with Sir Robert Anderson, Rev. Sholto Douglas, James E. Mathieson, and Dr. Bullinger as trustees.[1] Bullinger was also editor in chief of the

publication. It was originally conceived as a journal for the Prophetic Conferences, a series of gatherings that were

> . . . intended to be the beginning of a new movement
> which will, we humbly hope, embrace the whole world
> in testimony to our coming Lord.
>
> Such testimony has been borne now and again, here
> and there in recent years; but . . . no definite organiza-
> tion has been set on foot for this all-important subject
> until the arrangements were made for these. . . .
>
> It is clear that just as other Conferences and Subjects
> have their own organ, so these Conferences need, and
> should have, their own special organ.
>
> The promoters are unable to use any existing journal,
> and feel very strongly that such an organ ought not to be
> the private property of any individual, however excellent.
> Nothing will meet the case short of putting its property
> and its editorship under a Trust, so that the maintenance
> of fundamental truth may not be jeopardized; and that
> the profits may be devoted to the extension of the Con-
> ference work and the interests of the Truth alone. . . .
>
> After much thought, we have decided to make the
> basis of our new paper as wide as the Conferences them-
> selves. These embrace The Inspiration of the Scriptures,
> The Restoration of Israel, and the Personal Premillennial
> coming of the Lord Jesus. Our aim is to reach a large
> number of general Bible-loving readers, and to increase
> their love for the appearing of Christ—the *Living* Word,
> as they already love to find Him in the *Written* Word.
> We have therefore named our new journal THINGS TO
> COME: A JOURNAL OF BIBLICAL LITERATURE, with
> Special Reference to Prophetic Truth—The Official Or-
> gan of Prophetic Conferences.
>
> It will be addressed to all who love the Lord Jesus
> Christ in sincerity, who study His word, and wait for His
> glorious appearing.[2]

This journal was to contain special features such as "Conference Addresses," edited wherever possible by the speakers them-

selves; "Notes for Bible Study"; and, unique to this journal, "Illustrations of Bible-Structure." Each issue would also include three regular columns: "The Signs of the Times," "Questions and Answers," and "Notes and Notices."[3]

By 1898, the Prophetic Conferences were forced to close down for lack of funds. Bullinger was loathe to see his brainchild fold along with them, and with the consent of the other trustees, he assumed complete responsibility for continuing the journal.[4] The task proved to be considerable.

In March 1898, Bullinger wrote an open letter to his readers:

> In answer to the inquiries of some correspondents, it may be well to state that we have a large supply of questions. Our general rule is to take them in the order in which they are received, but when any are of special interest, and likely to be more generally useful, we give them precedence for the edification of the larger number of our readers. Some questions also demand more time than the Editor has at his disposal, for he has many other duties devolving upon him, and he carries on this magazine wholly in the interest of its readers, and without realizing any remuneration. He can only afford, therefore, to give the time which ought really to be taken for rest of mind and body.
>
> We are thankful to say that up to the present there has been no loss, and that our circulation is gradually increasing. Still, if any of the Lord's servants are able of their abundance to relieve us of all care, it would greatly encourage us to persevere against the weariness of the flesh, the opposition of "evil servants," and the worry and burden of business and financial arrangements, which we ought not to bear in addition to all the rest.
>
> The fewness of our reviews of books arises from the fact that the hours of the day are not sufficient to read them.
>
> We wish, also, that we had sufficient financial margin to enable us to dispense with all advertisements, so that we might devote the whole of our pages to Biblical matter.
>
> Were it not for the many letters of appreciation and

thanksgiving which we receive constantly from the poor of the Lord's flock in all parts of the world, we should often be tempted to give up this extra tax upon our strength.

We are tempted to say as much as this because we believe that very few are aware that the Editor has now the whole of the financial responsibilities and the business arrangements resting upon his shoulders, as well as the editorial labours.

We are making no appeal, but think it is more satisfactory that our readers should know and understand exactly what our position is.[5]

On May 7, 1898, Bullinger received a letter from Mr. Fred Newth, a reader from Sutton, Surrey, offering his services as bookkeeper and business manager for the journal. Newth also took it upon himself to set up a general fund to be used as working capital. He contributed the first £5, suggesting that twenty readers who were able should match that amount "of their abundance."[6]

Mr. Newth continued to manage the business affairs of *Things to Come* until his death on September 3, 1906. Although obituaries were not usually included in *Things to Come,* Dr. Bullinger made an exception in this case:

> From the moment we asked for help, on taking over the financial and other responsibilities of *Things to Come,* Mr. Newth *offered himself,* and kindly undertook to keep the accounts and attend to the business part of the work. His ripe experience and deep knowledge of Dispensational Truth has been, now, for some years, our constant comfort and help; and our almost daily intercourse was strengthening and refreshing. We are sure our many readers will sympathize with us; though it may not be possible for them to fill the gap which his death has made.[7]

After Mr. Newth's death, Dr. Bullinger was once again forced to grapple with the financial and business concerns of *Things to*

Come. As he shared with readers in October 1909, he looked to God to provide the finances and assistance he needed:

> If the Lord has further need of *Things to Come* He will, most assuredly make His will clear to us, and put it into, and lay it upon, the hearts of one or more of His stewards to find his or her joy in undertaking this service for His truth's sake.[8]

The increased workload and financial pressures notwithstanding, *Things to Come* provided the perfect vehicle for Bullinger's need to communicate. Different areas of life caught his attention, and *Things to Come* was the outlet to express his opinions on them. Nor was it without humor. Few others of Bullinger's many literary works give such a revealing glimpse of what his many friends knew to be an integral part of his personality: a piquant and lively sense of humor. The following sampling from the pages of *Things to Come* serve as an example:

SALAD BETWEEN SERMONS.
**Chicago Man Thinks He Has Solved Problem
of Gospel For the Million.**

"Chicago, Sept. 28.—Rev. John Boyd, of the First Presbyterian Church of Evanston, has solved, or thinks he has solved, the problem of filling the churches on Sunday evenings. He argues that a hot roast beef sandwich is better than much preaching; if beautiful women and splendid singing will not attract to the service, only one thing will, and that is a hearty meal. Consequently a new plan was tried. This was the programme of the church last evening:—

Hot roast beef sandwich; hymn No. 338, four stanzas; hot coffee, chocolate, tea; brief talk by elder; lobster salad, potato salad, shrimp salad; patriotic hymn; chafing dish indigestibles, prepared by beautiful girls; olives, pickles, radishes, young onions; Doxology."—

Mail Empire, Toronto, Sept., 1903[9]

A Baseball Service.

"A sensational preacher in the town of St. Louis, Central Michigan, has lately been startling his congregation by holding a 'baseball service.' The church was decorated with all the implements used in playing baseball, and in his sermon the preacher compared features of the game with phases of life. He spoke of the 'pitcher's' nerve, and likened him to the Christian soldier; said that the 'first base' was meditation, the second conviction, the third repentance, and the 'home plate' Heaven; he dilated on the qualities of the 'batsman,' the 'catcher,' and the 'shortstop.'"

But what we may notice as most significant, he said nothing about the "umpire." His judgement on all this is yet to come![10]

Igorrotes at Church Festival.
Head Hunters in Demand to Assist in Lifting Church Debt.

"The Bontoc Igorrotes are scheduled to appear in a new role, one which will greatly surprise their friends, and may be the means of getting them into bad odour with their orthodox pagan brothers now on the islands. They are to assist at a strawberry festival in aid of a fund to lift a debt from the church building of St. Charles Borromeo, of St. Charles, Mo.

Doctor Wilson yesterday received a pressing request from O. J. Martin, of St. Charles, in behalf of the church, to permit the savage head hunters to come, in all their native dress—or undress—to the church festival next Tuesday evening, to eat savory dog and dance and do the other merry stunts for which the Igorrotes are famed.

There is a debt of $2,500 on the church, and the parish committee believes that the *Igorrotes can do what nobody else has been able to do as yet–to lift it*. The church is willing to furnish baked dog, and to furnish a special car for the Igorrotes' journey to St. Charles, and *anything else in reason to get the popular savages*.

Doctor Wilson did not give his consent immediately, but it is probable that the matter will be left to the

Igorrotes themselves, and *if they are willing* to help the good cause along, they will be sent to the strawberry festival."

The above is from a St. Louis newspaper of June 10th, 1904.

These "Igorrotes" are part of the U.S.A. Government exhibit from the Philippine Islands, at the St. Louis Exhibition.[11]

Nor was it just religion gone rampant in the United States that came in for Bullinger's scorn. The following appeared in the August 1897 issue regarding a parish in London:

NEW-LAID EGG SERVICE!

And why not? And why stop at eggs? And why not every Sunday? If our God can be honoured and worshipped in this way, where is the limit at which to stop? Truly, as we have before said, wherever the *flesh* is concerned "the dose has to be increased"!

The Record, June 25, gives the following news quite seriously and gravely, and without comment:—

"A unique service was held at St. John's, West Streatham, last Sunday afternoon. For the past four years the Curate-in-Charge has asked for contributions of new-laid eggs at the afternoon service on Hospital Sunday. Last year 1,618 eggs were presented. This year, as Hospital Sunday fell on the day of national thanksgiving, this service was made as widely known as possible, as a *unique way of marking the Jubilee.* Altogether 300 donors were represented at the service, but of these no less than 257 made their offerings of new-laid eggs in person. The total number of eggs given or sent was 5,092, of which about a hundred were broken before they came to the service through the railway or parcel post, and only twenty after they reached St. John's."[12]

The appearance of increasing numbers of modern language Bible versions never failed to arouse pointed comment from the editor. One version, prepared by the feminist movement, evoked the following item.

THE WOMAN'S BIBLE.

Another New Bible! The object is to "revise" all the texts and chapters directly referring to women. Doubtless this New Bible is to be "revised" in order to bring it up to date. "The New Woman" decidedly requires a new Bible, for there is nothing about her in the old Book.[13]

As the Christian Science movement grew and spread in the early years of the century, traditional views of health, sickness, and medical services became a subject of discussion in religious circles. A review by Dr. Bullinger of two booklets authored by a friend, Philip Mauro, gave insight to his thinking on the subject:

It is asserted throughout the two booklets that, in all cases of sickness, a child of God should trust wholly in the Lord; and that it is a sin of the utmost gravity to consult a Medical Practitioner, or even to depend on the use of any "means" he may prescribe.

It is asserted that these latter gentlemen are all working in the special sphere of Satan's activities and works; and that it is not possible for any one of them to diagnose a physical disorder in a child of God. . . .

It is asserted that sickness among saints is one of the principal works of Satan. . . .

And further, that diseases in the people of God are really caused by some departure either individually or corporately, from the ways of God. . . . In proof of this latter proposition we are urged to "see Deut. 28.21,22,27,28,35,59,60,61."

But we are sure that no one can read those verses without seeing that they must refer exclusively to the People of Israel, and to the Land of Israel; for the promises and threatenings include one just as much as the other, and can have no possible general reference to Gentiles as such, or to the Church of God.

As to the *second* statement, it is contrary to the

experience of the vast majority of our readers. For we all know of many godly Physicians who must feel slandered by being spoken of as they are in these pamphlets (for we find no exception made in their favour).

Moreover, it is contrary both to fact and experience that they are "unable to diagnose a disease in a child of God. . . ." We are thankful that this is only the author's statement, and not the statement of God's Word, for it is contrary to our every day experience. Moreover, it is equally contrary to our experience as to *the cause* of disease among the children of God. We all of us know many of blameless life and sure and certain trust in God, of whom the statements made are wholly untrue. It is easy for one in robust health to write these hard things, but there are thousands of believers who will be saddened, and perhaps maddened by them. . . .

The writer fails to define the sense in which he uses the term *"Trusting God,"* but we are easily able to detect the only sense in which the expression is used; viz., that we are not to use any means whatever; any such use being wholly incompatible with any real trust in God. . . .

Our own definition of "trusting God" in this sphere is no different from that trust which we should have in Him "at all times" (Ps. 62.8).

When we have need of any supply and we trust in the Lord, He supplies *our need* by *His own means:* means which He employs, and which become ours when used by us.

If He supplies our own financial need, He does not give us the money miraculously, so that we put our hand in our pocket and find it there; but He employs means of *showing* us, in His own perfect way, and of guiding us (Ps. 32.8), what we are to do; or *showing* to a friend or even a stranger how he or she is to be His means in supplying that need.[14]

"Questions and Answers," a regularly featured column, was written by Dr. Bullinger himself. If his schedule did not allow time to prepare his answers, the column was postponed.

Dr. Bullinger's reply to a request for his views on "women's ministry" was indicative of the attitude of the day in regard to women:

> The sphere of women's ministry is clearly defined in the Word, and seems to be limited to what is personal and private, and not prominent or public. We look in vain for a Scripture which teaches otherwise.[15]

The answer he gave to an inquirer on where and with whom to worship proved so popular with readers that it was later printed separately and enjoyed a large circulation. Several years later, Bullinger summarized his original answer in response to continued interest by his readers:

> You ask, Where you are to worship? We reply wherever God is glorified, Christ is exalted, God's Word is honoured, the Holy Spirit's power is evidenced and man abased. Never go anywhere where you do not know more of God's Word than when you entered. Never be *in* any Body where you may be "turned out"; or have your name down where it may be scratched out. Be content with the membership which God has given you in the spiritual unity of the Body of Christ, from which no power in Earth or Hell can cut you off; and be content that your name was written in the Lamb's "book of life" before the foundation of the world, and from which no power in Earth or Hell can ever take it out. Do nothing to imply that you do not hold these priceless privileges to be of infinite value; or that they can be added to in the slightest degree by any of man's corporate unities.[16]

In reply to a serious query on what constituted prayer, Bullinger's answer was at once learned and charming:

> The answer to your question will be found in the definition of the term "prayer." What is prayer? Our hymn says truly, "Prayer is the Christian's vital breath." Or, it may be more accurately expressed by saying *Prayer is the*

breath of the new nature. Just as the natural breath is the
sign and evidence of physical life—so prayer is the mark
and sign of the possession of spiritual life. The analogy
is complete. Natural life commences with breathing and
the breathing produces a cry. It is so with the New Birth.
. . . From that moment the breathing continues as the
spontaneous outcome of the New Life. We require no
more rule for the one breathing than the other. No
knowledge of Physiology is required for the one, and no
knowledge of Theology is necessary for the other. Indeed one has often listened to discourses on Physiology
till one has exclaimed, "Pray say no more or I shall be
afraid to breathe!" So it is with the breathing of the new
nature. The moment it becomes the subject of discussion or of rule—its essence is gone. We are such formal-
ists by nature that we need nothing to encourage
formalism in our prayers. Our efforts should be used in
the opposite direction. The moment we reason about
prayer we make it artificial. But true prayer is *spontaneous*. Our business in natural life is to breathe and not to
think about it. Our business in spiritual life is to breathe
(*i.e.* to pray) and not to think about it. The moment we
begin to think about our prayer we are occupied with
the *means* and lose the *end*.

We are reminded of an old rhyme which we recently
heard, but which illustrates our meaning exactly:—

> "The centipede was happy quite
>   Until the toad, in fun
> Said, Pray which foot goes after which?
>   Which moved his mind to such a pitch
> He lay distracted in the ditch
>   Considering—How to run."

We immediately pointed the moral and put it into the
following form:—

> The praying soul was happy quite
>   Until someone did say

> Prayer must be *this,* and *that,* and *thus!*
> Which put his mind in such a fuss
> That here and there in vain he'd rush
> To find out—How to pray![17]

Two controversial questions much on the minds of his readers were infant baptism and speaking in tongues. On the first, he wrote:

> As to Infant Baptism (by immersion or otherwise) it has no Scriptural authority. The evidence from Archaeology is useless in face of the fact of the very early corruption which flooded the church.[18]

He said the following in answer to a question from the United States on the "tongue movement":

> It is very solemn, as you say, that the "tongue movement" is undermining the authority of the Word of God. This is a sure test of the origin of the movement. The Word of God is, and has been from Gen. iii.1 the object of the enemy's greatest enmity.
> When these "tongues" say "the Bible was the scaffolding to the building; and, now the revelation comes direct, there is no need of the written Word. The building is complete," we ask, Is any further test needed? "Try the spirits."[19]

Bullinger, however, did not always have the answers. He replied to one reader:

> We really cannot answer your question about Melchizedek. No one can know beyond what is written.[20]

The wide range of topics commented on within the pages of *Things to Come* attested to the editor's vital interest in current events. A special column to report on them, called "The Signs of the Times," was a regular feature. The first issue of *Things to Come* in July 1894 explained the purpose of the column:

We propose each month to give "the signs of the times" among the Jews and Gentiles, in order that the Church of God may "understand" them, and lift up its head.

Those who learn from the Scriptures what are the purposes of God, as recorded in His Word, can alone understand the events of the world as they are recorded in its News.[21]

"The Signs of the Times" was divided into separate categories: religious signs, political signs, spiritist signs, and Jewish signs. In these, Bullinger commented on such far-ranging subjects as the growth of crime in England and Wales and its impact in the educational system of the land, troubles in the Balkans, the new "medium" of the Russian czar, Christian Science, "Pseudo-Christianity," and the building of railroads in the Middle East.

Dr. Bullinger was especially interested in any current events that had bearing on the international Jewish community. On the one hand, he considered it the duty and joy of Christian believers to be witnesses of the resurrection of Christ and to reconcile all men, both Jews and Gentiles, to God. Thus he was a strong supporter of various programs aimed at converting Jews to Christianity. His friendship with such leaders of this work as Christian David Ginsburg; John Wilkinson, founder of the Mildmay Mission to the Jews; and C. T. Lipshytz, director of the Barbican Mission to the Jews was staunch and genuine. After Bullinger's death, Lipshytz was to say of him:

Dr. Bullinger's knowledge of Holy Scripture accounted for the depth of his interest in the cause of Israel. That interest, in turn, ensured his enthusiastic cooperation in the work of placing before the world the Hebrew New Testament prepared by the late Mr. Salkinson. And it is unnecessary to add that his warm support of the work of the Barbican Mission was the outcome of Biblical knowledge combined with practical observations as to the Jewish mind and heart.[22]

Yet Bullinger's interest in Jews was deeper still. His writings on the subject indicate that he viewed the Jews of his day as direct descendants of the Jews of Jesus' day—and therefore as a biblical entity quite separate from the Gentiles, or Church of God—a body that would play a vitally significant role in future events. As he wrote in *Things to Come* in February 1896:

> Events in the East are moving forward, and occupy the serious attention of all European Statesmen. Not less do they occupy the thoughts of Bible Students who see in them what may prove to be the beginning of the end.[23]

Although throughout the centuries many Jewish people had striven to integrate themselves into their respective western societies, there had always been those who favored the separation of Jews into their own national state. By the end of the nineteenth century, rampant hostility toward Jews in Europe caused increasing numbers of them to long for a homeland of their own. These desires found their expression in modern Zionism, the Jewish national movement that advocated the establishment of a Jewish homeland and the organized emigration of Jews to colonize it.[24]

Dr. Bullinger's deep concern for Zionism stemmed from the fact that he saw in this movement possible signs marking the beginning of events recorded in the book of Revelation. As he put it:

> God is not yet done with His people Israel. They are already, though in partial blindness (Romans xi. 25), feeling their way back to their land, and to a restoration of their national Polity. Since the year 1896, the Zionist movement has been at work to this end.[25]

Bullinger's interest in Zionism was also personal. Dr. Theodore Herzl, the man who has been called the father of modern Zionism, was a friend of his, and Bullinger frequently visited with him both in London and on the Continent. The following exchange between the two men was recounted in *Things to Come* a few months after Dr. Herzl's death in 1904:

> . . . during a brief visit to see him [Dr. Herzl] at Ischl [in Austria], where he was staying, we were walking together by the side of the beautiful, fast flowing river, he

remarked, "How is it that I get sympathy and friendship from Christians like yourself . . . but all my enemies are of my own people?" We replied, "It is the same in England, our worst enemies there are Christians like ourselves. The world and the Jews treat us with courtesy and respect as you do; but it is 'Christians' who bitterly oppose us and misrepresent us, and persecute us."[26]

In his book *The Apocalypse,* an in-depth study of the last book of the Bible, Bullinger further explained his position on the modern-day Jews. The distinct Hebrew character of the book of Revelation, both in its language and its prophecy, convinced Dr. Bullinger that the Jews, and not the Christian Church, were the subjects of that book. He stated:

> Our great fundamental proposition . . . is, that *The Church is not the subject of the Apocalypse.*[27]

He further explained,

> But . . . we ask whether the Church is likely to be the subject of prophecy in the Apocalypse, especially when its future is clearly foretold in the Epistles which contain the revelation of the Mystery. There we learn what is to be the future and end of the Body of Christ. The members of that Body are merely waiting to be "received up in glory" (1 Tim. iii.16). . . .
> But all this, we submit, takes place before the Apocalypse opens. There we have, not the coming of the Lord to take away His Church, but, the revelation of the events which shall take place after the Church has been "received up in glory."[28]

Another area that occupied Bullinger's attention was the rise of spiritualism.[29] He frequently voiced his strong opposition to this movement in the column "Spiritist Signs." "Are the dead really communicating?" one issue of *Things to Come* asked rhetorically. "No!"[30]

A later issue of the journal exposed the heart of the problem.

"Is Spiritualism a Fraud?"

Under this heading a long correspondence has been, and . . . is still being, carried on in the (London) *Daily Express*. It was started by the exposure of the celebrated medium Mr. Craddick in London. Many letters have appeared and challenges thrown down by writers on both sides. The fact is that both are wrong and both are right: for each has got a part of the truth. But each side, putting its part of the truth for the whole, hammers away at the other side. Exactly the same phenomenon is seen in students of Theology and Prophecy, as well as in other spheres.

Spiritualism Is Not a Fraud.

Though it has many Mediums who have been, and are, "Frauds": this is true of all Professions, not excluding Christianity itself. And we may say that wherever money passes between Mediums and their Clients there is reason to entertain grave suspicion. But Spiritism itself is not a "Fraud." There are manifestations of spirits and their doings which cannot be denied. Many, even of these, can be imitated by clever professional jugglers; but, none the less, the reality exists; and nothing is gained to the cause of truth by merely denying it. On the other hand,

Spiritism Is a "Fraud."

The spirits pretend to be what they are not. This has been confessed even by the spirits themselves. It is merely a pretence, emanating from the prince of demons himself in order to deceive mankind and afford the semblance of proof of the Devil's lie, *"There is no death."* This is at once the great *raison d'etre,* and the great objective of Spiritism. It exists for this end. This is its foundation and this is the cardinal point of its teaching.

God declares, "the wages of sin is death." The spirits give God the lie, and declare that there is no such thing as death. Death is only life in another form.

This logically leads to the denial of Resurrection. The

spirits teach that death is itself the first of many resur-
rections, each one conducting the dead man or woman
on to higher planes or spheres. . . . And Christians who
are deceived by these "lying spirits" may well believe the
same; for, if death be the entrance to glory, what need is
there for any resurrection?[31]

Another subject of Dr. Bullinger's criticism in the column
"Spiritist Signs" was the rapid dissemination of the theory of
evolution in England. This theory had revolutionized contemporary thought and brought about serious challenges to the
faith of many when Charles Darwin introduced it into nineteenth-century scholarship.[32] Regarding Charles Darwin himself, Bullinger reprinted, without comment, the following
remarks by C. H. Spurgeon, the well-known Evangelical preacher:

CARLYLE ON EVOLUTION.

The old man [Thomas Carlyle] eloquent, and hater of
all shams, expressed himself clearly on the fad which is
now taking possession of inferior minds.

"I have known three generations of the Darwins,
grandfather, father and son: atheists all. The brother of
the famous naturalist, a quiet man, who lives not far
from here, told me that among his grandfather's effects
he found a seal engraved with this legend, '*Omnia ex
conchis,*' everything from a clam-shell. I saw the naturalist not many months ago, and told him that I had read
his 'Origin of Species' and other books; that he had by
no means satisfied me that men were descended from
monkeys, but had gone far toward persuading me that
he and his so-called scientific brethren had brought the
present generation of Englishmen very near to monkeys.
A good sort of man is this Darwin, and well meaning,
but with very little intellect."[33]

But if Bullinger made light of Darwin himself, he did not
make light of the wholesale acceptance of the theory of evolution. In a pamphlet titled *The Fallacies of Evolution,* first published in *Things to Come,* he acknowledged the important role

played by Professor Thomas Henry Huxley in spreading Darwin's theory and giving it credibility:

> The late Professor Huxley became the exponent of Darwin's theories, and in his lay sermon preached on January 7th, 1866, he said, "Scepticism is the highest of duties; blind faith the one unpardonable sin."[34]

Bullinger went on to use Huxley's arguments against him:

> Professor Huxley goes on to say, "If the doctrine of evolution is true, living matter must have arisen from not-living matter." Thus we are, after all, landed in scepticism pure and simple; and we are expected to receive this assertion in "blind faith."
>
> But, like Elihu, we have something also to say on God's behalf; and a few facts will be worth whole volumes of *hypotheses* and *inferences*. They have been well set forth in "eight axioms," which jointly and severally prove that the doctrine of Evolution is untenable and fallacious.[35]

Bullinger then described eight scientific principles, including the permanence of species, the uniqueness of human blood, the lethal consequences of transfusing the blood of one genus to another, the many foods that nourish one species and poison another, and the law of reproduction, whereby every form of life reproduces "after its kind" and with offspring less developed than the parent.[36]

Although Bullinger was firm in his denunciation of those scientists who expounded the theory of evolution, he saved his bitterest attacks for so-called "Christian Evolutionists":

> . . . no one who holds the theory of evolution can be a believer in revelation, and is not worthy of the name of "Christian."
>
> Let our readers then beware of "accepting the theory of Evolution." It is destructive of the Bible and of Christianity. A "Christian Evolutionist" is a contradiction in

terms. We might as well speak of an "honest thief," or a "true lie."

If a man be the one, it is impossible for him to be the other. If he thinks he can be both, there never was a clearer case of self-deception. . . .

The necessity for our showing this, at the present moment, is very urgent, for the poison of evolution is working deeply and powerfully into the very vitals of the churches.[37]

From the first issue in July 1894 until his death in June 1913, Bullinger continued to leave his imprint on *Things to Come*. He wrote what he felt to be the truth regardless of the opinions of others, and he never shrank from a fight. The possibility of being misunderstood had long since ceased to worry him. He expressed his feelings in the following answer to one correspondent:

. . . it may be well to say that, when writing, it is absolutely impossible to guard against all the various ways in which words may be misunderstood. If we were to attempt to do this we might do nothing else, and never get forward at all.[38]

And to another person he wrote:

You ask "whether any important Theologian or writer endorses or agrees with *Things to Come*." We really cannot tell you, as it does not matter in the least whether they do or not. The all important question is—Does *Things to Come* agree with the Word of God, for there and there only "important writers" "spake as they were moved by the Holy Ghost."[39]

CHAPTER NINE

The Later Years

EARLY IN 1894, after the close of Brunswick Chapel, the Bullingers moved from London to Bromley, Kent, about ten miles southeast of London. Emma's failing health could have been one reason for the move back to the country. She was now in her mid-sixties, and her asthma had worsened. London's oppressive coal-dust-laden fogs and cold winters had become progressively more difficult for her.

In September 1895, Bullinger asked the Executive Committee of the Trinitarian Bible Society for a small room above their offices to use as an occasional bedroom.[1] It seems to have become a study room as well, for a few years later it was noted in a committee memorandum that his library was there.

Benjamin Josiah Hitchcock was also living on the premises at that time with his family. Hitchcock had been employed by the Society twenty years before as a young lad and had risen in responsibility to become stockkeeper and eventually cashier. Bullinger and Hitchcock became close friends during these years. Hitchcock's integrity and faithfulness on behalf of the Society were often noted by its secretary.

In 1896, after two years in Bromley, the Bullingers moved back to London, to 97 York Mansions, Battersea Park, one in a row of gracious new apartment houses near the Thames. Records indicate that Emma Bullinger did not now live in London during much of the year. During her aunt's long absences, Elizabeth Dodson, now in her early thirties, became her uncle's

BERNARD STRATTON, BULLINGER'S SECOND SON, FATHER OF
DOROTHY ROSEMARY.

housekeeper. Elizabeth divided her time between London and Llandudno, a lovely seaside town in northern Wales. Dr. Bullinger visited Llandudno many times and preached there on several occasions.

The whereabouts of the Bullingers' two sons, Ethelbert Augustine and Bernard Stratton Bullinger, during the years before 1896 are uncertain. Presumably they would have completed their educations at boarding school, as was customary for middle-class boys in Victorian England. By 1896 Ethelbert Augustine would have been thirty-four and his brother twenty-nine. As little or no mention of Bullinger's sons appears in any of his writings, correspondence, or the memoirs of his friends and colleagues, it is difficult to assess their relationship. This silence might point to an estrangement between father and sons; later evidence would seem to bear this out.

On July 29, 1896, Bernard, now twenty-nine years old, married twenty-six-year-old Miss Florence Sayer in the parish church of St. George, Hanover Square, London. One of the witnesses to the marriage was Emma Bullinger. A close affinity had always existed between Emma and her younger son. If the groom's father was present, no official note was made of the fact.[2] During this time, Bernard's career is listed a "motor engineer." Bernard and Florence were divorced a few years later, contrary to social customs of the time.

In 1902, when he was thirty-five, Bernard married again. His new bride was Miss Ellen Louisa Crosby, twenty-two, who had lived in the house next to his in Hammersmith, London. They were married in the registry office in Fulham, London, on May 24.[3] Bernard's profession was now listed as a "motor car dealer." He often spent his Sundays in Hyde Park, taking part in impromptu races with other car enthusiasts.[4] The couple continued to live in Hammersmith.

On May 6, 1898, Ethelbert Augustine, then thirty-six, enlisted as a sub-lieutenant in the Belgian *Force Publique,* the military police of King Leopold's army in Africa. His tour of duty was to be for three years. He was sent to the region of the Upper Congo, where Belgian, French, and English forces were engaged in the great adventure of the late nineteenth century—the exploration and subjugation of the Upper Nile. In March 1900, Sub-lieutenant Bullinger

ETHELBERT AUGUSTINE, BULLINGER'S OLDEST SON.

contracted malarial fever, a disease that had wreaked havoc among the non-native population. He was sent to a military hospital in Boma, near the western coast of Africa, to recuperate. Initially, he had seemed to respond to the treatment, but on May 2 he suddenly took a turn for the worse. He died on May 4 and was buried with full military honors in Boma on May 5, 1900, one day short of the second anniversary of his arrival in Africa.[5] The official letter of condolence from the Independent State of the Congo was sent, not to the father or mother, as was customary, but to the brother of the deceased, Bernard S. Bullinger.

Even with these difficulties and tragedies in his family, Dr. Bullinger persevered in his research and writing. The years after 1894 saw increasing numbers of books and pamphlets issuing from his busy pen. His research method was microscopic in its thoroughness. Again and again, he would isolate a subject, develop it, and present it for inspection, study, and admiration.

As he once wrote:

> The Word of God may, in one respect, be compared to the earth. All things necessary to life and sustenance may be obtained by scratching the surface of the earth: but there are treasures of beauty and wealth to be obtained by digging deeper into it. So it is with the Bible. "All things necessary to life and godliness" lie upon its surface for the humblest saint; but, beneath that surface are "great spoils" which are found only by those who seek after them as for "hid treasure."[6]

This deep appreciation for the wealth of detail in the Bible can be observed throughout Bullinger's works. In *"Also": A Biblical Study of the Usage of This Word in the Gospels and New Testament*, published in 1895, Bullinger explained the reason for this minute study:

> When the word "also" occurs in a sentence, the sense of the passage entirely depends on its position, and it is impossible to read (especially aloud) correctly and intelligently without knowing the particular word it is intended to emphasize.

In the Greek this is never in doubt, but in English literature, including both the Authorized and Revised Versions, there seems to be no definite law as to the position of the word "also," and no uniformity as to its usage.

In the Greek the word *kai,* when it means "also," is placed always immediately *before* the word which it emphasizes; while in English usage it is placed either before or after the word.

In the Authorized and Revised Versions it is sometimes placed before and sometimes after the word, in which case it is ambiguous; but in many cases it is placed in connection with quite another word, in which case it is misleading.[7]

"Also" was followed in 1899 by a mammoth work titled *Figures of Speech Used in the Bible: Explained and Illustrated.* This book was unique and so comprehensive that at the time of this writing it continues to stand alone in its category. In the preface, Bullinger noted:

John Vilant Macbeth (Professor of Rhetoric, etc., in the University of West Virginia) has said:—

"There is no even tolerably good treatise on Figures existing at present in our language—Is there in any other tongue? There is no consecutive discussion of them of more than a few pages; the examples brought forward by all others being trivial in the extreme and threadbare; while the main conception of what constitutes the chief class of figures is altogether narrow, erroneous, and unphilosophical."[8]

Bullinger then listed every known work bearing on the subject of figurative language in the Bible, from *Philologia Sacra* by Solomon Glassius, written in 1625 in Latin but never translated into any other language, to incomplete treatises dealing with small parts of the whole field. He added:

Translators and commentators, as a rule, have entirely ignored the subject; while by some it has been derided. There is great need, therefore, for a work which shall deal exhaustively with the great subject of Figurative Language; and, if possible, reduce the Figures to some kind of system (which has never yet been completely done either by the Ancients or Moderns), and apply them to the elucidation of the Word of God.[9]

Bullinger started by explaining the meaning of the term *figure* and relating the importance of figures to the correct understanding of the Bible.

A figure is simply a word or a sentence thrown into a peculiar form, different from its original or simplest meaning or use. These forms are constantly used by every speaker and writer. It is impossible to hold the simplest conversation, or to write a few sentences without . . . making use of figures.[10]

The lack of literature on the subject of figures, let alone figures in the Bible, caused Bullinger a number of difficulties from the outset. First, there existed no proper English names for the figures. He solved this problem by transliterating their Greek and Latin names and adding English equivalents. Second, the sheer number of Greek and Latin figures posed a considerable challenge. Bullinger isolated more than two hundred distinct figures, many of which had a number of variations, totaling more than five hundred figures.[11] The most serious difficulty, however, proved to be the complete lack of classification. If figures of speech had ever been arranged by the Greeks, no knowledge of the system survived, so Dr. Bullinger undertook to classify them himself. He divided them into three main categories:

1. Figures which depend for their peculiarity on any OMISSION. . . .
2. Figures which depend on any ADDITION, by REPETITION of words or sense. . . .

3. Figures which depend on CHANGE, or alteration in the usage, order, or application of words.[12]

Figures of Speech was originally published in ten separate parts, which caused some difficulties. Dr. Bullinger explained to the readers of *Things to Come* when the announcement of the publication of the final part was made in 1899:

> The body of the work is printed and consists of 1022 pages, without the Introduction, Contents, and Indexes.
> The Figures of Speech defined and illustrated number 217, and the passages of Scripture explained amount to nearly 8,000.
> Not knowing how many pages the work would make (the ground being wholly untrodden), the earlier parts were made too large; the consequence is that there are only ten parts instead of twelve as was originally reckoned. This means that those who have taken it in parts will have paid only 18/- instead of £1, notwithstanding all the extra expense entailed in doing up the parts, printing covers and order forms, and the postage on each part![13]
> When we add to this the serious loss entailed by those who have taken some of the parts and not the whole, thereby spoiling so many complete volumes and making the rest of the parts waste paper, we shall have the sympathy of many friends, who will, we are sure, do their best to make the work known.[14]

Figures of Speech was received with great acclaim, and the number of Bullinger's avid readers multiplied. A friend wrote:

> Bullinger's treatment of figures is masterly—his classification superb; no one else touches it! . . . Thank God for such thrilling new light on His Word![15]

Writing and study were not the only items on Bullinger's busy schedule. He continued to travel frequently for the Trinitarian Bible Society, visiting auxiliaries throughout Great Britain and

Ireland, many of which he had founded himself. Bullinger was a well-known preacher, and auxiliaries strove for the privilege of having him at their meetings. A typical speaking schedule, published in *The Trinitarian Bible Society Quarterly Record* for January 1899, lists thirty-six different engagements during a three-month period.[16]

Dr. Bullinger also traveled to the Continent at least twice a year to visit members of the Society in France, Spain, Italy, the Netherlands, Belgium, Germany, and Hungary. His purpose was not only to visit auxiliaries but also to make arrangements with printers and agents of other Bible Societies to publish and distribute foreign language translations funded by the Trinitarian Bible Society.

Dr. Bullinger undertook most of these journeys alone by train. The long hours were not wasted, however, as he spent many of them working. He had also developed the ability to rest on trains so that he could arrive at his destination ready for whatever lay ahead.[17] Steadfast and determined, Dr. Bullinger refused to postpone or curtail any of his itineraries; not even the widespread fear of terrorist acts, which kept many would-be travelers home in the last year of the century, deterred him.[18]

In early October 1899, Dr. Bullinger went to Rome to attend the Twelfth Congress of Orientalists. The International Congress of Orientalists, of which he was a member, had been founded in Paris in 1873 and was composed of individuals and learned societies from all over the world whose particular interest was Oriental studies. These studies included archaeology, linguistics, geography, history, and ethnography of the peoples of the Far and Middle East, as well as the native peoples of Asia, Africa, and America.

An excerpt from the opening address of the second meeting of the Congress, held at the Royal Institution in London in 1874, shows some of the reasons for the awakening interest in these studies:

> The nineteenth century has seen the revival of Oriental learning, and the great discoveries made throughout the East, in Mesopotamia, Egypt, India, and Persia, have thrown an entirely new light on the ancient monarchies,

religions and languages of the Eastern world as it existed forty centuries ago. This has been due to several causes, chiefly to the improved facilities of access, by which travelers and others have visited these countries and their monuments, and have excavated their remains, and partly to the advance made in Europe itself, which has enabled the monuments discovered to be more accurately copied. The extensive excavations made throughout the East and the continuous explorations of modern travelers have left no accessible monument unoccupied; and the quantity of the material now placed at the disposal of the student is consequently immense. With the increased number of texts of the old East has come the more accurate knowledge, based on the power of comparison now given to the student. These materials were unknown to inquirers of the previous century. Empires have been exhumed, and for the first time a contemporary history of recorded events has been found.[19]

Dr. Bullinger attended the Congress in 1899 with his friend Dr. Christian David Ginsburg. Both men had been asked to present papers for the section on Semitic Languages and Literatures—Bullinger on "The Law of Correspondence as Exhibited in the Hebrew Bible" and Ginsburg on "Abbreviations in Hebrew mss."[20]

After the Congress, Ginsburg was given a special introduction to the chief librarian of the Vatican library and was granted time to study its collection of Hebrew manuscripts. He requested that Dr. Bullinger be allowed to accompany him. Later, Bullinger recorded some of his thoughts while touring the library.

After exploring several special objects in the Library, and while Dr. Ginsburg was examining all the Hebrew Manuscripts in the Library, our Secretary was examining the ceiling, which was arched and was very gaudily painted with pictures of all the Councils of the Church, from the Council of Nicaea to that of Trent. The Rev. James Wall had called his attention to these pictures, and he noted a matter of great importance in connection with them.

In the first, that of the Council of Nicaea (325 A.D.), no prelate or potentate occupies the chair. The Bishop of Rome and the Emperor Constantine both declined to preside, and the Bible is placed on the chair.

In the succeeding pictures man becomes more and more prominent, and the Bible more and more insignificant.

In the second, it is placed by the side of the chair; and it gets smaller and smaller; until, at the Council of Trent (1545), it vanishes altogether.

This is (though doubtless undesigned) a fitting symbolical representation of the relations between the Church and the Bible! As the one increases in authority, the authority of the other decreases.[21]

Dr. Bullinger rarely missed an opportunity to point out to his readers and listeners what he perceived as the corruption of the Roman Church. One reason for this could have been the increasing influence of the High Church movement, with its Roman Catholic bias, within the Church of England.[22]

A few years after the visit to the Vatican library, Bullinger took a trip to Spain with other members of the Trinitarian Bible Society. He wrote an account of this trip that was published by the Trinitarian Bible Society and included photographs of Inquisition buildings and their torture chambers.[23] His keenest criticism, however, was leveled at the ease with which he and his party of four had been able to purchase indulgences, no questions asked, outside of a cathedral in Spain. As he reported:

One [indulgence] was to enable the purchaser to eat meat on fast-days.

Another allowed sins of uncleanness; but for this a priest had to pay more than a layman.

A third allowed the purchaser to steal up to £200!

The fourth . . . is called *"Composition."* . . . A "Composition" means that, if a person has wrongfully acquired goods or money, he may (if he cannot find the owner) continue in possession of them for a consideration! The consideration is that he may keep a part provided he pays a part over to the Church. The limit is £30.

Beyond this he must apply personally to the Pope's Commissary through his Father Confessor.

An Indulgence means that if the person purchasing it commits the sin named, he need not *confess* it or *do penance* for it, as he has settled that by payment beforehand.[24]

Dr. Bullinger's trips to the Continent almost always included a stay with Pasteur LeCoat in Tremel. In the years since their meeting, great advances had been made in the Tremel mission. By the beginning of the twentieth century, an orphanage, a boys' school, a girls' school, a cottage for indigents (homeless men were a common sight in those days, on every road and at every door), a dispensary, and a chapel had all been built. In 1902, an old flax mill was bought to make the mission financially independent. Many of Dr. Bullinger's friends, such as Fleet-Surgeon R. A. Mowll, R.N., and his son, R. R. Mowll, M.D., were active in these endeavors and donated their services to the dispensary. Amy Manson, another close friend, went to Tremel frequently. (It was Miss Manson who had made the original drawings for Bullinger's book *The Witness of the Stars*.) Miss Manson was the daughter of one of the original owners of Christie's, the famous London auction house. A contemporary of Dr. Bullinger's, she was a woman of formidable energy as well as considerable wealth. Maurice Golby, who had been employed by the Trinitarian Bible Society for a few years as a clerk, was another friend who actively contributed to the work in Tremel. He became the second honorary secretary of the Breton Mission after Dr. Bullinger.

Dr. Bullinger had a large circle of friends. Two prominent men who were very close to him were Sir Robert Anderson and Rev. Sholto Douglas, both of whom shared his strong stand on Protestantism and his interest in prophetic studies. They had been among the original trustees of *Things to Come*, and they frequently spent time with Bullinger on weekends and holidays.

Sir Robert Anderson was born in Ireland in 1841. His father was the Crown Solicitor for Dublin and his mother was a member of the nobility. Although Sir Robert was called to the Irish Bar in 1863 and the English Bar in 1870, he never practiced law but instead became involved in public service. He rose to be assistant commissioner of police and head of the Criminal Investigation Department in London, retiring in 1901 after a distinguished career.[25]

Following his retirement, Sir Robert devoted himself to writing and teaching, principally on biblical subjects with particular emphasis on prophecy. A frequent speaker at the Mildmay Conferences and the Prophecy Investigation Society, Anderson also chaired and spoke at the Annual Meetings of the Trinitarian Bible Society. Although not personally active in the work of the Society, Anderson gave his time and lent his prestige to these meetings out of respect for its secretary. As he said at one, "As a prefatory word, I may say that any dislike I feel to being in the chair is overborne by the pleasure of standing beside my friend Dr. Bullinger, and of doing anything, no matter how little, to help him in the great work in which he is engaged."[26] Sir Robert was one of the earliest members of the National Club, a private social club in London founded by men holding strongly evangelical views. Dr. Bullinger was an honorary member.[27]

Of Sir Robert's literary efforts it was said:

> The quality in Sir Robert Anderson's books, as well as in his numerous other writings, which appealed with special force to many people, was the strength and certainty of his own beliefs and the clearness of their expression. . . . "Your writings are specially helpful to me," wrote a very old friend . . . "there is always in every chapter that which you *must* either accept or reject. You must stop and think, and not pass on unheeding."[28]

Dr. Bullinger once wrote to Sir Robert about one of Sir Robert's books: "I feel I have a fuller, better and deeper knowledge of 'my Lord and my God,' and praise Him and bless you for it.[29]

At times, Dr. Bullinger and Sir Robert collaborated in their literary efforts. In Anderson's book *The Buddha of Christendom,* written in 1899, he noted that Bullinger had not only prepared the index but also assisted him further by reading the manuscript proofs.[30]

The two men did not always agree on biblical matters, however, as can be seen by the following letter:

Dear Bullinger,

I am deeply touched by the graciousness and cordiality of your notice of "Forgotten Truths." I know well how unreservedly you sympathise with very much there is in it, and your praise of that element is not stinted.

But I am fully aware that on certain matters respecting which you feel strongly I have gone counter to you. But on whatever side is the truth—yours or mine—there is no doubt on which side is the grace!

R. Anderson[31]

Rev. Sholto Douglas, officially Rev. Lord Blythswood, was one of very few ordained ministers among the nobility. Despite his great wealth and prestige, Douglas spent most of his ministry serving in populous and poverty-stricken districts. A deeply religious man, his ministry was principally one-to-one teaching and counseling. He published only two works, "Order of Events in Our Lord's Second Coming" and "The Anti-Christ," both of which were featured in *Things to Come*.[32] Like Bullinger, Douglas was vitally interested in the conversion of the Jews and served as Vice President of the Barbican Mission to the Jews in London.[33]

In 1887, Douglas moved to his ancestral home in Scotland and undertook a pastoral charge in St. Silas Church, Glasgow. During the summer, he and his wife would stay in the Highlands, in Balmacara House on Loch Alsh. This lovely spot was the scene of many weekend gatherings, with Dr. Bullinger and Sir Robert and Lady Agnes Anderson as frequent guests.

Many years later, reminiscing about his father, Arthur Anderson wrote the following about one of those holidays:

I shall never forget a holiday many years ago in the Highlands, when the Rev. Sholto Douglas (afterwards Lord
Blythswood) and Mrs. Douglas, with their house party,
including Dr. Bullinger and my father, met daily for Bible
study. (Our hostess divided the company into great
prophets and lesser prophets!) The hours spent in this
way made the beauty of mountain and loch and island
seem all the more perfect, the same God revealing Himself in these as in the Book.[34]

Arthur Anderson's biography of his father includes the following accounts of other peaceful times at Loch Alsh, described
by Mrs. Douglas. One of them makes note of Bullinger's nick-
name within that close circle of friends:

Another letter in July 1896, to my father, speaks of all the
hills being lit up with lights such as are *only* to be seen at
"Bal[macara]" or in Heaven; "and we *groaned* that you
were not with us; we are having a proper honeymoon this
time, expecting no one except you or Bully. . . ."[35]
. . . We will let you do *exactly* what you feel inclined for
from morning to night; unlimited tea, fresh made! What
other inducements can we offer? Absolute rest of mind
and body. If you care to join us in Biblical researches
you shall; but we promise not to be scandalized if you
snooze on the beach instead, for we have great sympathy with what *must* be your longing to think of nothing
but food and air.[36]

Late in 1903, the Scottish-born Rev. James Christopher Smith,
a former minister of the Free Church of Scotland, became a
member of the General Committee of the Trinitarian Bible
Society. He had long been interested in the subject of biblical
prophecy and had been a featured speaker at the Prophetic
Conferences; his writings were regular features in *Things to Come*.
In October 1904, he was appointed as the first assistant secretary
of the Trinitarian Bible Society. At that time, he was described
as "an able and attractive speaker and peculiarly qualified to
advocate the principles and claims and needs of the Society."[37]

Smith's abilities as a public speaker were put to use; he began to accompany Dr. Bullinger on his journeys throughout England and Ireland. They often shared the platform and sometimes alternated between conducting the meeting and speaking. Their relationship developed into a warm friendship.

Yet, while Dr. Bullinger enjoyed a circle of valued friends, he was also the target of a shrill chorus of criticism that increased with the years and often came from the Plymouth Brethren. The more he wrote, the louder the criticism became. As he once wrote:

> God's prophets were men who could never swim with the stream, they were never popular, they could never make popularity their aim, they could never look on success as their end. And it is the same to-day with God's spokesmen and witnesses. . . . If any of you do not believe it, try it! Be a faithful witness for God; dare to stand alone with Him, and you will soon see that you will have to "suffer persecution."[38]

In a letter written in 1908, Bullinger shared with a friend his manner of dealing with those who opposed him:

> I have long said "Lord I am going to delight myself in Thee and in Thy Word and Thou must look after all who 'oppose themselves.' I will try and instruct them (in meekness) but Thou canst deal with them as I can not and may not."
>
> From that time I have enjoyed great peace. Some opponents He has chastened. Some He has turned into my best friends and zealous defenders!! (I could not do either!!)[39]

In 1902, Bullinger published a pamphlet—*The Rich Man and Lazarus: or The Intermediate State*—on the state of the soul after death. He began by affirming once more the authority of Scripture over tradition.

> In dealing with this Scripture [Luke xvi.19–31], and the subject of the so-called "intermediate state," it is important

that we should confine ourselves to the Word of God, and not go to Tradition. Yet, when nine out of ten believe what they have learnt from Tradition, we have a thankless task, so far as pleasing man is concerned. We might give our own ideas as to the employments, etc., of the "departed," and man would deal leniently with us. But let us only put God's Revelation against man's imagination, and then we shall be made to feel his wrath, and experience his opposition. . . .

There are several matters to be considered before we can reach the Scripture concerning the rich man and Lazarus; or arrive at a satisfactory conclusion as to the State after death. It will be well for us to remember that all such expressions as "Intermediate State," "Church Triumphant," and others similar to them are unknown to Scripture. They have been inherited by us from Tradition, and have been accepted without thought or examination.[40]

To the question, "What does God in His Word reveal concerning death?" Bullinger answered from Psalm 146:4: "His breath goeth forth, he returneth to his earth; in that very day his thoughts perish."[41] He then cited corroborating verses and concluded with Ecclesiastes 12:7, "Then shall the dust *return* to the earth as it was: and the spirit shall *return* unto God who gave it."[42]

Where Scripture is silent, we may well be silent too: and, therefore, as to the spirit and its possibilities between dying and resurrection we have not said, and do not say, anything. Scripture says it will "return TO GOD." We do not go beyond this; nor dare we contradict it by saying, with Tradition, that it goes to Purgatory or to Paradise; or with Spiritualism, that it goes elsewhere.[43]

The Rich Man and Lazarus was received with much comment and debate. William Hoste, a regular critic of Bullinger's and a member of the Plymouth Brethren, had the following to say in his own pamphlet titled *The Intermediate State: A Reply to Dr. E. W. Bullinger:*

> Though not a student of this author's general works, I know a few of his controversial writings. Anyone hoping to find therein accuracy of statement, or logical sequence, will be greatly disappointed. His references to the original Greek cannot be accepted without great reserve; indeed in such matters as Greek rules and renderings, he may well be described as "a law unto himself."[44]

In *The Church Epistles: (Romans to Thessalonians): Their Importance, Order, Inter-Relation, Structure, Scope, and Interpretation,* first published in *Things to Come* from 1898 to 1901, Bullinger wrote:

> When the Apostle Paul preached the good news concerning Christ and His Church, at Ephesus, his ministry continued in Asia for the space of two years (Acts xix.10). We read that the Word of God grew mightily and prevailed, and that "all they which dwelt in Asia heard the word of the Lord Jesus." And yet, at the close of his ministry, and of his life, he writes his last Epistle to Timothy, when he says "I am now ready to be offered, and the time of my departure is at hand" (2 Tim. i.15): "This thou knowest that all they that be in Asia have turned away from me." We are told, on every hand, to-day, that we must go back to the first three centuries to find the purity of faith and worship of the primitive church!
>
> But it is clear from this comparison of Acts xix.10 and 2 Tim. i.15, that we cannot go back to the first century. No, not even to the apostle's own life-time!
>
> This turning away could not have been merely personal; but must have included his teaching also. . . .
>
> It was Pauline truth and teaching from which all had "turned away." . . .[45]
>
> The four Gospels and the Sermon on the Mount are taken as the essence of Christianity, instead of the Epistles specially addressed to Churches.[46]

On the number and order of the church epistles, Bullinger explained:

> Seven churches were addressed as such by the Holy Spirit. *Seven* being the number of spiritual perfection. . . .
>
> Not only is the *number* of these epistles perfect, but their *order* is perfect also.
>
> The order in which they come to us is no more to be questioned than their contents. But what is that order?
>
> Is it chronological? No! Man is fond of arranging them according to the times when he thinks they were written, but God has not so arranged them. . . .
>
> In all the hundreds of Greek manuscripts of the New Testament, the order of these seven epistles addressed to churches is exactly the same.[47]

On the subject of the mystery, Bullinger wrote in 1903:

> There is no subject of greater importance to the Church of God than that which, in the New Testament, is called "The Mystery."[48]

Bullinger defined the word *mystery* as "secret" in its biblical application and went on to explain those Scriptures in which the "great secret" is specially and formally revealed— Colossians 1:24–27; Romans 16:25, 26; and Ephesians 3.[49]

> . . . [T]his was the secret: that a people should be taken out from among both Jews and Gentiles, who should with Christ be made *(sussomos)* a joint-body in Christ (Eph. iii.9)—a peculiar ecclesiastical word which occurs only here: it does not mean that there was a body already previously in existence and that others became afterwards in due time members of it, a Body of which Christ should be the glorious Head in heaven, and His people—the members of that body on the earth—"one new Man."
>
> This was the secret which was revealed to God's "holy apostles and prophets by the Spirit," and which had never

entered into the heart or mind of mortal man—CHRIST
MYSTICAL.[50]

Bullinger's study of the Scriptures dealing with the "Mystery"
led him to conclusions that were unusual for his day. One such
conclusion was what he believed to be "the true place of Pentecost":

> Pentecost thus is shown to have nothing whatever to do
> with the Church; and all the modern talk about
> "pentecostal blessings," and "pentecostal enduement," etc.,
> and the awful heresy of the "Pentecostal league" are all
> based on a scripture which does not refer to the Church
> of God at all; and those who so base it are those who so
> greatly neglect the teaching of the Holy Ghost in the
> Pauline Epistles, which are expressly given for the guid-
> ance, teaching, blessing, and building up of the Church.
> All that Christians need of teaching concerning the work
> and power of the Holy Spirit is fully contained and re-
> vealed in the Epistles, which are written for that purpose.[51]

By 1907, Bullinger had modified some of the views on the
order of the church epistles that he had espoused in 1898. His
willingness to change if he felt he had gained added insight can
be clearly seen in an article titled "The Pauline Epistles" in *Things
to Come:*

> Most of our readers are acquainted with the special im-
> portance of the "Pauline" Epistles.
> We have shown, both in the pages of *Things to Come*
> as well as in our separate work on the Church Epistles,
> that they are given to us in the *Canonical order* in which
> we are to study their truth and learn their teaching (sub-
> jectively in our own selves).
> But there is also something to be learned from the
> historical or *Chronological order* in which they were
> written. . . .
> The truth flowing from this is so important that, if it
> should compel us to revise our own views in some particu-
> lars, or even to re-write certain matters, let us together

thank God for the light that reveals further truth, and for the grace which enables us to receive, believe, and use it.[52]

The following appraisal of Dr. Bullinger and some of his critics was given years later by others who continued to study his teachings on the importance of the church epistles and on the mystery:

Dr. Bullinger had no misgivings as to the manner in which his teachings, as well as his personality, would be treated. He well knew that at no time in the history of the Church has new intellectual and spiritual light, no matter how clear, succeeded without hindrance in obtaining entrance into the minds and consciences of men and women. He realized that new interpretations of the Word required the aid of time and repetition to force general attention and to become accepted as foundational truth, and so, he was content to labour on despite misunderstanding, misrepresentation and slander.

Dr. Bullinger suffered much from tyrannous criticism, ridicule and every mode of biting sarcasm, to which, strange to say, were added unfounded accusations and calumny. He received from an energetic circle of opponents reproach, scorn and hatred, instead of that encouragement and approval which he merited.[53]

But Bullinger was ever ready for a good fight, and he took on his worst critics among the Plymouth Brethren in the pages of *Things to Come* in July 1902:

What is there to be replied to in criticisms of this kind? Nothing, except to say that the charge of "alteration" of God's Word is very serious and malicious, as is the charge of *dishonesty* in the same article. But it is peculiarly appropriate as coming from a school whose past history and present position is the lamentable result of "strife about words." It began with them about sixty years ago, and its fruits are seen to this day in the breaking up of

assemblies and in the breaking of hearts, instead of building up the one Body of Christ.[54]

On February 14, 1907, a special meeting of the executive committee of the Trinitarian Bible Society was called to discuss the
crisis that had arisen as a result of the "sudden indisposition" of
Dr. Bullinger, now sixty-nine years old. A letter was read from
Dr. Risien Russell, his attending physician, confirming his
patient's need to have at least two months of complete rest. The
question of who would carry on Dr. Bullinger's work during his
illness was important because he, as secretary, had supervised
every phase of the Society's operations. Two men had to step in
to replace him.

The committee appointed Rev. F. Cecil Lovely—a member of
the general committee since 1897—as secretary for four months
with the responsibility of conducting all correspondence dealing with contributions and all Bible orders. James Christopher
Smith was elevated to "Association Secretary," a newly formed
position with charge of all correspondence relating to existing
auxiliaries, the formation of new ones, and all arrangements
for the annual meeting. The committee granted Dr. Bullinger a
two-month leave of absence with pay, with extensions if necessary. The sum of £50 was given to him from the general fund to
help with extra expenses. In addition, the following message
was composed:

> It is with deep gratitude that they record their convic-
> tion that the growth and present position of the Society
> are, under God, largely due to the ability, zeal and untir-
> ing energy with which he has conducted its operations.
>
> The Committee offer their warm congratulations to
> Dr. Bullinger on having held his office for so many years
> with such manifest success and on having acquired the
> esteem and friendship of the supporters and friends of
> the Society.
>
> They pray that he may speedily recover from his
> present indisposition; that he may be fully restored to
> his usual health and long continue to fill the position he
> has so ably and faithfully maintained.[55]

E. W. Bullinger with granddaughter Dorothy Rosemary.

Dr. Bullinger replied that the kind words of sympathy, cheer, and appreciation had touched him deeply. He also requested another month, until the middle of May 1907, in which to recuperate fully.

By April, he had recovered enough to once again take up his correspondence. In a letter dated April 11, 1907, and addressed to A. E. Knoch in the United States, he wrote:

My dear brother

I am now able to write one or two letters. I have not heard from you since my niece sent you my news. . . .

Writing and reading are my trials but all is well. If I had overworked my arm I could put it in a sling. But I cannot do that with my brain. I can rest *that* only occupying it with other and different subjects, [it] is very difficult.[56]

The secretary was not present at the annual meeting of the Trinitarian Bible Society in April and, as was noted in the report, "his well-known form and genial manner were much missed at the Social Gathering [before the meeting], and on the platform." His absence was all the more regretted on May 1, 1907, which was the fortieth anniversary of his tenure as secretary to the Trinitarian Bible Society.[57]

By June of that same year, Dr. Bullinger was back and able to attend to some of his duties. Rev. F. Cecil Lovely, who had been secretary *locum tenens* during his absence, was now named his assistant secretary. James Christopher Smith continued to do most of the traveling, but by the end of the summer Bullinger felt ready to follow his usual Continental itinerary himself.

Whatever his illness had been, his recovery seems to have been complete. On this trip he visited Hungary to negotiate copyrights for the printing of the New Testament; Bohemia [in present-day Czechoslovakia] with regard to the Bohemian and Polish New Testaments; and Berlin, where he saw the directors of the Prussian Bible Society to arrange for a supply of suitable New Testaments.[58]

Dr. Bullinger's illness did, however, have important consequences.

Later in the year, Elizabeth Dodson left Llandudno and came to London to find and establish a home for her uncle. That it was her decision and initiative can be seen by the fact that she herself bought the home they were to share, a rare occurrence in Victorian England. There is no evidence that Emma Bullinger ever lived there.

The house that she found had been built early in 1907 on North End Road, Hampstead, in northwest London. Close to Hampstead Heath, it was situated in a rapidly growing area of spacious, semi-detached houses so familiar to that city.

Although originally sold by the builder in March 1907, the house had come on the market again in the autumn. Elizabeth bought it in November for £1,050, with the help of £500 that two friends loaned to her.[59] Taking immediate occupancy, she and her uncle promptly renamed the house Bremgarten after the Swiss village that had been the birthplace of Heinrich Bullinger.[60] That same month, Bullinger was happily sharing with the readers of *Things to Come* his thanksgiving to God for the restoration of his health, and his prayers for abundant increase and continued blessing on his labors.[61]

There was other happy news that year. On September 3, 1907, a daughter, Dorothy Rosemary Stratton Bullinger, was born to Bernard and Ellen Bullinger. As she grew up, the little girl became a frequent visitor at Bremgarten and was a source of constant joy to her grandfather.

CHAPTER TEN

Life at Bremgarten

IN SEPTEMBER 1907, Dr. Bullinger published the book that to many has remained his most endearing work: *How to Enjoy the Bible*. In the preface, he recounted the circumstances leading to its writing:

> In the autumn of 1905 I found myself in one of the most important of the European Capitals. I had preached in the morning in the Embassy Chapel, and at the close of the service, my friend, His Britannic Majesty's Chaplain, expressed his deep regret at the absence of two members of his congregation, whose disappointment, he said, would be very great when they discovered they were away on the very Sunday that I was there.
>
> As it was a matter which I could not possibly alter I was compelled, perforce, to dismiss it from my mind with much regret, and returned to my hotel.
>
> In the afternoon a visiting card was brought to my room, announcing a gentleman holding a high Government position.
>
> In explaining the object of his visit he began by saying that he had been brought up as a Roman Catholic; and that, a few years ago, there came into the office of his department a copy of *The Illustrated London News*. As he was learning English at the time, he was naturally interested in reading it. The number contained an account

of the funeral of the late Charles Haddon Spurgeon, the illustrations of which attracted his attention. The letterpress made some reference to Mr. Spurgeon's sermons and the world-wide fame which they had obtained. This led him to procure some copies of the sermons, and these, by God's grace and blessing, were used for his conversion.

He was at the time thinking of marriage, and felt the importance now of finding a Christian lady for his wife. At the same time he began to attend my friend's English Services, and before long he found an English lady, residing at that time in _____, and in due course the engagement ended in marriage. . . .

After their marriage they began to read together the sermons which had proved, under God, so great a blessing to himself; and, before long, the same happy result took place in his wife's case, and they rejoiced together in the Lord.

They soon however began to find that they had much to learn. Reading the sermons and the Word of God they felt that there were many subjects in the Bible which they found little of in the sermons. True, they found the same sound doctrines and useful teaching, and spiritual food; but, they found also the absence of other truths which they longed to know.

They spoke to my friend their minister, and told him of their trouble. He lent them my book on *The Church Epistles*. This book they began to study together, and as the husband told me, "we went over it, three times, word by word." This they did to their great edification. "But," he said, "we soon discovered that *you* did not tell us everything, and there were many things which you assumed that we knew; and these we naturally wished to learn more about. So, a few weeks ago, we resolved to take our holiday in London; find you out; and talk over with you the things which filled our hearts. . . .

We found, to our disappointment, that you were here, in the very place from which we had set out to seek you.

So we returned here at once, and arrived only last

night, but were too tired to get from our suburb to the service this morning."

Not till that moment did I discover that these were the same two persons to whom my friend the chaplain had referred when he spoke of his regret at their absence from the service that morning, and of the disappointment which he was sure they would experience.

"I have lost no time in searching you out (he said), and am delighted to find you. You must come out to us and see us in our home to-morrow." . . .

I . . . said we would gladly go out to him on the morrow.

At this he was very pleased; and spoke, now, freely, of the great desire of himself and his wife to know more of God's Word.

"We want (he said) to study it together, and to be as independent as possible of the teachings and traditions of men. In fact,

WE WANT TO ENJOY THE BIBLE.

We want to read it, and study it, and understand it and enjoy it for ourselves!"

This, of course, sounded very sweetly in my ears; and it was arranged that he should come into the city, the next morning early, and fetch us out to his home in the suburbs.

He arrived soon after 8 o'clock, and by 9 o'clock we were sitting down together over the Word of God. There we sat till noon! . . .

On my journey home to England I thought much, and long, and often, of my pleasant intercourse with my new friends: and I was impressed by the thought that *what they needed, thousands needed;* and that the vast majority of Bible readers who were filled with the same deep desire to "enjoy the Bible" were beset by the same difficulties in attaining that desire. . . .

This explanation of the origin of this work will show that no better title could be chosen, or would so well describe its object, and explain its end. My prayer is that the same Spirit who inspired the words in the Sciiptures of Truth, may also inspire them in the hearts of my readers and may cause each to say (with David), "I rejoice in Thy words as one that findeth great spoils [*sic*]" (Ps. cxix. 162): and to exclaim (with Jeremiah), "Thy words were found and I did eat them, and Thy Word was unto me the joy and rejoicing of my heart" (Jer. xv.16).[1]

Bullinger further explained:

The Root of all the evils which abound in the spiritual sphere at the present day lies in the fact that the Word and the words of God are not fed upon, digested, and assimilated, as they ought to be.

If we ask the question, Why is this the case? the answer is, The Bible is not enjoyed *because the Bible is not understood*. The methods and rules by which alone such an understanding may be gained are not known or followed; hence the Bible is a neglected book. . . .

The cloud that now rests over its intelligent study arises from the fact that it is with us to-day as with the Jews of old—"The Word of God has been made of none effect by the traditions of men" (Matt. xv.1–9).[2]

To Bullinger's mind, it was the reliance on tradition instead of on the study of the Bible that prevented people from understanding and enjoying it. To assist readers, he introduced an inductive method of study similar to that used in the natural sciences. Bullinger had the following to say about the method of study:

But our object is to "Open the book"; to let it speak; to hear its voice; to study it *from within itself;* and have regard to other objects and subjects, only from what it teaches about them.

The method of the "Higher" criticism is to discredit a Book, or a passage on *internal evidence*. Our method is to establish and accredit Holy Scripture on internal

Bullinger with his niece Eveline at Bremgarten, North End Road.

evidence also, and thus to derive and provide, from its own pharmacopoeia, an antidote to that subtle and malignant poison.

This method of study will reveal more convincing and "infallible proof" of inspiration than can be adduced from all the reasonings and arguments of men.[3]

Dr. Bullinger also suggested that small groups could be an effective way to study the Bible, so that "each point could be made clearer and more profitable by mutual study and conversation."[4] To assist those who wished to study in this manner, he posed the following five principles for interpretation:

It must be affirmed, and it will be conceded by all Bible Students, that an interpretation of a passage to be satisfactory:—

(1) Must take all the words in their natural meaning and Scriptural usage.
(2) Must be uniform and consistent in its translation.
(3) Must give due weight to the inexorable laws of grammatical construction.
(4) Must give the passage its logical place in the context.
(5) Must harmonize the passage with the general teaching of the whole book, and not merely cleverly explain it as though it were an isolated passage.

If an interpretation can comply with these demands then it may challenge criticism, and commend itself to general acceptance.[5]

How to Enjoy the Bible was received with much praise and continues today to be one of Bullinger's most popular works. As one reviewer said:

This is a book of facts and principles, set forth in a manner that shows reverence for the Book and loving devotion to the God of the Book.[6]

Now, with restored health and settled comfortably in his new home, Bullinger in November 1907 shared his thoughts on the coming year with the readers of *Things to Come*:

> May He, who has done such things for us, do still more, and add the needed gifts of wisdom, and knowledge and patience that *Things to Come* may be still carried on without looking for the "praise," or heeding the "fear," or begging for the help of man.[7]

On December 15 of that year, Dr. Bullinger celebrated his seventieth birthday. Not tall in stature, he was by then quite portly with a full head of white hair and a white beard. He had kindly eyes and a puckish smile that lit up his whole face. His closest friends described him as "bright, buoyant, cheerful, merry."[8] Others said, "he had a large heart; he was always accessible; there was nothing mean or unworthy in him; with a large fund of humour, he was always a most delightful companion."[9] A friend summed it up well: "He had an intense belief in the unchanging love of God which supported him through all and gave him a pleasure in life it was refreshing to witness."[10]

The years at Bremgarten were the happiest in Bullinger's life, and without a doubt Elizabeth Dodson helped to make them so. Theirs was a relationship which mutually sustained and refreshed. He called her "Lizzie" and referred to himself as "P.U." (Pet Uncle).[11] A letter that was written to her by a friend after Dr. Bullinger's death, is illuminating:

> You knew our dear Friend better than anyone because you lived with him and saw him in adversity and prosperity and from what he told me in June last year, when we dined together, he was enjoying the most peaceful part of his life.[12]

Another friend wrote at the same time,

> Was there ever such an uncle and niece; I never knew of any. What a comfort it will be to you when you are able to think that no devotion could have exceeded yours,

BULLINGER'S STUDY WITH DESK MADE ESPECIALLY FOR HIM.

and that it was given unceasingly. I am sure you will be
glad that Llandudno was given up that you might make
a home for him and be such a strength and comfort to
him.[13]

And Lizzie was exactly that—a strength and a comfort. She
managed the household with efficiency and good humor; she
was an expert hostess, always ready to entertain friends and
associates; and she was also an astute business woman who helped
with the publication and distribution of his work.[14]

Their home, Bremgarten, looked out on North End Road, a
broad avenue that began at the village of Golders Green and
proceeded up a long hill toward Hampstead Heath, one of the
largest parks in London. The house was spacious and comfortable. There was a dining room in the front and a parlor in the
back, with glass doors opening out to the garden. The garden
was a favorite place in nice weather. They often had tea by the
back hedge with its tumbling cascades of creamy white roses,
Bullinger's favorites.[15]

Upstairs, the front of the house was dominated by the doctor's
study, with its great bay window overlooking the street. It was
furnished with an imposing desk that had been specially made
so that he could refer to multiple books at the same time. The
walls of the study were lined with bookshelves. His library was
extensive, including the works of all known contemporary writers of biblical scholarship as well as volumes on history, orni-
thology, botany, gazetteers, puzzle books, word games, and, of
course, music. He was described as an avid and rapid reader
who "digested with ease the thoughts of others."[16] Behind the
study was Dr. Bullinger's bedroom, a small and simply furnished
room at the back of the house. Over his bed hung a plaque,
painted for him by a friend. It read, "I rejoice at thy word, as
one that findeth great spoil. Psa. cxix.162."[17]

Music was part of life at Bremgarten. Dr. Bullinger frequently
played the piano or the violin after dinner. True to his childhood promise to his father not to neglect music in the life he
had chosen, Bullinger had continued to play and to write music
throughout his adult life. While in Walthamstow he had once
won first prize at the Stratford Music Festival for a tune to a

hymn he composed on the spot. When there was no organist for services at St. Stephen's, he would step off the pulpit to play the organ and then carry on as reader and preacher.[18]

Throughout the course of his life, Bullinger composed more than seventy hymns. These were published in at least three known collections: *Hymns for the Waiting Church, Fifty Original Hymn Tunes,* and *Twenty-One Original Hymn Tunes.* In addition, *Sixty-Six Old Breton Tunes* was published separately for the use of the churches of the Breton Evangelical Mission. "Our Hymn of Deliverance," composed by Dr. Bullinger in September 1883 to words written by Dr. Horatius Bonar, was adopted by the Luther Commemoration Committee for the celebration of the fourth centenary of Martin Luther's birthday.[19]

Dorothy Rosemary, Bernard and Ellen Bullinger's little daughter, was a frequent guest at Bremgarten. Her visits were happily anticipated by everyone, including Kaffie, Dr. Bullinger's smooth-haired fox terrier. The words, "Dorothy's coming!" would send Kaffie barking to the front windows. Many years later, those happy times at Bremgarten were still vivid to Dorothy. She fondly remembered sitting with her grandfather by the front window on bank holidays, watching "the Pearlies," the street merchants of London, riding their goat carts up the hill to Hampstead Heath. At the head of the colorful parade rode the "pearly king and queen" with their huge feathered hats and jackets studded with pearl buttons. Dorothy also recalled piggyback rides up and down the stairs on her grandfather's back, balloon games in the parlor, songfests by the piano, and tea parties in the garden with rounds of extra-thin currant bread and butter.[20]

Dr. Bullinger enjoyed words and often used puns. He loved word games, puzzles, conundrums, and enigmas. In a special notebook, he collected many of his own puzzles. The following is a small sample of typical brain teasers:

From "Enigmatical List of Birds":

1. A child's plaything. [Kite]
2. What we all do at every meal. [Swallow]
3. Nothing, twice yourself, and fifty. [Owl]
4. Equality and decay. [Parrot]
5. An instrument for raising weights. [Crane]

E. W. BULLINGER WITH GRANDDAUGHTER

From "Vegetables or Herbs":

1. A small coin and whatever belongs to a Queen. [Penny-royal]
2. A cooking utensil, the first letter of the alphabet, and part of the foot. [Potato]
3. To be on an equality and to cut short. [Parsnip]
4. A bank to confine water, and what everyman must be. [Damson]

From "Charades":

1. My first I would venture for; my second I would venture in; my whole is more talked of than practised. [Friendship]
2. My first a slice affords so nice; My second discomposes. My whole's a bed where honour's head devotedly reposes. [Hammock]
3. My first is a plaything; my second few play with; my third plays with nobody. [Rattlesnake]
4. My first is an obligation; my second is inevitable. My whole is slavery. [Bondage]
5. My first a man will often take; he hopes my next to share. But he who shall possess them both, will find them hard to bear. [Misfortune]

And "Enigmas":

1. Why is a glass cutter the most likely to make the alphabet gallop? [Because he makes decanters]
2. My master left me at home without a doubt. And though I've no legs, he found me gone out. [Fire]
3. What word is there in the English language that by adding a syllable you make it shorter? [Short]
4. I am never into respectable society but in a gang of gypsies and beggars make a principal figure. I generally take up my abode at the extremity of a village. I am never seen in the day but always make my appearance in the middle of night. From the description I have given of myself you will probably take me for a pick-pocket or a

thief; but I am neither and as a proof of it I never was in
a crowd and I no sooner appear before one than I am
gone. [The letter "G"]

5.   Who was the oldest woman? [Antiquity][21]

He wrote and collected poetry of different kinds, including
nonsense rhymes, a style very popular then. It is unclear if Bullinger
wrote the following rhyme, but it certainly was a favorite of his
and was found among the notes in his Bible at his death:

Pussy cat lives in the servants hall
    She can sit on her back and purr,
The little mice live in a crack in the wall
    But they hardly dare venture to stir.

For whenever they think of taking the air
    Or filling their little maw maws,
The pussy cat says, "Come out if you dare
    I will catch you with all of my claws."

Scrabble, scrabble, scrabble went all the little mice
    For they smelt the Cheshire cheese,
The pussy cat said, "It smells very nice
    Now *do* come out, if you please."

"Squeak," said the little mouse. "Squeak, squeak, squeak!"
    Said all the young mice too.
We never creep out when cats are about
    Because we are afraid of you.

So the cunning old cat lay down on the mat
    By the fire in the servants hall,
If the little mice peep they'll think him asleep
    So she rolled herself up in a ball.

"Squeak," said the little mouse, "we'll creep out
    And eat some Cheshire cheese."
        "That silly old cat is asleep on the mat
            And we may sup at our ease."

Nibble, nibble, nibble, went the little mice
  And they licked their little maws,
Then the cunning cat sprang up from the mat
  And caught them with all of her claws![22]

On a more serious note was this poem adapted from one he found in a newspaper:

When you've got some work to do
  Do it now.
If its work you wish were through
  Do it now.
If its work you do not like
  Don't sit down and groan, or strike
Do it now.

Don't put off that piece of work
  Do it now.
Or its disagreeables shirk
  Do it now.
And then when that is done,
  The rest will quickly run
And you will have some fun
  Do it now.[23]

"He Gives in Sleep" is the title of this poem, written by Dr. Bullinger and conveying so much of his loving attitude towards God:

How wondrously He gives! E'en while we sleep:
  When we from all our "works" have ceased, and rest;
And He our life doth mercifully keep.
  Then, without works, are His beloved blest.
Yes! "His beloved!" Loved—not because
  Of any work which we have ever done:
But loved in perfect grace "without a cause,"—
  This is the source whence all our blessings come.

He gives in sleep! In vain we toil, and strive,
  And rise up early, and so late take rest:

> But, while our powers in sweetest sleep revive,
>   And we abandon all our anxious quest—
> Then He bestows His gifts of grace on us,
>   And where we've never sown, He makes us reap
> A harvest full of richest blessing. "Thus
>   He gives to His beloved while they sleep."[24]

Throughout the years, Dr. Bullinger had been active in a secret society known as the Orange Order. This organization was formed during the last years of the eighteenth century by Irish Protestants dedicated to combating their constant adversaries, the Roman Catholics. It was named in honor of King William III, Prince of Orange, whose accession to the throne of England in 1689 established Protestantism as the state religion.[25] In the early nineteenth century, the Order traveled across the Irish Sea to England, carried by the large waves of Irish immigrants and British soldiers who had served in Ireland. Soon, lodges of Orangemen sprang up in many urban centers, particularly in the Midlands.[26]

The battle in England, however, was not a physical one. As years went by, the English lodges took on the aspect of benevolent societies that supported the fight of their brothers across the Irish Sea. In one area, however, all of the lodges were united— in their relentless hostility against Roman Catholicism.

When exactly Bullinger first joined the Orange Order is unknown. It is known, however, that his lodge was situated in Walthamstow and that by 1881 he had risen to the position of Worshipful Master, or head of the lodge. The love and respect of his fellow lodge members for him is attested to by the following letter, written to Elizabeth Dodson after his death:

> Most of us in this Lodge feel that we have lost a real friend, for we looked to your dear Uncle as our Father in Christ. We had but an imperfect knowledge of the glorious truths of God's Word until by God's gracious Providence, we were brought in contact with Dr. Bullinger, who opened up to us the glorious truths of Holy Writ, for which we shall always love and revere his memory.

Of few could we feel so sure that he will hear from his Beloved Master the welcome "Well done, good and faithful servant," for few have laboured so hard and so consistently in the service of his Lord.[27]

In 1908, the year following the move to Bremgarten, Bullinger published *The Chief Musician: or, Studies in the Psalms, and Their Titles,* an explanation with practical application of research work done by James W. Thirtle. Dr. Thirtle, a friend of Bullinger's, had in 1904 published a work titled *The Titles of the Psalms: Their Nature and Meaning Explained,* which was hailed as a landmark in the understanding of the book of Psalms.[28] With the author's encouragement, Bullinger undertook to rework the material in a simpler style, "referring those who seek for further and deeper knowledge, and more exact evidence, to Dr. Thirtle's own work."[29]

Although Bullinger's associations with friends and coworkers seem to have been for the most part friendly, one relationship that began amicably ended painfully. *The Quarterly Record of the Trinitarian Bible Society* records the public account of what happened.

In October 1909, *The Quarterly Record* contained a lengthy report by Dr. Bullinger explaining certain difficulties that had arisen between Dr. Christian David Ginsburg and the Society regarding the publication of the second edition of Ginsburg's great work, the *Massoretico-Critical Text of the Hebrew Bible.* When the Society had published the first edition in 1894, an agreement between the Society and Dr. Ginsburg gave the copyright to the Society in return for a remuneration plus royalties to Dr. Ginsburg. Although the Society had never totally recouped its original financial investment in the Bible, the publication had nevertheless been considered a spiritual success and had been distributed extensively to Jews both in England and on the Continent. In 1904, when the edition was almost sold out, Dr. Ginsburg contacted the Society with regard to preparing a new edition with amendments.

At first, it seemed as if the new edition would go ahead as planned. For unknown reasons, however, negotiations soon broke down. In June 1905, Dr. Bullinger met with Dr. Ginsburg. What took place was not recorded, but the result of the meeting was a decisive split between the two former collaborators and friends. The Trinitarian Bible Society reluctantly decided not to proceed further with the new edition of the Hebrew Bible. Sometime later, they published a reprint of the first edition.

Nothing more was heard about this regrettable affair until January 1909, when a leading article in *The London Times* called attention to the forthcoming publication of Dr. Ginsburg's new edition of the Hebrew Bible to be put out by the British and Foreign Bible Society. A few days later, *The Times* printed a letter from John Ritson and Arthur Taylor, secretaries of the British and Foreign Bible Society, describing Dr. Ginsburg's proposed work and adding that three scholars of international renown—Professor Strack of Berlin, Herr Kahan of Leipzig, and Professor Eberhard Nestle of Maulbronn—had been hired by the Society as proofreaders.[30]

Dr. Bullinger, acting in his official capacity as secretary of the Trinitarian Bible Society, wrote immediately to *The Times:*

> NEW EDITION OF THE HEBREW BIBLE.
> To the Editor of 'The Times'
>
> Sir,—After the article and leader in your journal of Saturday last, and the letter of the secretaries of the British and Foreign Bible Society, which appeared on January 27th, it is only right that you and your readers should be placed in possession of the following facts, as no subject can be correctly represented or understood unless all the *data* necessary to that end are available.
>
> The "New Edition" in question will be precisely the same, as far as the text is concerned, as that prepared by Dr. Ginsburg, and recently published by the Trinitarian Bible Society (of 7, Bury Street, Bloomsbury), at an expense of over £2,000.
>
> As that Edition was running out, Dr. Ginsburg approached the committee of the Trinitarian Bible Society in view of their bringing out a Second Edition, in which the only difference would have been certain additional marginal readings, discovered since the completion of the First Edition.

The Committee of the Trinitarian Bible Society did not see their way clear to proceed any further in the matter, and printed a Second Edition from the plates of the First, which is still on sale at a greatly reduced price, and on which royalties continue to be paid. A Third Edition is being prepared in which there will be an appendix of several pages of typographical errors.

The "New Edition of the Hebrew Bible," referred to in your journal of the 23rd and 27th inst., will be the Edition that was declined by the Trinitarian Bible Society, and has since been taken in hand by the British and Foreign Bible Society.

It ought to be generally known that, so far as the text is concerned, this "New Edition" will be precisely the same as the other two, *minus* the before-mentioned corrections.

I may add that the copyright of this work is the sole property of the Trinitarian Bible Society, and it is quite an open question whether the proposed additional notes will constitute this a "New Edition of the Hebrew Bible" without infringing this copyright.

Yours faithfully,
E. W. Bullinger, D.D., Secretary.[31]

Bullinger's letter caused no small stir, and consequently both Professor Nestle and Professor Strack wrote articles in leading journals, lamenting the position in which the British and Foreign Bible Society had placed them in the whole affair.

In the meantime, the Trinitarian Bible Society had decided to seek legal counsel from their solicitor, Mr. Vyvian G. Hicks. He advised that, to settle this affair as privately as possible, a letter be sent to the British and Foreign Bible Society setting forth the matter of copyright infringement and requesting a certain remuneration to help recoup some of the original expense, with a small royalty on future sales.

Solicitors corresponded for several months over the matter, but the committee of the British and Foreign Bible Society declined to propose any compensation and refused to submit the matter to friendly arbitration. Not wishing to go to court, the Trinitarian Bible Society reported the facts in the *Quarterly Record* and left the issue "not to a judge and a jury, but to a larger tribunal: to the Committee and members of the British and Foreign Bible Society . . . and, to the still larger body of Christian supporters of that Society"—and, finally, to the public.[32]

But from Dr. Ginsburg they heard nothing. His royalties were held for him at the Trinitarian Bible Society's offices as he had always requested. Eleven months later he had yet to collect them. It is not known if he ever did.[33]

CHAPTER ELEVEN

The Companion Bible

In November 1910, Bullinger shared the following with the readers of *Things to Come:*

> Our appeal in October, 1909, brought forth so many letters from hitherto unknown friends that we were overwhelmed with praise and thanksgivings.
>
> We had no idea of the extent to which God is using *Things to Come* for the instruction and blessing of his people in the remotest parts of the earth until we made that appeal.[1]

It was certainly true that *Things to Come* carried Bullinger's work farther afield than any of his other publications. Its readership had spread throughout Europe and reached as far as the United States, Canada, Australia, New Zealand, and Africa.

It was Mr. William Barron of Gisborne, New Zealand, a devoted reader of *Things to Come,* who first suggested the concept of *The Companion Bible* to Dr. Bullinger. Mr. Barron had been introduced to *Things to Come* early in the century and shortly afterward had begun a correspondence with Dr. Bullinger. During a trip to England in 1907, Barron went to see him in London. Later, he described their meeting:

> Five years ago [in 1907] I went home to see my Mother and relations and also Dr. Bullinger with whom I had

been corresponding for six or eight years. This proved
to be the beginning of "The Companion Bible." For three
years previous to this I had been writing and trying to
show forth the need of such a work, in which he could
bring forth all that the Lord had been pleased to give
him.

Until we met we could not understand how this could
be done apart from a new translation (which no doubt
would have been excellent) but which never could have
taken the place of the A.V. amongst the Common people.
"The Companion Bible" will be the gathering together
of all his great labours, and the crowning part of all his
works while it will bring much glory to God even our
Father and much help to his dear ignorant and misguided
people.[2]

With Barron's promise of financial support, Bullinger set to
work immediately, characteristically undaunted by the immense
task before him—the compilation of a lifetime of biblical study.
Beginning with the word studies that had been the genesis of
the *Lexicon and Concordance* in the late 1860s, the new Bible
would also contain Bullinger's research on figures of speech,
Old and New Testament chronology, the spiritual significance
of numbers, the stars, weights and measures, meanings of proper
names, definitions of terms, historical records, and explanations
of Eastern manners and customs. Contemporary biblical scholarship, including Ginsburg's *Massoretico-Critical Text of the Hebrew Bible* for the Old Testament and for the New Testament,
and textual critics such as Griesbach, Lachmann, Tischendorf,
Tregelles, and Alford would be cited. Places where the biblical
text had been altered by the translators were to be noted, as
well as recent archaeological discoveries in Assyria, Egypt, and
Palestine.

Bullinger decided upon a system of marginal notes wherein
the reader could have the explanation side by side with the text.
Items of particular importance or difficulty requiring more space
were to become separate appendixes.

Two special innovations in *The Companion Bible* were the extensive use of the information in the Massorah, never before

presented in any text of the Authorized Version, and the first systematic attempt to indicate and analyze structure.[3]

Dr. Bullinger was careful to explain why he had chosen the name *The Companion Bible:*

> It is called THE COMPANION BIBLE because its wide margin is intended to be a Companion to the Text; and the whole is designed as the Companion of all readers of the Bible.
>
> The human element is excluded, as far as possible, so that the reader may realize that the pervading object of the book is not merely to enable him to interpret the Bible, but to make the Bible the interpreter of God's Word, and Will, to him.
>
> To the same end this BIBLE is not associated with the name of any man; so that its usefulness may neither be influenced nor limited by any such consideration; but that it may commend itself, on its own merits, to the whole English-speaking race.
>
> It is NOT A NEW Translation.
> It is NOT AN AMENDED Translation.
> It is NOT A COMMENTARY.[4]

Bullinger did not want his name associated with his new project because he did not want it printed on the title page of the Bible. He wanted to avoid *The Companion Bible* ever becoming known as "Bullinger's Bible." He was content, he said, to let the crowning achievement of his life's labors stand on its own merits.[5]

His strong convictions can be seen in a letter he wrote to a friend in 1909:

> I am on a very great work at this present moment. It will take 2 years more to complete.
>
> When I write again I will send you a prospectus. Part I (of 4 parts) will be out by Xmas. Till then all is private. After then it can not be too widely *known*. But *my name* is *never* to be associated with it. But is given and is to be kept in *strictest* confidence.[6]

He did not waver in this desire. Three years later, still working on the Bible, he made the following request in a letter to
the same friend: "Please respect my desire for anonymity in
respect to this!"[7]

It is interesting to note that, in choosing the format for the
Bible, Bullinger went counter to the third rule of the Trinitarian
Bible Society's "Laws and Regulations," which stated that the
Society would circulate only Holy Scriptures without note or
comment.[8] This regulation prevented the Society ever acquiring the copyrights or being able to use their own channels for
its distribution. Nevertheless, the Society would eventually profit
from future sales of *The Companion Bible* because of the terms
of Bullinger's will.

Anxious to get the Bible into print quickly, Bullinger decided
to issue it in four parts with each volume priced as inexpen-
sively as possible. Mr. Henry Frowde, a well-known publisher
connected with Oxford University Press, agreed to publish the
Bible.

The task facing Bullinger was formidable. Though an early
riser since his youth, he now rose even earlier and by four in the
morning was already at his desk.[9] Activities he had formerly
enjoyed, especially his extensive, hand-written correspondence
with people all over the world, were now set aide. In 1909 he
wrote to a close friend in the United States: "No one under-
stands better than you how pressed I am, and how I avoid all
unnecessary penmanship."[10]

Relief from some of the workload came from two very different men: Henry Charles Bowker and Charles Welch.

Henry Bowker, a seventy-year-old retired schoolmaster, moved
to Northwood, Middlesex, a few miles northwest of London in
1909. By 1910, he had become a member of the committee of
the Trinitarian Bible Society and a member of its finance sub-
committee as well. Sometime after his coming to London,
Bowker began giving Dr. Bullinger editorial help with *Things to
Come* and *The Companion Bible*. A quiet, unassuming man, he
kept himself severely in the background. It was said of him:

> He gave up much in his early days for truths which he
> held strongly; but was patient with all men, and slow to

strive, for, as he frequently said, "all of us err somewhere, and I may be erring here." He was a ripe scholar, and a Christian gentleman.[11]

Charles Welch was born on April 25, 1880, in Bermondsey, London, in the shadow of Mary Magdalene Church, the site of Ethelbert Bullinger's first curacy twenty years before. Like so many other families in Bermondsey, Welch's family was poor and his father often unemployed. They were not churchgoers. Charles went to the neighborhood school until the age of fourteen, when his family's scanty resources made it necessary for him to stop and seek employment. Despite their poverty, the family was stable. Reminiscing about his early years, Welch recalled:

> I have before indicated that while we were as a family "without God in the world," we were a happy family, kindly, generous, tolerant and rigidly honest. My father was quick tempered, so quick, that before he was half through some explosive utterance, he would be all apology. I remember some hard words being uttered between my two parents, but in the night he came where I was sleeping to assure me all was well, and that he was forgiven.[12]

One day in November 1900, while Charles was walking in London, someone handed him an announcement about a forthcoming meeting on "Skeptics and the Bible." Curious, he went to the gathering. For the first time in his life, he came across people who actually believed the Scriptures were true. The following night, Romans 10:9 was taught, and he confessed Jesus as Lord in his life. The skeptic had become a believer.

Now, aged twenty-one and at a crossroads in life, Welch sought to learn all he could about the Scriptures. In 1904, he became associated with the Bible Training College in London. During his time with this group, he acquired much knowledge, but he resigned in 1906 following doctrinal disputes with the leadership of the college. In the years that followed, he continued to study the Bible, giving particular emphasis to the dispensations, or the different time periods of God's dealings with mankind. It was during this time that, through friends who were readers of *Things to Come,* he became acquainted with Bullinger's work and was prompted to suggest a meeting. As recounted by Welch in his autobiography:

> Toward the end of 1908 I felt moved to write to Dr. Bullinger. . . .
>
> After some delay, the Doctor granted me an interview at the offices of the Trinitarian Bible Society, Bury Street, London, and that hour's interview proved to be the most critical turning point in my life and ministry. The Doctor invited me to say what was troubling me, and I feared, that after all, he would smile indulgently, pat me on the shoulder and tell me to go home and forget all about it. Again I plucked up courage and here is a transcript of our conversation.
>
> Myself—From your writings Doctor, I believe I am right in saying that you do not believe "The Church" began at Pentecost, but rather, that the Dispensational Boundary must be drawn at Acts 28?
>
> Dr. Bullinger—That is so. I have made that quite clear.
>
> Myself—Well, what seems to me to stultify the position you have taken regarding Acts 28, is, that you nevertheless treat the whole of Paul's epistles as one group, starting with Romans, ending with Thessalonians, with Ephesians somewhere in the centre.
>
> To my amazement and joy, the Doctor looked at me for a moment, then slapping his thigh with his hand said:
>
> "That scraps half the books I have written. But we want the Truth, and the Truth is there in what you have said."
>
> I felt that here was indeed "grace." Dr. Bullinger was a man of world repute, a scholar and an elder. I was a

young man of twenty-eight years and unknown. We spent
the remainder of our brief interview in considering the
dispensational implications that arise from observing the
relation of Paul's epistles to the boundary line of Acts
28 thus:

Acts 28.

Epistles Before.	Epistles After.
1) Galatians	1) Ephesians
2) 1 Thessalonians	2) Philippians
3) 2 Thessalonians	3) Colossians
4) Hebrews	4) Philemon
5) 1 Corinthians	5) 1 Timothy
6) 2 Corinthians	6) Titus
7) Romans	7) 2 Timothy

At the close of this important interview, Bullinger said:

"I will now let you into a secret. I am just commencing what I feel sure will be my last work, *The Companion Bible*. I have prayed that someone be sent along to relieve me of some of the pages in *Things to Come*. You're the man."

At first I demurred. I felt that the standard set by the articles in *Things to Come* was above my attainment, and I was also rather intimidated as I visualized the calibre of its readers. . . .

However the Doctor persuaded me that the call was of the Lord, and so in March 1909 there appeared an article entitled "The Unity of the Spirit (Eph. 4:3). What is it?"[13]

After Welch's first article for *Things to Come* in March 1909, he commenced a series titled "Dispensational Expositions," which became a regular feature.[14]

With Bowker and Welch's assistance, Dr. Bullinger was able to proceed swiftly on *The Companion Bible*. By the end of 1909, *Part I, The Pentateuch,* with fifty-two appendixes, was released. It caused considerable stir among Christian circles and prompted reviews, many of them enthusiastic, in leading publications.

In *The Record,* April 8, 1910, reviewer W. St. Clair Tisdall wrote:

This is the first volume of a new edition of the English
Bible, to be completed in four parts. Nearly half of each
page is devoted to notes, which are short and very much
to the point. In many places these notes are lucid and
admirable. They will be found by the ordinary reader to
clear up many difficulties. The volume does not bear
the name of the commentator, but he is evidently a good
Hebraist. The amount of work devoted to the book must
have been immense. In many places great use has been
made of Dr. Ginsburg's Massoretico-critical Hebrew text,
and all the really important various readings are given.
Places in which the Authorised Version is clearly wrong
are corrected in the notes. Reference is made to recent
archaeological discoveries. No praise can be too great
for the reverent as well as scholarly way in which Holy
Scripture is dealt with.[15]

Another periodical, *The Sword and Trowel,* commented:

This "Companion Bible" is "the Authorized Version, with
the structures and notes critical, explanatory and suggestive," and it is really a capital production. The short
pithy notes are most valuable, and what is specially refreshing in these days, they are on the side of the orthodox faith and give no countenance to the vagaries of
"Higher Criticism."[16]

The prevalence of higher criticism, is reflected in the following review from the London paper *The Daily News:*[17]

This is the first part of a new edition of the Authorised
Version of the Bible of 1611, with the structures and
notes, critical, explanatory and suggestive. The various
readings and alternative renderings are fully given in
the broad margins, and for the first time the facts and
phenomena treasured up in the Massorah are given in
connection with the Authorised Version.
  While we have nothing but praise for the care and
skill which are manifest on every page, we doubt whether

there is a wide-spread demand for a book built upon a conception of Biblical interpretation which includes the dogma of verbal inspiration. "The record of the dates and periods stated in the Bible are as much inspired as any other portion of it. . . . They must be as unreservedly received and believed as any other statements contained in its pages." Evolution is ruled out in a sentence. The story of the fall is accepted in bare literalness. "In Genesis III, we have neither allegory, myth, legend, nor fable, but literal historical facts set forth and emphasised by the use of certain figures of speech."

Many other instances could be given in which the interpretation is hopelessly at variance with the results of modern Biblical criticism.[18]

Other reviews were critical also. From *The Inquirer,* dated March 26, 1910, came the following:

We regard the appearance of this elaborate work as a very melancholy phenomenon, and we should have thought that at this time of day the publication of such a book was impossible.[19]

Negative comments notwithstanding, *Part I* of *The Companion Bible* sold very well and was widely distributed. The following review, from the *New York Observer* of May 12, 1910, attests to the enthusiasm with which the Bible was received from readers overseas:

"The Companion Bible" is a new edition of the English Bible. . . . It is a self-explanatory Bible designed for the general use of all English readers throughout the world. It has an amount of information, much of it hitherto inaccessible to the ordinary English reader, in its wide margins not to be found in any edition of the Authorized Version extant. . . . It is called "The Companion Bible" because its wide margin is intended to be a companion to the text, and the whole is designed to be the companion of all readers of the Bible. The human element is excluded, as far as possible, so that the reader may realize that the pervading object of the book is not merely to enable him to interpret the Bible, but to make the Bible the interpreter of God's Word, and will, to him.[20]

Part II, Joshua to Job, became available in September, 1910. It was issued with the following notice:

In compliance with several requests, it has been decided to issue the Old Testament in four parts instead of three. As many have expressed the desire to have the Psalms at an early date, arrangements have been made to issue the Psalms, Proverbs, Ecclesiastes, and Song of Solomon (with their twelve Appendixes) as Part III, and the Prophets as Part IV.[21]

In one review of *Part II* of the Bible for the *Expository Times,* February 1911, an ironic statement must have brought a wry smile to Bullinger's face. It was underlined in his copy:

So conservative are the notes and appendixes that if they are right the great bulk of the Biblical scholarship of our day has been wasted labour.[22]

CHAPTER TWELVE

The Last Years

IN THE DECEMBER 1910 issue of *Things to Come,* Bullinger announced the features planned for the coming year:

OUR PROGRAMME FOR 1911

will (D.V.) include a series of articles on a subject entirely new to most of our readers.[1]

It will be a privilege and honour to be the first Magazine to make known these precious things on this side of the Atlantic.

We have had personal correspondence with the author Mr. Ivan Panin. . . .

The purport of Ivan Panin's papers will be to show that our Bible, *like all the other Works of God* is perfect, and is constructed on the same marvellous *numeric design* running through its every conceivable detail. . . .

We propose to say more of Ivan Panin personally, introductory to his first paper, which we hope will appear in our January number.

The Rev. J. Christopher Smith will commence a series of the Bible Word Studies, and will specially include such words as are vital to a clear understanding of the Word.

Mr. H. C. Bowker, M.A., will contribute some papers on "The Gospel of the Glory of Christ."

The Dispensational Expositions will be continued by Mr. Charles H. Welch.[2]

An English picnic, May 1910. Bullinger in center, Elizabeth Dodson at right with the dog.

With such expert and trusted help, Bullinger could free himself somewhat from the pressure of deadlines to work on *The Companion Bible* and other projects. As he entered his seventy-fourth year, he seems to have also continued his heavy travel schedule. In early January he was in Italy visiting with the agents of the Trinitarian Bible Society. He then went on to Paris before returning home by the middle of the month.

On February 17, 1911, Dr. Bullinger's younger son, Bernard, died suddenly at the age of forty-four. The death certificate specified "respiratory failure." He had been the owner of *The Rose and Crown,* a pub across the street from St. Bartholomew's Hospital in London. Bernard was survived by his widow, Ellen, and his daughter, Dorothy Rosemary, then four years old.

Within a month of the death of the son to whom she had been so close, Emma Bullinger died also. Her whereabouts during the final years of her life are uncertain. Prior to her death, of asthma and chronic bronchitis, she had been staying at the home of one Arthur Samuel Markes of 29 Stockfield Road, Streatham, in southwest London. Mother and son were buried together in Highgate Cemetery in London.

The "little old queen" was gone as well. Victoria had died on January 22, 1901, a few short years after her triumphant diamond jubilee. Her reign of sixty-three years had been the longest in British history as well as one of the most prosperous. She was succeeded by her eldest son Edward, who reigned as Edward VII until his death in 1910. He was then succeeded by his son George, who reigned as George V.

In April 1911, King George was presented with a special Bible by the Trinitarian Bible Society. It commemorated two important events: his coronation and the tercentenary, or three hundredth anniversary, of the Authorized (King James) Version of the Bible. Dr. Bullinger noted the following:

> We rejoice to think that from the religious and secular press the Authorized Version of our English Bible has been most highly commended, and that the King has spoken in the highest terms of it.
>
> Truly it is a worthy heritage which the Translators have handed down to us. We cannot speak too highly of

the privilege we have enjoyed during the last 300 years
of an open Bible—a Bible that could be read and understood by the people.[3]

Perhaps gratitude for this heritage was on Dr. Bullinger's mind
when he first conceived the idea of a monument to honor William Tyndale, a man to whom all English-speaking people who
love the Bible are deeply indebted.

William Tyndale had been born in England about 1490 and
received a B.A. degree from Oxford in 1512. He distinguished
himself as a brilliant scholar with great knowledge of the Scriptures. After graduating from Oxford, Tyndale became a tutor
in the home of Sir John Walsh, a man who often entertained
both nobility and church dignitaries. Tyndale witnessed such
lack of knowledge of the Bible among Sir John's many visitors
that he began to teach it to all who were interested. He became
known for his goodness and sincerity as well as for the straightforwardness of his teaching. Straightforwardness, however, was
often confused with heresy in those days, during which Roman
Catholicism was the only religion in England. It was not long
before Tyndale found himself at odds with Church authorities
and embroiled in controversy.[4] In one encounter with a priest,
who argued that the common people could live better by Church
laws than by the Bible, Tyndale made this memorable reply:

If God spare my life, ere many years, I will cause the boy
that driveth the plough in England shall know more of
the Scripture than thou doest.[5]

Gutenberg's invention of moveable type in 1456 had initiated
the printing of Bibles, but these texts were scarce, accessible to
scholars and clergy only. Moreover, they were printed in Latin,
making them unintelligible to the unschooled lower classes.

Tyndale set out to translate the Bible into English, the language of common people. He started his work in London but
was forced to flee to Germany in 1523 to escape imprisonment
by Church authorities. While in Germany, he visited Martin
Luther at Wittenberg and completed his English New Testament, which was printed there and then smuggled back to En-

gland. This very first printed edition of the New Testament in English was greeted with joy by believers but denounced by Church officials; copies were confiscated and burned wherever they were discovered. Tyndale, now living in obscurity on the Continent and working on the Old Testament translation, became a marked man. He was captured in 1535 in Antwerp, Belgium, which was then under Spanish rule, and imprisoned in the fortress at Vilvorde for almost two years before being burned at the stake on October 6, 1536.[6]

On a trip to Belgium in May 1911, Dr. Bullinger visited Vilvorde. He was dismayed to find that, although there were statues honoring Tyndale in England, no monument stood at this spot, the place of his execution. Together with Monsieur L. Valat, secretary of the Belgian Bible Society, Dr. Bullinger inquired in the town and found considerable interest in this distinguished Englishman who had been imprisoned in the Castle of Vilvorde and had died a martyr's death. At the town hall they were received graciously and were encouraged to begin making plans for a monument.

Leaving Monsieur Valat to make the necessary arrangements in Belgium, Dr. Bullinger returned to London and, with his usual enthusiasm and energy, set about designing the monument and raising the necessary funds. He wanted the following to be inscribed on the monument in English, French, Flemish, and Latin:

> William Tyndale, who suffered martyrdom under Spanish rule on Oct. 6th, 1536, was first strangled and then burnt in the Grande Place de Vilvorde. Among his last words were these:
>
> "Lord, open the eyes of the King of England."
>
> This Prayer was answered within a year by the issue, under Royal Authority, of the whole Bible in English.[7]

At the time of this writing, the monument still stands in a small park somewhat outside the modern city center of Vilvorde.

In July 1911, *The Companion Bible, Part III, Psalms to Song of Solomon*, was issued. *The Christian* had the following to say about it:

> The great undertaking known as THE COMPANION BIBLE proceeds apace, and with Part III the reverent student of Holy Scripture finds himself led through one of the most attractive divisions of the Word, namely, the Book of Psalms, the Book of Proverbs, Ecclesiastes, and the Song of Solomon. Those who have consulted the earlier Parts will know what to expect in this—a treatment which is at once in harmony with the high claims of the Inspired Book and designed to enable the Word to explain itself. In days when ancient error and modern speculation are only too frequently *read into* Scripture, it is no small privilege to submit oneself to the guidance of those who, in the fear of God, come to the Bible as learners, and bow to its teaching as disciples of Christ should do.[8]

By autumn, Dr. Bullinger had yet another book ready for the printers: a compilation of his articles on Hebrews 11 that had originally appeared in *Things To Come*. Lack of capital had prevented its publication, so he had appealed to those readers who wanted to see the book in print:

THE "GREAT CLOUD OF WITNESSES."

Under this title the Editor proposes to reprint the Editorials on Heb. xi, which were concluded in the October number.

Many readers have desired it, and others have enquired concerning it.

As the Editor has no capital he hesitates to give the order to the printer. But if he were assured that a sufficient number of friends would order copies he would proceed with it at once. The work makes about 460 pages and will form a handsome and suitable present.

The money need not be sent with the order, except where it is desired to save extra trouble and expense later on in postages for notices and receipts, etc.

If orders are sent *at once* it may be possible to get it
out before Christmas.[9]

The appeal was successful. In December, Bullinger was able
to announce that copies of *The Great Cloud of Witnesses* were
promised by the printers for December 14, 1911, "which will be
in ample time for the season's presents, and will relieve many of
our readers from the difficulty of deciding what they shall give."[10]
Bullinger commenced the book with an analysis of the structure of the entire epistle of Hebrews for the following reasons:

> We trust that our readers are by this time duly impressed
> with the fact that we must not give an interpretation of
> any passage of Scripture, or even a chapter, apart from
> its context.
>
> We have learnt also that the *Scope* of the passage must
> be gathered from its *Structure*. In other words, we must
> know what it is all about before we can find a clue to the
> meaning of the words: and we can find this out only by
> getting the *Structure* of the whole context.
>
> As our subject here consists of a complete chapter, it
> will be necessary for us to see the exact place in which it
> stands in relation to the Epistle as a whole.[11]

The message of *The Great Cloud of Witnesses* concerned believing God:

> None can hope in vain who believe God.
>
> This is why the common question, Do we believe? is
> so senseless. The real question is, not Do we believe? but
> WHAT do we believe? or rather, WHOM do we believe.
>
> We believe many things that man says, and that man
> promises. But the question is, are they true?
>
> It is not a question of the *sincerity* with which we be-
> lieve, but of the *truth* of what we believe.
>
> The more sincerely we believe what is not true, the
> worse it is for us. This holds good in every department
> of life. If what we hear be not true, then, to doubt it,
> means our safety.

When we give ear to man, we can never be certain that what he says is true. But when we give ear to God, we can set to our seal that "God is true" in what He says; and that "He is faithful" in what He promises. Faith is hearing God and believing what He says. This is the simple definition.[12]

The Great Cloud of Witnesses was well received by the growing numbers of Bullinger's followers. According to one review:

Chapter eleven of the Epistle to the Hebrews is a mine of precious gems to all believers. Dr. Bullinger in *The Great Cloud of Witnesses* takes each gem and polishes it to a splendour not before appreciated, and digs down to find many more to add to that galaxy so that his reader feels compelled to say with the Psalmist: "O how love I thy law! it is my meditation all the day."[13]

In the autumn of 1911, Dr. Bullinger also wrote a short editorial in *Things to Come* to clarify one of his newer scriptural positions: the dividing of the Pauline Epistles with respect to Acts 28:28. Bullinger had been reworking the question of the canonical versus the chronological order of the Epistles since his meeting with Charles Welch in 1908. He began teaching his findings early in 1911 at Trinitarian Bible Society meetings. In October, Bullinger wrote:

We have had several letters from our readers asking questions concerning difficulties which they have met with in connection with the dividing of the word of truth, at Acts 28. . . .

We must not forget that difficulties must need arise in cutting the tether of traditions in which we have all been so long bound and tied. Some are almost afraid to use their liberty so newly found; others are in danger of using it too freely.

Some stand still for fear of moving in a wrong direction; others go forward stumbling, for fear of standing still. . . .

This being so, we propose, in our Editorials commencing next month, to examine the very FOUNDATIONS of Dispensational Truth; and endeavour to place them so truly, and fix them so firmly that, once we are well grounded in them, we may build upon them with such certainty that our difficulties will be removed, and our readers will find themselves in a position to answer all their own questions as they may afterwards arise.

What we ask for now, therefore, is *patience.* Let us hold all questions as to this or that *particular* difficulty in abeyance until we are grounded in the great *general* principle.

We are not "directors of the conscience," but "ministers of the Word," and our desire is, so to minister it as to leave individual readers to direct their own consciences by the Word.[14]

The editorials continued in *Things to Come* for almost two years. Later, they were published in one volume titled *The Foundations of Dispensational Truth,* the last book to bear Bullinger's name as author. In it he wrote:

When we come to the Epistles of Paul, we have to treat them chronologically, and to divide them into two categories—earlier and later.

The earlier series was written before Acts xxviii., and the later written after the formal rejection of the proclamation of the offer of the King and the Kingdom by Peter and the twelve during the Dispensation covered by the Acts of the Apostles. These two series are of equal importance; but, at the same time, they are distinct and separate. . . .[15]

. . . the Dispensation of the Acts of the Apostles is not the present Dispensation of the Mystery, in which the Spirit of Truth Himself is guiding us through the Scripture of truth.[16]

He emphasized the significance of the order of the Epistles, an order unchanged in every Greek manuscript:

This fact tells us that, whatever may be the teaching of the chronological order, *i.e.,* the order in which they were written, the order *for us* to-day is none other than the canonical order (beginning with Romans and ending with 2 Thessalonians). It is not that one order is right and the other wrong. Both are right; neither is wrong.

Both are important, but not equally so: for while the chronological order is full of most important information for all who would understand Dispensational truth, the canonical order is full of deepest instruction as to doctrinal and experimental truth. . . .

For those who first received them, the chronological order was of greater importance—in fact, all-important. But for us to-day, since the rejection of the testimony of "them that heard Him" and the consequent postponement of the Kingdom, the canonical order is the more important.[17]

Bullinger concluded the series by stating his convictions about the present time—convictions that to many were highly controversial:

We have come into a new Dispensation, where the old things have passed away; where all things are become new; where all things are of God. That which is perfect has come. "Signs and wonders, and divers miracles, and spiritual gifts" have here no place. The gift of prophecy has failed, as foretold in I Cor. xiii.8.

The gift of tongues has ceased.

Knowledge *(gnosis)* of the mysteries has no place (I Cor. xiii.8; cp. verse 2 and xiv.2).

That which was partial and incomplete has been done away.

All these things had their appointed place and service in that Dispensation to which they belonged. They were to be sought and used and controlled; but we are now in a Dispensation where all is perfect. The word "perfect" means that we have come to the end, or the last Dispensation.[18]

On July 6, 1912, Dr. Bullinger celebrated the silver jubilee of his ordination in the Church of England. Throughout his career he had often written and taught doctrines foreign or contradictory to established Church of England doctrine. Yet he had never sought separation from it. While officially remaining in the Church of England, he was aptly described as "a *free* Christian, who, without distinction of denominations, desires only to see all Christians preaching Christ and Him crucified."[19] Another friend once remarked, his "sympathies [were] not limited by the bounds of denomination, nor his influence by the borders of a parish."[20]

Appendix 19 of *The Companion Bible*, "The Serpent of Genesis 3," indicates that Bullinger's straightforward criticisms, regardless "of the praise of man or the fear of man,"[21] could also be leveled at the church:

> The history of Gen. 3 is intended to teach us the fact that Satan's sphere of activities is in the *religious* sphere, and not the spheres of crime or immorality; that his battlefield is not the sins arising from human depravity, but the *unbelief* of the human heart. We are not to look for Satan's activities to-day in the newspaper press, or the police courts; but in the pulpit, and in professors' chairs. Wherever the Word of God is called in question, there we see the trail of "that old serpent, which is the Devil, and Satan." This is why anything against the true interests of the Word of God (as being such) finds a ready admission into the newspapers of the world, and is treated as "general literature." This is why anything in favour of its inspiration and Divine origin and its spiritual truth is rigidly excluded as being "controversial."
>
> This is why Satan is quite content that the *letter* of Scripture should be accepted in Gen. 3, as he himself accepted the letter of Ps. 91.11. . . .
>
> This is his object in perpetuating the traditions of the "snake" and the "apple," because it ministers to the acceptance of his lie, the hiding of God's truth, the support of tradition, the jeers of the infidel, the opposition of the critics, and the stumbling of the weak in faith.[22]

How Anglican Church authorities may have felt about Dr. Bullinger, especially during the latter part of his ministry, is unknown. He remained among the ranks of their clergy, and no record seems to exist of any official censure. For the most part, the criticism he received came from smaller independent Christian groups such as the Plymouth Brethren; from the Anglican Church, whether High Party or Low, there seems to have been only silence. It was a time of comparative freedom for Anglican clergy, and this may be one reason for the silence. The church's attitude was that it "could not rein its teachers so tightly, and must allow room for individual conviction of truth."[23] One contemporary critic, however, blamed the Church of England's lax attitude on its own "weak government, with tangled jurisdictions, crossfire of law-courts, [and] elastic articles. . . ."[24]

The following excerpt from *The Great Cloud of Witnesses* gives Bullinger's insights into the nature of "religion" and religious intolerance:

> . . . *the subjugation of the conscience,* and *the extinction of liberty* . . . are, and ever have been, the two aims and objects of religious persecution.
>
> The spirit of them is seen in the religious intolerance of modern Christian and so-called Protestant sects, who suffer not their members to worship outside their own bodies, without making them feel certain pains and penalties, often resulting in excommunication, and extending as far as surveillance of the private life and associations which bring "a visit" from those who assume and usurp an authority in defiance of the simplest laws of Christian liberty. Even those outside, like ourselves, are made to feel the secret power of religious boycotting which is as rife and rampant in some "Christian" sects as in the political sphere.
>
> Let a member of such sects dare to learn and discover some new truth from the Word of God, which happens to be different from what has been determined on by the sects themselves, and at once he is made to experience the worst features of "religion," and to realize, even in his

private life, the power of a secret inquisition, which is as real as that of Rome, and whose tortures, though not physical or in the body, are as acutely felt, and may have after-effects on bodily health and mental powers. . . .

The irreligious world has formulated its Eleventh Commandment. A breach may be made and tolerated in any or all of the other ten; but "Thou shalt not be found out," is more important than all, in the eyes of the world and is certain to bring down the world's condemnation.

It is the same in the religious world. It has its Eleventh Commandment: "thou shalt not differ in opinion." All else will be tolerated; but once this command is broken, the unpardonable sin has been committed.[25]

The autumn of 1912 saw the publication of *The Companion Bible, Part IV, Isaiah to Malachi*, the final section issued during Dr. Bullinger's lifetime. *The Record* gave it an enthusiastic review:

We welcome with great cordiality this fourth part of a truly valuable work. It will prove a mine of wealth to the thoughtful reader and student who wish to know the contents of the Old Testament prophetic books. In addition to the careful analysis giving the literary structure of books, and sections of books, the notes in the right-hand column of the page opposite the text are at once clear, abundant, and suggestive, while the appendixes add material which will be of great service. It reveals an almost incredible knowledge of the Bible, and we do not hesitate to say that it will be one of the best helps to the study of the Scripture; a true "companion." With this fourth part the Old Testament closes, and there remains the New Testament, which, if treated in the same proportion, should need at least two more volumes.[26]

It was Bullinger's custom toward the end of each year to write an open letter to the readers of *Things to Come*, summarizing and looking ahead. He wrote the following in November 1912:

Dear Friends,

Through the grace and goodness of God we have been
enabled to complete our eighteenth volume of *Things to
Come*.

We have had abundant showers of blessing in letters
from many of our readers in all parts of the world; and
we heartily thank them for their encouraging words.

It humbles us when we learn how God has deigned to
own and bless our efforts when all we have done is only
through His own gifts, material as well as spiritual.

We have been preserved in health and strength, notwithstanding the many demands on our time and
strength by other work which press upon us, almost beyond measure.

We ask for your continued prayers and help, so that
we may be kept without care in our service for you and
for God.

Yours in "that blessed hope,"
E. W. Bullinger[27]

This letter would prove to be his last to his thousands of readers throughout the world. Throughout the years, he had often
shared both his successes and his needs with them; he had rejoiced to hear from them and assured them of his steadfast commitment. Now he asked for their prayers and help, admitting
that the demands of his work were "almost beyond measure."

Dr. Bullinger's actions in the new year of 1913 indicate a determination to settle his affairs with care. On January 9 he made
his last will and testament, which seems to have been drawn up
without legal help. He appointed Mr. Vyvian G. Hicks, solicitor
for the Trinitarian Bible Society, and Mr. Maurice Edward Golby,
the Honorary Secretary of the Breton Mission and an old friend,
as executors and trustees.

His estate was to be left to Elizabeth Dodson with the exception of £150 allocated for the education of his granddaughter,
Dorothy Rosemary Bullinger, and £1,000 to be given to Dorothy at Elizabeth Dodson's death.

The executors were given full power to carry on the publication of his works or to dispose of both plates and copyrights—at their discretion and in consultation with Sophie Louisa Fairfield, a neighbor and very close friend of Elizabeth's, and Benjamin J. Hitchcock, the young employee of the Trinitarian Bible Society who had gained Bullinger's respect many years before.[28]

The Companion Bible was dealt with separately. He wrote:

> As to the Companion Bible (the account of which with balance) is with the London County & Westminster Bank Lothbury. The balance with any additional donations received for the same is to be held in trust for the completion of the same (should I leave it unfinished).
>
> If I live to complete it I shall make further Testamentary instructions dealing with the subject, it being my wish that all profits, after providing a sufficiency for the maintenance of Elizabeth Dodson should go to the Trinitarian Bible Society provided it is carried on without any departure from its original and fundamental lines.[29]

The will was witnessed by two old friends and associates, Henry Charles Bowker and Frederick Cecil Lovely.

On January 10, the day after his will was signed, Dr. Bullinger left Charing Cross station in London, bound for a lengthy journey on the Continent. He returned on March 5, having revisited friends and coworkers in France, Italy, Spain, and Belgium.

Bullinger's first destination on his final itinerary was Tremel, where he arrived on January 13. Pasteur LeCoat had been in failing health for some time, and it must have been a poignant visit indeed between these two men who had shared so much during their thirty-year friendship.

Bullinger's last stop was in Belgium, where he discussed the proposed Tyndale monument with Monsieur Valat. Both men had been disappointed with the initial response to the fund appeal, and they now sought other ways to raise money. They also decided to make the monument simpler and therefore less expensive.

Bullinger's health suffered during this long journey. Upon his return to London on March 5, he received a letter from the

BULLINGER WITH ELIZABETH DODSON AT HOME IN BREMGARTEN, NORTH END ROAD, GOLDERS GREEN, LONDON.

committee of the Trinitarian Bible Society expressing sympathy and granting him a leave of absence until the eve of the annual meeting on April 29.

The following day, March 6, he replied:

> Dear Mr. Chairman and Brethren,
>
> I am writing to thank you all very sincerely for your kind expression of sympathy at your last meeting forwarded to me by Mr. Lovely.
>
> I am feeling much better, but am acting on your most kind desire that I should take a further rest from exciting business.
>
> I have not neglected anything vital in connection with the Society.
>
> I have seen Mr. Bowker this afternoon, and have asked him to kindly report the result of my visit to Charleroy and Vilvorde on my return this week.
>
> Again thanking you, believe me.
> Yours most gratefully
> E. W. Bullinger
>
> P.S. Mr. Lovely will report a gift of £50 for any purpose I please, and I have handed it over to the T.B.S. with much pleasure for the Tyndale Memorial Fund.[30]

Bullinger had told some friends that he wanted to travel with Elizabeth to the southern coast of England, and on March 20 they left for a long Easter weekend in Margate. March 26 saw him off to Dublin, Ireland, the last time he would visit there.

Throughout the month of April, Dr. Bullinger remained in London working on *The Companion Bible*. During this crucial time, many decisions had to be made, not least of which was whether to divide the New Testament into two parts. This was a departure from the original agreement with William Barron, who was largely financing the work. Sometime during the month, Bullinger wrote to William Barron in New Zealand, informing him of his decision to publish the Gospels separately.

As the end of his leave of absence approached, it became clear that Dr. Bullinger could not yet resume his duties at the Trinitarian Bible Society. He declined with regret to occupy his usual place on the platform of the annual meeting, noting that there had been very few times in the past forty-six years that he had not been present for the meeting.[31] Instead, he and Elizabeth went again to the country, this time to Worthing.

He returned on May 10 feeling refreshed and stronger. The work on the Bible proceeded, but on Sunday, May 25, Dr. Bullinger complained of having lost power in his right arm. He also experienced momentary failure of speech. The doctor prescribed special food and more rest. On Wednesday, while having tea in the garden with his very close friends, the Mowlls, Dr. Bullinger suffered a convulsive attack in the throat. The patient was put to bed with absolute quiet, and a nurse was engaged to attend him. Elizabeth wrote to many of their close friends, asking for their prayers. The intense, uncharacteristic heat that engulfed London that spring made matters worse for everyone, especially for Bullinger, who had always suffered discomfort in hot, humid weather.[32]

Later, at the request of friends, Elizabeth recounted the last days with her beloved uncle:

> As the days passed, the attacks occurred again and again; and on Tuesday, June 3, a specialist was called in. He expressed a hope that Uncle would get better; but it was only a hope, and there seemed to be little real comfort in his words.
>
> "What did he say?" was the inquiry immediately. I returned to the room after the specialist had left.
>
> "You may get better."
>
> "But shall I be able to do my work?"
>
> Ah, it was his work he was thinking about. I knew his thoughts, and was certain that if he got better he would be at his work, so I made reply:
>
> "If you get better, we know you will do your work."
>
> The specialist's report gave some relief, and that night, the first time for a week, I was able to get a little rest.
>
> Early the next morning, that is, on Wednesday, Nurse told me that the night had been one of great restless-

ness. Thereupon, going to his room, I inquired what sort of night he had had.

"I have been dreaming."

"What have you been dreaming about?"

"I have been trying to get things right in Daniel. It has been worrying me much, and I could not get the notes right."

Still he was occupied with his work on the "Companion Bible," notwithstanding the painful restlessness!

Just afterwards he asked if there were any letters. I had to remind him that it was only about six o'clock. On some further remark on my part, he put his hand to his mouth to let me know that he could not speak. From that time he said very little; the power of speech seemed to have left him.

On the evening of Wednesday, June 4, he became unconscious; and, except for brief intervals, remained so up to the time of his death two days later. The intervals were noted on the following day—Thursday. About ten o'clock in the morning, a few of us, filled with anxiety and sorrow, were standing round his bed. All at once he opened his eyes, and said very quietly: "You are all there." He seemed to experience some satisfaction in knowing that those who represented the various interests of his life and had helped in his work were then present. Later on, I was at his bedside with our faithful maid, and then again he opened his eyes, and made a sign of recognition; but he was unable to speak.

The days of consciousness were days of prayer—not petulant request, but trustful communion. Some three days before the end, he said to his niece: "I want you to take down a prayer I have been offering ever since I came to bed." She said she would get paper and write; but he stopped her, saying: "Not now, to-morrow will do." On the following day he could not speak, so the words were never taken down.

At the same time he said that on the page of the Bible upon which he had last been at work there was a little "Structure" of some passage which he hoped Mr.

Lovely would kindly have copied out and sent to some friends. . . .

It was at this point that the laborious worker laid down his pen. His task on the "Companion Bible" came to an end with a full-orbed contemplation of the grace of the Good Shepherd. From this inspiring starting-point his like-minded successors will carry the work to a conclusion, in harmony with his plans and purposes.

Not only did Dr. Bullinger think much of his work in the earlier days of his illness, but at that time he was his old self in faithful testimony for Christ. As is well known, he viewed with profound grief the tendency to place human "religion" where Gospel truth should be, and this feeling was with him to the last.

At the close of the first week of illness, the nurse, after temporary absence from the room, said that she had heard from a friend who had been reading some of his books. He asked if she herself had read any of the books, and received the reply: "No, I never read religious books." Weak as he was, he was roused by these words, and he almost rose from the bed as he said:

"I never write religious books. Religion may mean anything. What you and I want is *not* religion, but Christianity. CHRIST."

The declaration was characteristic, and the energy with which it was made, when his life was drawing so rapidly to its close, was very impressive.[33]

The end came on Friday, June 6, 1913, at about midday. Dr. Bullinger fell asleep, in perfect peace. He was seventy-five.

CHAPTER THIRTEEN

Afterward

Tremel June 6, 1913

Dear Miss Dodson,

How is dear Dr. Bullinger getting on? Since Mr. Grubb has told us about him we are very anxious.

I have again these days great difficulty to breath. Elsewhere I can do a line of my work; but I am every day and every hour thinking of my dear friend that has been so kind, so good to me. Oh may the Lord spare him many years more and restore him to health is the earnest prayer of your Tremel friend.

G. LeCoat[1]

But the dear friend was no more. Pasteur LeCoat's note, written with shaky hand, arrived in Bremgarten just as Elizabeth, Henry Bowker, Sophie Fairfield, and others were communicating the news of Dr. Bullinger's death by telephone calls, letters, and newspaper announcements.

Shocked and saddened, people responded quickly.

7th June 1913

My own darling Lizzie,

I have just got your card and like you I feel stunned.
You see till Tuesday I did not even know of his illness. I
have scarcely had you both out of my thoughts since.
What it must be to you I cannot realise only in so far as
I compare it to my mother's death, and its meaning deso-
lation to me. . . .

What a memory uncle leaves, such a genial large
hearted loving soul, such a worker, and working to the
last. . . .

All my love and my prayers dear
Your
Maggie[2]

The executive committee of the Trinitarian Bible Society hastened to issue a formal statement:

. . . The Committee, having in remembrance the active
part taken by our late lamented and honoured Secretary, the Reverend Ethelbert W. Bullinger, DD in the
work of this Society since his appointment thereto in
1867; his fearless avowal and steadfast maintenance of
its distinctive principles; and the many services rendered
by him to its cause, desires to record its sense of the
great loss sustained by the Society through his death.[3]

The committee voted to continue Dr. Bullinger's salary until
August 13, and they gave an additional £100 to Elizabeth Dodson.
They further requested that letters of condolence be sent to
Miss Dodson and Mrs. B. Bullinger, Dr. Bullinger's daughter-in-
law.[4]

Friends and colleagues shared their sympathy and grief.

Sunday June 8th 1913

Dear Miss Dodson,

The post has just brought me the news of your and
our great loss. Our grief is altogether beyond words,

BULLINGER'S STUDY AND HIS DOG, KAFFIE.

but I just want to offer you on behalf of my wife and self our most sincere and heartfelt sympathy.

I cannot say more but I can understand something now of what Timothy must have felt at the death of Paul.—so much did we love our dear friend who has now fallen asleep.—how much more must you feel the loss of so dear a relative.

Yours in mutual sorrow,
G. W. Taylor[5]

By Monday, June 9, the news had already reached the Continent. It prompted a quick reply from George Crichton, whom the Doctor had visited in February.

Monday eve. June 9, 1913
Villa San Silvestro,
Bordighera, Italy.

Dear Miss Dodson,

I cannot properly express to you with what sorrow we read this morning in "The Times" of Saturday the news of the death of your dear Uncle.

After the letters which you were good enough to ask Mr. Bowker and Mrs. Fairfield to write to us the sad issue was, of course, not unexpected nor unlooked for. All the same it is very terrible—and the final collapse and break-down was certainly far from our thoughts, at least so soon. Just about 14 or 16 days ago I had a short letter from him in which he told me that he was feeling more like himself, his old self, again than he had done, and he was evidently in good and cheerful spirits. And now!

Our hearts are full of sympathy for you—and all that we can think for you is that by God strengthening you will be graciously sustained.

As for myself words fail to tell how tremendously I feel myself indebted to the teaching of Dr. Bullinger.

The Bible has become a new book to me—a vitally living book—and to the end of my days and throughout Eternity I shall have cause to thank God that I fell in with the writings and finally made the acquaintance and friendship of such a Bible man as was your Uncle. What had formerly been un-understandable became understandable and my love for my Bible—for I always loved it—increased a thousandfold. . . .

And may God be with you in your sorrow—a sorrow shared by, I am sure, thousands of others.

Very faithfully and truly yours, shared in by my dear Wife,

George Crichton[6]

Close friends took note of the special relationship between niece and uncle, as shown in the following letter:

We are in a better position than many for realising how overwhelming your sorrow must be in face of this heavy bereavement that has come upon you, and we have been entering very fully and sympathetically with you into this great trial.

We recall your devoted attachment, and tireless service for the one who has been taken from us, and we know that you allowed your life to be so absorbed in his interests that the wrench cannot but be of the most painful.[7]

Dr. Bullinger's church associates wrote Elizabeth to offer their services for the funeral arrangements. She selected six of them, all members of the general committee of the Trinitarian Bible Society. The funeral was planned for Wednesday, June 11, at 2:30 P.M. in West Hampstead Cemetery, not far from North End Road, where Dr. Bullinger and Elizabeth had lived.[8]

By the day of the funeral, the unusual heat had not yet diminished. The weather was bright, clear, and hot. About forty people gathered at the house and followed the funeral procession to the cemetery, where another two hundred people were gathered. The small chapel on the grounds of the cemetery was incapable of holding such a crowd, and many mourners stayed by the grave site during the service.

Elizabeth had planned each detail of the service. It was simple in the extreme, without tributes, eulogy, or flowers. The opening prayers were read by Rev. F. C. Lovely, one psalm by Rev. A. Griffith, another psalm by Rev. J. C. Smith, and the "Lesson" by Rev. T. A. Howard. At the graveside, "Committal Prayers" were read by Rev. Sydney Thelwall and "Concluding Prayers" by Rev. J. J. Beddow.[9]

As the weeks went by and the news spread, the pile of mail waiting for Elizabeth's attention grew into a mountain. Letters came from Wales, Ireland, Italy, France, and Germany as well as from all over Great Britain. Later, Elizabeth heard from the United States, Canada, and China. Many pieces of Dr. Bullinger's life came together in the rush of sympathy—the Trinitarian Bible Society, the Breton Mission, the Bullinger Loyal Orange Lodge, the National Club, the Barbican Mission to the Jews, old friends from former parishes—each in its own way a testament to the life of this remarkable man. The following letter from a former parishioner in Walthamstow is typical:

> I cannot believe that the dear old friend of so many years has gone. The man of the big heart and tender sympathy, as well as of the wonderful brain.
>
> He has entered into and understood all our joys and sorrows without the telling of them, and this for almost all our lives.
>
> Dear Lizzie, with you we are all of us wondering how the world will get on without him, it has not another with a more sincere and child-like sense of duty and desire to be of use to others.[10]

Time and again letters, editorials, and tributes confirmed that the knowledge of the Bible that Bullinger had passed on to others became, after his death, their most joyful remembrance of the man. The following is a letter that was reprinted in *Things to Come:*

The news of the death of Dr. Bullinger will fall as an announcement of grievous loss upon a large number of thoughtful Christians. May I be permitted to offer a word or two as to the great value of the work that God granted him to do, and as to the attractiveness of his personality?

Though gifted with unusual powers as a deep scholar and thinker, he was simple, affectionate, and conspicuously free from pretension of any kind; but the feature which made him pre-eminent was his greatness as a teacher of the Scriptures. His aim was to delight himself in the word of God, and to pass on that supreme happiness to others.

It was his constant practice to be up in his study, over his Bible, at about 3 to 5 A.M., and there, day after day, he stored his receptive mind with masses of Scripture knowledge, which made him a giant in apprehension of the Mind of God. He cared little for the mind of *man;* but was unvarying in his search after what the Bible says of itself.

With thankfulness, I should like to testify that through his teaching, the Word of God is an entirely new Book to me; and as I tell others what I have learned through him, again and again I am told, that they have never heard such truth before, and ask why teaching of this kind is not general. It was never Dr. Bullinger's habit to set forth an isolated text or thought, and then deliver his opinions on it. That is often done, but he counted it of little value. He would set forth a text or thought, and then gather together all that he could find in the whole Bible bearing on the subject; and, laying the accumulated evidence side by side, differentiating those passages that appeared to treat of the same matter (but which really belonged to another category), he opened up the secret of "proving things that differ," and so, rightly "divided the Word of Truth."

Beloved Dr. Bullinger! Thank God for his life and his works.

I pray that his books may long remain in circulation, and that so, "being dead, he may yet speak" to many who may thus be led to follow him in delighting in God's Word.

Yours sincerely,
James B. Delap.[11]

Correspondence aside, it soon became clear that Elizabeth had pressing decisions to make. On July 29, the long-delayed answer from William Barron arrived concerning Dr. Bullinger's decision to publish the Gospels in *The Companion Bible* separately. It stated, "Advise including Acts with Gospels."[12] But it was, of course, too late. The work on *The Companion Bible* was put into abeyance while Elizabeth wrestled with the question of its continuation. Conflicts that could have been related to this question arose regarding her uncle's will.

On August 13, 1913, more than two months after Dr. Bullinger's death, with his will not yet probated, Elizabeth Dodson was granted Letters of Administration, which allowed her to proceed with the settlement of the estate. For reasons that are unknown, Vyvian G. Hicks and Maurice E. Golby had refused to act as executors.

Pressures regarding *The Companion Bible* surrounded Elizabeth on all sides. William Barron, when he heard of Dr. Bullinger's death, immediately sent her a telegram saying, "Put [Charles] Welch on to the Epistles."[13] Others wrote urging great care in making the decision:

My daily prayer now is, that someone fit and worthy to complete his great work may be raised up to do so. But, oh! I was so looking forward to having your dear Uncle's own work on The Epistles.[14]

One letter introduced a note of caution:

As soon as you feel able perhaps you would grant me a few minutes. I desire to learn what arrangements are made concerning the Doctor's crowning work.

There may be an effort to mar or wreck it. Much will
depend upon you his faithful and patient helper whom
he would expect to faithfully and jealously guard it.[15]

In the end, Elizabeth decided not to follow Barron's instructions but to proceed with the help of H. C. Bowker, using the
material left by her uncle at the time of his death. She said, "We
do not know what Dr. Bullinger *would have written,* we can only
go back and adopt what he has already written."[16]
Welch was dismayed. He claimed that Miss Dodson was looking to future sales when she rejected his editorship and the
unpopular positions he might introduce, namely, dispensational
questions regarding the beginning of the church in the book
of Acts. He cited Bullinger's last book, *The Foundations of Dispensational Truth,* to support his arguments. Elizabeth, however, was adamant. From New Zealand, Barron withdrew his
name from the project and terminated all financial support.
Charles Welch had no further involvement with *The Companion Bible.* He continued to contribute his "Dispensational Expositions" in *Things to Come* until its end, but for the most part
he now concentrated his energies upon his own journal, the
Berean Expositor.
It was Sir Robert Anderson who quietly stepped in at this
juncture to oversee the completion of this project.[17] It is probable that he also made up for the loss of financial resources.
Henry Bowker took over the day-to-day work of *The Companion
Bible* and *Things to Come.*
Exactly how much of the final portion of *The Companion Bible,
Part VI, Acts to Revelation,* was Dr. Bullinger's work has been a
matter of speculation over the years. The evidence, however,
strongly indicates that, although unfinished at the time of his
death, it was, in the main, Dr. Bullinger's work. A letter written
to Elizabeth in October 1913 by W. T. Broad of Carlisle, England, for many years Bullinger's close friend and faithful supporter, sheds light on this subject. The two men had shared the
platform at the Prophetic Conferences, and Broad had been a
contributor to *Things to Come.* At the time of Bullinger's death,
Mr. Broad was in Canada.

12 Oct. 1913
Calgary, Alberta, Canada

Dear Miss Dodson,

Since the end of June I have been away in British
Columbia for some months and I have recently come
back. The news of your uncle's death came to me as a
sad and terrible blow. Of course I read the account in
"Things to Come" which I get regularly. To me the Doctor was a real spiritual father. I owe it to him that my
eyes were opened, and a diligent study for years of the
treasures he has brought out of God's Word, has resulted in untold blessing to me and others. . . .
"The Companion Bible" to me is a veritable "Magnum
Opus," a vast treasure. I do hope he was able to complete
the Mss. of the New Testament. I see from T. to C. the
Vol. on the Gospels and Acts is to be out in October. I
will send this week for a copy. Kindly tell us in T. to C.
about the last volume. If unfinished cannot some one put
it together from what is published in his other works.
From what he told me, I gathered the last part of the N.T.
was almost done before the 1st vol. was started.[18]

Further confirmation that the preparation of the material in
Part VI was Dr. Bullinger's work comes from the working notes
and papers left in his Bible at the time of his death. These indicate that Dr. Bullinger continued to review and rework topics
vitally important to the final volumes of *The Companion Bible* and
their accompanying appendixes right up to the end of his life.[19]
    Also, C. T. Lipshytz, director of the Barbican Mission to the
Jews and Bullinger's friend and confidant of many years, indicated in his review of *The Companion Bible, Part V, The Gospels*
that Bullinger had already done the work for the New Testament at the time of his death.[20]
    On October 26, 1913, a large crowd gathered in Vilvorde, Bel-
gium, for the unveiling of the monument honoring William
Tyndale, a project that had been very dear to the heart of Dr.
Bullinger. Rev. F. Cecil Lovely, now the secretary of the Trinitarian

Bible Society, took part in the ceremony as did Monsieur L. Valat, secretary of the Belgian Bible Society and representatives of religious societies in France, Belgium, England, Norway, Sweden, and Finland, as well as Belgian civil authorities. The vital part played by the late Dr. Bullinger in the project from its beginning was noted repeatedly by many of the speakers.[21]

During the month of March 1914, both Pasteur LeCoat and Dr. C. D. Ginsburg passed away. Although so different in background and lifestyle, they had each touched Bullinger's life in profound ways.

Weakened by his long illness and saddened by the death of his longtime friend and supporter, Pasteur LeCoat spent his last months largely incapacitated. On March 1, he died peacefully at home. The Trinitarian Bible Society issued the following obituary, adapted from Tremel newspaper accounts:

> All who knew Pasteur Lecoat knew what a worker and fighter he was. He translated the Bible into the Breton tongue. In 1872 he succeeded, in spite of the greatest difficulties and desperate opposition, in opening a school for boys at Tremel. In 1888 a girls' school was inaugurated. These schools have furnished all the workers of the Breton Mission—evangelists, colporteurs, school officials, etc.
>
> Few men have done as much in the cause of education as Pasteur LeCoat, and we are pleased to think that he received, shortly before his death, the well-merited decoration of "Officier d'Academie."[22]

The Trinitarian Bible Society Quarterly Record, in a later issue, described LeCoat's funeral, a singular event that bore witness to the power manifested by the life of this uncommon man:

> He [LeCoat] was buried on Wednesday, March 4th, in the Cemetery at Tremel. Such a sight as his funeral had never been seen there before; from all parts the mourners came; the nobles of the land mingled with the peasants round his grave. More than a thousand people were there.

The Maire [Mayor] of Tremel, a Roman Catholic, sent
a message to Madame LeCoat, asking that he and the
Councilors of Tremel might have the privilege of carry-
ing him to his last resting-place. . . .

At the grave Monsieur Scarabin, a preacher of the
Gospel, spoke to the people of the life of Pasteur LeCoat,
and said that what would make him immortal in Brittany was his translation of the Bible. . . .

Then a Roman Catholic, Monsieur Jaffrennou, a
Breton poet and author, spoke in Breton. He, too, traced
Pasteur's life. He said that the faith he had in Jesus Christ,
and the courage he had shown in His cause, had given
him the victory over all his enemies. He was an evangelist and one who loved his fellow-men. Even those who
opposed him had to admit how true he was to his principles, and how difficult it would be to find any wrong-
doing in his life. He was a Breton born, and a Breton he
died, and all his life was spent in Brittany.[23]

On Saturday, March 7, 1914, Dr. C. D. Ginsburg died in his
home in London at the age of eighty-three. *The Trinitarian Bible
Society Quarterly Record* printed an announcement of the death
and eulogized him with the following words:

We regret to announce the death of the distinguished Hebrew scholar, Dr. Christian David Ginsburg, who died on
Saturday morning last at his residence at Palmer's Green.

Born at Warsaw on Christmas Day, 1831, he was educated in the Rabbinic College in that city, but became a
Christian in 1846. He came to England, and was for a
time connected with the Liverpool branch of the London Jews Society; but as time went on he devoted himself more and more exclusively to literary work. . . .

The great work of his life was the publication and
explanation of the Massorah. In 1894 he published, in
two volumes, a "Massoretico-Critical" edition of the
Hebrew Bible, based upon the text of Jacob ben Chayim,
with footnotes, containing various readings of Mss. and
early printed Bibles, and also, from time to time, read-

ings presupposed by the Ancient Versions. This edition, which was published by the Trinitarian Bible Society, was also accompanied by a most valuable "Introduction to the Hebrew Bible."

Dr. Ginsburg was a most laborious and painstaking student, whose minute researches in a highly technical department of linguistic learning placed scholars under a heavy debt for the stores of exact knowledge with which he furnished them. . . .[24]

It is not known if Ginsburg and Bullinger had ever met again after their disagreement in 1909. But of the 242 letters written to Elizabeth Dodson after her uncle's death that have been preserved, there is none from Dr. Ginsburg. No mention is made of a representative from the Trinitarian Bible Society at Dr. Ginsburg's funeral. Later, it was the British and Foreign Bible Society that acquired Ginsburg's valuable collection of old Bibles in various languages, including a complete series of old German printed Bibles.[25]

Fourteen months after Dr. Bullinger's death, in August 1914, World War I engulfed Europe. England, in the heart of the conflict, grappled with the seemingly never-ending casualties and with the realization that the world she had known was totally gone. The pride and sense of national security, so characteristic of Victorian England, expired in the graves of a generation of young men. Many people thought that the end of the world must be near. The September issue of *Things to Come* featured an editorial on the tragic events.

WAR!

The terrible war which is now raging in Europe is emphatically a sign of the times, indicating that the times of the Gentiles are rapidly running out, and running out in social ruin and disorder. At the beginning of August the newspapers spoke with bated breath of the opening of the great "battle of Armageddon"; and from time to time since then they have been delineating incidents and aspects of a truly awful conflict, involving several "Christian" nations.

Of course, such language as the newspapers employ is not that of Apocalyptic exegesis in the true sense of the word; but rather it is an accommodation of Biblical phraseology to the description of scenes which are without parallel in the history of war. So to speak, the kings of the earth and their armies are gathered together; and a woeful gathering it is, with instruments and engines on sea and land, and in the air above, such as have never before been used for the destruction of man and all his works.[26]

By December 1914, the next volume of *The Companion Bible* was ready. It was advertised thus in *Things to Come:*

THE COMPANION BIBLE.
Vol. V.—The Four Gospels.

It is with great satisfaction that we announce the publication of Part V of *The Companion Bible*. In a beautiful volume, uniform with those that were issued during the life-time of the late lamented Editor, we have the Gospels as prepared (in substance) by Dr. Bullinger, and since his death completed by those who laboured with him in opening up the Sacred Word.[27]

Part V of *The Companion Bible–The Four Gospels* was greeted with scant comment; other projects were now drawing the reviewers' attention. One of those who did hail its publication was finally candid on the subject of the editor's identity. In March 1915, *Watchword and Truth* stated:

It is no breach of confidence, now that the author of this monument of devout scholarship has passed away, to say that it is the work of the late Dr. Bullinger. He published many books of which he was the author, but in none of them is there seen such marks of versatility of talent, patient investigation, accurate scholarship, and fearless independence, as is seen in the five volumes making this marvelous work. We had been informed that Dr. Bullinger left the notes for the present volume almost complete for publication. These "notes" have fallen into the hands of a distinguished scholar so that we can discover no decline in the value of the book.[28]

Things to Come continued to be published, but rising prices for paper and other wartime needs, coupled with the death of old subscribers, forced the editor repeatedly to ask for financial help. In October 1915, he made the following appeal to readers:

The accounts for 1914 closed with a deficit of over £23, and though we gratefully acknowledge an increase in the Publishing Fund, we are still faced with the prospect of a deficit in December next.

Never self-supporting, the Magazine has always had to depend upon the gifts of its readers. The decease of old subscribers, the war and other causes have so curtailed the incomings, that there is no prospect of its surviving to another year unless the help hitherto given is considerably increased.[29]

In November, H. C. Bowker issued the following letter:

Dear Friends,

With this volume *Things to Come* concludes its testimony after a little over 21 years' service, its first number having appeared in July, 1894. It is with sorrow that we take leave of our readers, but we believe it is manifestly the Lord's will.

Throughout these years hundreds of letters have testified to the blessing brought by this little monthly witness, an expression frequently used in them being, "The Bible has become a new book." No appeal has ever been made to man's authority, doctrines, or traditions. Its motto has always been, "Study to show thyself APPROVED UNTO GOD."

As many have expressed a wish to know some particulars about the editorship during the last two years, it may suffice to say that the undersigned, who was closely associated with the late beloved Dr. Bullinger, conducted the magazine for three or four months after his death, when one of considerable literary ability and experience, who wished to remain anonymous, undertook the work. He, however, was obliged to resign it in the spring of the present year, when the former arrangement was resumed, a valuable colleague being found in one who also was closely associated with the Doctor's work, but who wishes his name to be withheld.

We would here repeat the thanks due to him and other helpers and sympathizers which we have endeavoured to express on the last page of the volume.

It only remains, in taking leave of our readers, to "commend them to God and to the word of His grace." That alone can build them up.

All man's efforts have an end. Things human pass away. One abides.

"THEY SHALL PERISH, BUT THOU REMAINEST."
Yours in "that blessed hope,"
H. C. Bowker[30]

Now relieved of the concerns of *Things to Come,* Bowker continued to ready the sixth and final volume of *The Companion Bible, Acts to Revelation* for publication. But other issues would need to be resolved before this could become a reality. Under the terms of Dr. Bullinger's will, Vyvian Hicks and Maurice Golby were the only ones with full power to carry on publication of his works (in consultation with Sophie Fairfield and Benjamin Hitchcock); and as they continued to refuse to help in the finishing of *The Companion Bible* or in the publishing of his other books, the situation seemed to be deadlocked.

On December 24, 1918, a month after the war's end, Elizabeth Dodson took action to clear up matters. Because of the refusal of Vyvian G. Hicks and Maurice E. Golby to act, Elizabeth became the administratrix of her uncle's will. With the consent of Sophie Fairfield and Benjamin Hitchcock, she deeded all rights of *The Companion Bible* and Dr. Bullinger's other literary works to Thomas Henry Hilken and Frederick William Carter, old friends from Walthamstow. For their part, Hilken and Carter agreed to publish the remaining volume of *The Companion Bible* and to procure the necessary funds to continue printing it, as long as was deemed necessary, along with any other of Dr. Bullinger's works. All proceeds from these sales were assigned to Mr. Hilken and Mr. Carter, with the proviso that they would make certain payments, as required, to Elizabeth Dodson and the Trinitarian Bible Society.[31]

The team of Thomas Henry Hilken and Frederick William Carter was an excellent choice to handle Dr. Bullinger's affairs. Not only were they leading business men but also they were loyal both to the late Dr. Bullinger and to Elizabeth. Thomas Hilken, who had settled in Walthamstow as a young man, was a prominent shipbroker in London. He had joined the committee of the Trinitarian Bible Society in 1910 and later had authored a history of St. Stephen's Church in Walthamstow that contained many details of Bullinger's vicarship there.

Frederick Carter had grown up in Walthamstow and had known Dr. Bullinger all his life. His father, H. W. Carter, who had acquired considerable wealth in the London Stock Exchange, was among the first church wardens of St. Stephen's and served throughout Dr. Bullinger's vicarship. Later, the Carters moved to Red Hill in Surrey but remained close to their former pastor. It was Frederick's sister, Mabel, who thought of constructing a memorial stone to be placed over Bullinger's grave the year following his death.

In March 1919, William Barron, who had helped to finance *The Companion Bible,* wrote a letter to Charles Welch. His comments indicate that some of the difficulties that plagued Elizabeth with regard to her uncle's will might have been linked to her original decision to countermand Barron's instructions and take Welch off *The Companion Bible* project.

> Had Miss Dodson fallen in with our request that you should be identified with *Mr. Bowker* in the *Companion Bible* work all the present trouble which has arisen would not have occurred.[32]

Whatever the conflict had been, the way was now clear for the completion of the last section and the publication of the

Bible as a whole. It was to be H. C. Bowker's last work. He died on April 29, 1920, at his home in Northwood, Middlesex. The Trinitarian Bible Society issued the following obituary:

> With sincere sorrow we record the death of Henry Charles Bowker, M.A., which took place in his house after a long time of weakness on 29 April last, in his 81st year. Mr. Bowker was a member of the Trinitarian Bible Society Committee for some years, and was a regular attendant at the meetings, and took a great interest in the work of the Society. For a number of years he was a helper of the late Dr. E. W. Bullinger, and after the Doctor's death, with another coadjutor, carried on the work of completing the Companion Bible; the last volume being now in the press.[33]

The Companion Bible, Part VI, Acts to Revelation was published late in 1921. It was followed in 1922 by the complete Bible in one large volume. Like the previously published individual parts, the whole attracted much attention, some of it negative. *The British Weekly* of December 14, 1922, labeled it "The Eccentric Bible";[34] *The Witness Watch Tower* in February 1923 called it "A Dangerous Bible."[35] But for the many who had eagerly anticipated the completed Bible and who had known the man behind it, faultfinding was unthought of and praise unnecessary. *The Christian,* December 14, 1922, stated it thus:

> Many will give a hearty welcome to this beautiful volume. Originally published in six parts, some of them already out of print, it now appears in one volume, and thus takes its place as a new edition of the English Bible. In all lands there are men and women who waited with patience for the succeeding parts, and have learned to treasure them for the wealth of information which they contain. For such Bible students there will be no need to describe the complete book, as now issued. . . .
>
> As is well known, this Bible was projected by the late Dr. Bullinger, and when he passed to his rest, in 1913, the work was well in hand for completion. Thereupon

scholars who had helped the projector found delight in doing what remained, and they did it in the same spirit of devotion to Holy Scripture. Hence, here is an edition of the Bible, in the preparation of which unbelieving criticism has had no hand. The editors themselves had no doubts, and no words or thoughts of that nature will be found in the 2,150 pages of the book.

Another observation is permissible. Here is a great and noble enterprise, which occupied its editor and his helpers for many years, but nowhere is there sign or indication as to the personnel of the workers. They said they worked for God, and with Him they left their labour. Here and there the name of some scholar is mentioned, as demanded by the necessities of the case, but Dr. Bullinger and his learned friends kept severely in the background; their monument is in the *Companion Bible,* now given to the world in a single volume, which supersedes the several parts issued during recent years.[36]

Elizabeth Dodson remained at the house on North End Road for almost twenty years after her uncle's death. She never married but lived with a female companion and frequently had friends stay with her for prolonged periods of time. Dorothy Rosemary, Dr. Bullinger's only grandchild, was a frequent visitor. Dorothy's wedding to Mr. Leslie Fielder on September 29, 1928, took place at Bremgarten.

As the twenties neared their end, friends urged Elizabeth, now in her sixties, to move to smaller quarters, but she did not want to leave Bremgarten. Finally in 1931 Elizabeth sold the house and moved to a smaller one in Worthing, outside of London.

During her uncle's lifetime his interests had formed the primary concern of Elizabeth's life, and so it continued after his death. She became the principal link with what he had left behind. She wrote to people in many countries who were interested in Dr. Bullinger and filled orders for his works. The publishing trust continued to be managed by Frederick Carter and Thomas Hilken until the latter's death in January 1930.

On January 6, 1933, Frederick Carter approached the

executive committee of the Trinitarian Bible Society to discuss the possibility of transferring the copyright of *The Companion Bible* to them and of their taking over its publication. This arrangement would, he said, "avoid the inevitable transfers, and consequent expenses on deaths of Trustees."[37] The Society declined, however, claiming that, "it was felt that, in view of our constitution as a Bible Society, it would be better if the Copyrights were not held by the Trinitarian Bible Society Trust."[38] The stumbling block seems to have been law number three of the Society's constitution, which stated that the Society would circulate the Holy Scriptures, "without note or comment."[39]

In 1934, a new trust was formed, with Frederick Carter and Mr. Wilfred Petty of Westcliff-on-Sea, Essex, named as trustees. As before, the trustees assumed all rights to Dr. Bullinger's works and all income from the sales. They agreed to continue paying royalties to both Elizabeth Dodson and the Trinitarian Bible Society as stipulated by the previous trust. In the event of Elizabeth's death, her income was to revert to Dorothy. If the Trinitarian Bible Society were to, in the estimation of the trustees, depart from "its original and fundamental lines," the benefits given to the Society "shall cease and the same shall from time to time thereafter be paid or applied by the Trustees to or for the benefit of such one or more charitable institutions or organizations, having as one of its or their primary objects the dissemination of the Scriptures."[40]

Elizabeth tried to remain current with what was being said about her uncle. A letter in 1931 from Dr. Bullinger's old friend, Dr. J. W. Thirtle, now editor of *The Christian*, showed that sentiments about Bullinger were still heated many years after his death:

Dear Miss Dodson,

Some stupid man in America has been having a growl about our dear friend the Doctor. I thought you would like to see the statement. Quite as you might suppose, it is unsigned. These brave folks that would put the whole world right, generally keep their names in the background.[41]

The term "Bullingerism" was coined by Bullinger's critics to designate those positions with which they did not agree. Generally speaking, "Bullingerism" denoted Bullinger's stand against water baptism and the Lord's Supper as not being intended for the church age; his distinctions between the church of the bride found in the Gospels and the church of the body recorded in the Pauline epistles; his views on death and what happens to the soul after death; and the study of biblical future events. The most important objection to Dr. Bullinger's teaching, however, was usually with regard to his stand on what was labeled "Dispensationalism." It was his claim that the Christian church commenced after Acts 28:28, as outlined in his book *The Foundations of Dispensational Truth,* instead of on the Day of Pentecost.

Algernon Pollock, a member of the Plymouth Brethren and one of Dr. Bullinger's persistent critics, said:

> All through Dr. Bullinger's writings, as far as we have seen, he seems to take a delight in differing from every-body, and in so doing is constantly being driven into such tight corners that he has again and again to contra-dict *himself.* The most charitable critic cannot attribute to him humility, and he cannot escape the charge of excessive and conceited dogmatism. He is right and ev-erybody else is wrong.[42]

Yet Bullinger was not without his supporters. One in particu-lar was Harold P. Morgan, an Englishman who had emigrated to the United States. In 1936, Morgan wrote the following to Elizabeth Dodson:

> Two of our outstanding Fundamentalist leaders in the United States have designated me "The High Priest of Bullingerism in America" and the "Chief exponent of Bullingerism." Now I do not object to be thus desig-nated though I would prefer to have them acknowledge that my teaching, as was Dr. Bullinger's, is based on a correct understanding of the Pauline economy. . . .
>
> I feel that the time is near when Dr. Bullinger's worth will be appreciated.[43]

In 1943, Morgan wrote a series of papers titled "Dr. Bullinger: the Man and His Work," which were published in his journal *Questions and Answers*. Running in four successive issues, the articles opposed the slander and misrepresentation so rampant against Bullinger while pleading for a more precise understanding of his teachings. Morgan asked his readers to consider the testimonies of Bullinger's contemporaries, and then to judge for themselves:

So much has been written about Dr. Bullinger and so much of it worthless, prejudiced or misinformed that one now opens with intense diffidence any work offered in criticism or appreciation of that able scholar's teachings and aims. Notwithstanding all this, I shall endeavour to present a judicious appraisal of both the man and his work.

That Dr. Bullinger attained considerable intellectual acumen seems to be conceded by the stoutest of his opponents. Now, while it is true, that the English scholar rarely came off second best in the conflicts fought out in the controversial arena, I would urge the consideration of another and higher standard by which to measure a man's full worth and the right to a permanent place in the hearts of his fellow Christians.

I am inclined to the opinion, after years of observation in Great Britain, Europe and large areas of the American continent, that the merely intellectual man is perhaps the sorriest of all human misfits. Unusual mental abilities are greatly admired by people as a whole, much in the same way as the traveller enthuses over the high lights and changing colours of an iceberg as it floats into the rays of a midsummer sun. As seen from a distance both are spectacular, but the hard fact remains that closer proximity introduces one to colder atmosphere.

It was my lot in early years to be thrown into the society of a number of highly intellectual people, whose stunted emotional life was a constant source of bewilderment to me. Since then I have met with other extremely intelligent people whose circumscribed lives no longer puzzle me. As one grows older he realizes that it is not altogether unusual to find in one and the same person a highly developed intellect and a shrivelled, self-centered soul. How vastly different was Dr. Bullinger from all this. Indeed, it was this marked difference in outlook which first intrigued me. The place Bullinger held in public esteem may be brought into still clearer view by the record of those who had the inspiration of his counsel and friendship. To those who enjoyed a personal fellowship, more or less intimate, belongs the right to pay tribute to this balanced personality. The following appraisals, selected at random from a score or more testimonies, (written by men and women in all walks of life in widely separated parts of the world), tell in simple, direct fashion of the high regard in which this richly endowed servant of Christ was held generally. One cannot but note the similarity in testimony, each one, in his own way, magnifying the power of God's grace which shone forth conspicuously in this warmhearted man of God.

". . . Dr. Bullinger was a great spirit and a constant source of inspiration in my own life. . . . The radiancy of his life will go on and on. . . ." "He was a man to love and admire . . . a great and good man whom to know was to love. . . ." "Not Great Britain and the English speaking world only have lost a great soul, but the entire Christian world. . . ." "A large number of our leading Evangelical ministers have been benefitted by his instruction and blessed by his life . . . the whole Church contains no nobler man than Dr. Bullinger. . . . The warmth of his handclasp, the light in his eye, and the genial smile, created at once a feeling of friendship"; "Dr. Bullinger was a benediction to countless men and women the world over . . . as a steadfast, sympathetic, and understanding friend in sunshine and shadow, there have been few to compare with him. . . . A finer man and truer friend than Dr. Bullinger I have never known. . . . He was a brave and gentle soul who loved goodness and revered God's Holy Word. . . . He preached the genuine gospel of God's grace with rare power and charm. . . . He was a warm personal friend, an understanding comrade, an able teacher greatly beloved"; "Great as he was intellectually he impressed me as one of the most modest men I have known. Chivalrous, courtly, refined, he seemed to possess all the attributes of a truly great man. He served his generation with rare fidelity and I count myself favoured to have been regarded as one of his friends."

Happily it is not our province to pass judgment on fellow-Christians. Nevertheless, as a meditative man in the quiet of his study, I have occasionally pondered the question, "To which one of Dr. Bullinger's aggressive critics could any or all of these high tributes be paid in very truth?" The question, perhaps, was prompted by a consideration of another question, spoken by the Lord Himself, "Do men gather grapes of thorns, or figs of thistles?"

The outstanding lesson as I conceive it, to be learned from a review of Dr. Bullinger's life and labours, is the exemplary way in which this gifted teacher met and overcame abuse and calumny, and the strenuous opposition to the proclamation of reclaimed truths—brought to light in large measure by his own prayerful, diligent study of the Holy Scriptures.[44]

Elizabeth Dodson died on December 27, 1950, at the age of eighty-six. Her last years were spent in her home in Worthing where, as a semi-invalid, she was cared for by a companion. Dorothy, married and the mother of three children, remained in close contact. When Elizabeth died, it was Dorothy who decided to bury her with her uncle.

Doctor Bullinger's gravestone, once standing alone, was now surrounded by many others in the expanding cemetery. It had been engraved: "In loving memory of Ethelbert William Bullinger, D.D." A large replica of an open Bible placed at the head of the grave had been the memorial decided upon by Elizabeth, Mabel Carter, and a group of friends in the months following his death. Elizabeth had selected her uncle's favorite verses to be engraved upon it:

"That I may know him, and the power of his resurrection."
Phil.III.10.

"I rejoice at thy word, as one that findeth great spoil."
Psalm CXIX.162.

"Study to shew thyself approved unto God, a workman
that needeth not to be ashamed, rightly dividing the
word of truth."
2 Tim.II.15.

Now Dorothy added the final memorial: "Also his beloved
niece Elizabeth Dodson. 27th December, 1950. Aged 86."
The monument was fitting.
For Elizabeth Dodson, who in her life had helped, sustained,
and loved her uncle—it was right. And for Ethelbert Bullinger,
who all his life had opened the Book, known his Lord, and
studied and rejoiced in His Word—it was right.

Epilogue

In 1978, IN AN ARTICLE titled *Some Present-Day Errors,* Dr. Henry Grube, well-known American pastor, religious speaker, and Bible conference leader, wrote the following:

> Dr. E. W. Bullinger presents a problem: (1) because believers on one hand esteem him for his works' sake, honor him for his faithful defense of the great evangelical truths of the Word of God, and admire him for his zeal and scholarship. While (2) some of his writings must be condemned, and some of his teachings have been proved to be contrary to the correct interpretation of Scripture. A former president of one of our leading fundamental Bible institutes wrestled with this problem, when he said, "Bullinger would be called a fundamentalist were he now on earth, for he was an able defender of the inspiration of the Bible, the deity and virgin birth of Christ, the substitutionary atonement, the premillenial coming, and all that. But he was an extremist, some would call him a faddist on dispensational truth, and he was unscriptural, we believe on future retribution." It is no secret that practically all present day Bible scholars realize the debt they owe to E. W. Bullinger, J. N. Darby, W. R. Newell and others who presented to this generation the wonderful truth of the Church, which is the Body of Christ, the dispensational interpretation of the Scriptures, and the way to rightly divide the Word of Truth.
> It is regrettable that Mr. Bullinger's writings must be

"sifted" for it must be conceded that he did make several serious errors in his writings. This "tragedy" however, is quite the natural thing for it seems that God in His sovereign dealings with men, has never permitted any of His children to be absolutely perfect in his writings. From the record of all human authors, it seems that God has "allowed" them all to make one or several terrible blunders just in order that *not one* would ever have his writings classed as "infallible." Search the records. Every great Bible scholar has failed at some point, has gone astray in some way and has made a blunder somewhere along the path he has trod.[1]

It is always unfortunate when a scholar's so-called blunders are allowed to obscure the rest of their work in the eyes of posterity. For many contemporary Bible critics and scholars, such has been the case with E. W. Bullinger. The large body of material he authored is often pushed out of sight while criticism of his more controversial works receives the spotlight. If Bullinger were alive today, this would probably not surprise him. In 1902, he wrote:

Very few care to be thought peculiar, and therefore they like to have some names to appeal to. But this is the very reason why the mists of tradition have been allowed to take the place of independent research.[2]

This reliance on independent research rather than religious orthodoxy remains for many the hallmark of Bullinger's work. It is quite certain that this firm attitude of intellectual (and spiritual) independence has earned for him his most severe criticism, for out of this independence were born his most controversial viewpoints. Yet at the same time Bullinger's characteristic independence is valued by many for its ability to challenge and stimulate. Warren W. Wiersbe, in his foreword to the 1979 edition of Bullinger's *The Gift and The Giver,* phrased it thus:

We may not agree with him, but at least we have the opportunity to examine our own convictions in the light of his thinking. It has been well said that he who knows only his own position does not know even that. . . . We may not agree with all that Dr. Bullinger has written, but we must confess that he stimulates us to give our very best to the study of the Word of God.[3]

Many students of the Bible use Bullinger's books with enthusiasm and gratitude. To them, the vast treasury of his works provide inspiration and assistance in the often difficult task of understanding and applying the Bible to modern-day life. The following remarks are characteristic:

> E. W. Bullinger's life was devoted to the detailed analysis of the Scriptures, rooted in his foundational beliefs that they are truly the written word of God, that they are entirely sufficient unto themselves, and that as such they must be allowed to interpret themselves. A perfectionist in his analysis and a prolific writer, his volumes shed light not just upon the Scriptures but upon the compendium of tools that give power, persuasion and meaning to the written word. The body of work he created is thus of great value not just to the student of the Scriptures, but to any student of language, communication or persuasion as well. . . .
>
> That so many of his works remain in print is testimony enough to the thoroughness, clarity and value of his unique perspective.[4]

But we must allow Dr. Bullinger himself to have the last word. In *The Apocalypse*, he wrote with humility and vision of those who would come after him:

> None are more cognisant of imperfection and failure than ourselves; and, after all we have done, there is still much left for others to do.
>
> We do not exhaust the book; and may, after all, have only laid out a road on which others may follow with far greater success. We claim only one thing—an earnest desire to believe God; and to receive what He has said,

regardless alike of the praise of man or the fear of man; and quite apart from all traditional beliefs or interpretations.

May the Lord own and use and bless our efforts for His own Glory and the good of His people.[5]

Chronological List of the Works of E. W. Bullinger

PUBLICATION DATA ARE given for works currently known to be in print. All others are out of print at publication date.

All items denoted as "articles" were published in *Things to Come*.

Although it is assumed that Dr. Bullinger wrote most, if not all, of the editorials in *Things to Come*, we have in this list attributed to him only those that can be verified as his work.

-1872-

(Editor)   *Portuguese Reference Bible*. Trinitarian Bible Society.

-1880-

Pamphlet   *The Importance of Accuracy in the Study of Holy Scripture*.

Music   *Hymns for the Waiting Church*.

-1881-

Music   *The Stars Are Shining Bright and Clear*. Carol (for Christmas), The Parish Choir, no. 150, p. 598, Medford, 1881.

-1887-

Book   *A Critical Lexicon and Concordance to the English and Greek New Testament*.

Pamphlet	*Ten Sermons on the Second Advent* (later title: *Minor Works*). Sermons preached in Oxford, November 1887.
Pamphlet	*The Second Advent in Relation to the Jew. Ch. VII of Minor Works.*

-1889-

Pamphlet	*God's Purpose in Israel: In History, Type and Prophecy.* Address at Mildmay Conference, London, October 1899.
Pamphlet	*The Name of Jehovah in the Book of Esther.*
Music	*Fifty Original Hymn-Tunes.*
Music	*Hymns for Bible Readings.*
Music	*Hymns on the Second Advent.*
Music	*Sixty-Six Old Breton Tunes* (also titled *Chants Chrétien*).

-1890-

Pamphlet	*The Inspiration and Authority of Holy Scripture.* Address at National Protestant Congress, London, 1890.
(Editor)	*A Key to the Psalms,* by Rev. Thomas Boys, M.A.

-1891-

Pamphlet	*The Spirits in Prison: An Exposition of I Peter III:17–IV:6.*

-1892-

Pamphlet	*Christ's Prophetic Teaching in Relation to the Divine Order of His Words and Works.*
Pamphlet	*The Kingdom and The Church: or, The Seven Parables of Matthew XIII.*
Pamphlet	*The New Creation and The Old: or, The Ways of God in Grace.* Address at Mildmay Conference, London, June 1892.
Pamphlet	*The Ways of God in Grace, Illustrated by the Ways of God in Creation* (A Bible Reading . . . June 23, 1892).

-1893-

Book   *The Witness of the Stars*. Kregel Publications, Grand Rapids, Mich.

Pamphlet   *Things to Come: An Epitome of Prophetic Truth.*

(Editor)   *Rome's Tactics: or, A Lesson for England from the Past*, by William Goode, D.D.

-1894-

Book   *Number in Scripture: Its Supernatural Design and Spiritual Significance*. Kregel Publications, Grand Rapids, Mich.

Journal   *Things to Come: A Journal of Biblical Literature*. vol. I–vol. XXI.

Articles   *The Epistle to the Romans and the False Gospels of To-day.*

Articles   *The Names and Order of the Books of the Old Testament.*

Article   *The Purpose of the Ages*. Address at Nottingham Conference, May 1894.

Article   *Rightly Dividing the Word of Truth*. Address at Carlisle Conference, May 1894.

Article   *The Seventy Weeks*. Address at Glasgow Conference, June 1894.

Articles   *Tatian's Diatessaron.*

-1895-

Pamphlet   *"Also": A Bible Study on the Usage of This Word in the New Testament*. American Christian Press, New Knoxville, Ohio.

Pamphlet   *Sunday School Lessons*. 1st, 2d, 3d Series.

Article   *Fulfilled Prophecy: Edom*. Address at York Conference, May 1894.

Articles   *The Mystery.*

Article   *The Practical Power of Our Hope*. Address at Liverpool Conference, November 1894.

Article   *The Rights of the Lord Jesus*. Address at Dundee Conference, June 1894.

Article   *The Use of the Divine Titles: A Proof of Inspiration*. Address at Keswick Conference, July 1895.

Poem   "He Gives in Sleep" (in *Things to Come*).

-1896-

Pamphlet	*Holiness: God's Way Better Than Man's.*
Pamphlet	*The Man of God: II Tim. III:16,17.*
Pamphlet	*Sunday School Lessons.* 4th Series.
Articles	*The Divine Names and Titles.* Jeffrey S. Bowman, 17692 Flintstone Lane, Huntington Beach, Calif.
Article	*Was Peter Ever at Rome.*

-1897-

Pamphlet	*The Massorah.*
Pamphlet	*Sunday School Lessons.* 5th Series.
Article	*By Me Kings Reign.* Sermon preached at St. Stephen's Church, Walthamstow, Trinity Sunday Morning, 1886.
Article	*First and Last Words in Scripture.*
Articles	*The Hope of His Calling.* Address at Mildmay Conference, October 1896.
Articles	*The Structure of the Books of the Bible.*
Article	*The Structure of the Books of the New Testament.*
(Editor)	*Holy Scripture: The Sole Authoritative Expositor of Divine Truth,* by William Goode, D.D.

-1898-

Book	*Figures of Speech Used in the Bible.* Baker Book House, Grand Rapids, Mich.
Pamphlet	*Intoned Prayers and Musical Services: Are They in Harmony with the Worship of God "in Spirit and in Truth"?* Address at Evangelical Protestant Union, Manchester, October 1898.
Articles	*The Church Epistles.* Chapters 1, 2, and Conclusion. The Word Inc., G.P.O. Box 450, Adelaide, South Australia.
Article	*The Fixing of Dates.*
Article	*The Last Seven-fold Command of Christ.*
Article	*The Seven Church Epistles As a Whole: Their Interrelation.*
Article	*The Sufferings and The Glory: or, The Transfiguration and Its Lessons.* Address at Prophecy Conference, Keswick, July 1895.

Article	*This Is My Body.*
Article	*What Is the Spirit Saying to the Churches?*

-1899-

Article	*Anglo-Israelism: The Root of Its Error.* Address at Prophetic Conference, n.d.
Article	*Be Perfect.*
Article	*The Dispensational Position of John's Gospel: or, The Fig, the Olive, and the Vine.*
Article	*The Guilty by No Means Cleared.*
Article	*Made Meet.*
Articles	*Rationalism and Its Relation to Romanism.* Address at National Protestant Congress, Manchester, November 1899.
Article	*The Royal Road to Holiness.*
Article	*Sanctification.*
Article	*Where We Ought to Worship.*

-1900-

Pamphlet	*The Vision of Isaiah: Its Structure and Scope.* Jeffrey S. Bowman, 17692 Flintstone Lane, Huntington Beach, Calif.
Article	*Far Off and Made Nigh.*
Articles	*Papers on the Apocalypse: Fifteen Preliminary Points.*
Article	*Perfection.*
Article	*Truth for Times of Trouble.*
Article	*Where Is He?*
Music	*Hymns for Christian Conferences.*

-1901-

Article	*Knowing Christ after the Flesh.*
Articles	*Papers on the Apocalypse.*
Article	*The Paulicians: A Lesson from the Past.*
Article	*The Zionist Medal and What It Teaches Us.*

-1902-

Book	*The Apocalypse or, The Day of the Lord* (see Articles, 1900, 1901; new title: *Commentary on Revelation*). Kregel Publications, Grand Rapids, Mich.

Book	*The Church Epistles* (see Articles, 1898).
Pamphlet	*The Rich Man and Lazarus: or, The Intermediate State.*
Articles	*The Christian's Greatest Need.* Berean Pub. Trust, Brittania Warehouse, Cranleigh, Surrey.
Article	*The Great Conflict of the Ages: Gen. 3:15–Rev. 20:10.* Address at Mildmay Conference, London, 1902.
Articles	*The Potter's House.*
Article	*Sheol.*

-1903-

Article	*A Bible Acrostic.*
Article	*The Darius Papyrus.*
Article	*The Divine Plan of the Ages.* Address at Mildmay Conference, London, 1902.
Article	*The Fallacies of Evolution.*
Articles	*Hades.*
Articles	*The Oldest Lesson in the World: or, The End of the Lord as Seen in the Book of Job.* Scripture Research Inc., P.O. Box 518, Atascadero, Calif.
Articles	*"S" and "s": The Use and Usage of the Word "Pneuma" (Spirit) in the New Testament.*

-1904-

Pamphlet	*Four Prophetic Periods: A Key to the "Things Which Must Shortly Come to Pass"* (rev. ed.).
Article	*Christian Evolution.*
Articles	*The Gospel of the Kingdom: As Set Forth in the Parables of the Sower, the Dinner, and the Supper.*
Articles	*The Titles of the Psalms.*
Articles	*The Two Prayers in the Epistle to the Ephesians.*

-1905-

Book	*The Giver and His Gifts* (see 1903, *"S" and "s"*; new title: *Word Studies on the Holy Spirit*). Kregel Publications, Grand Rapids, Mich. Chap. 1, 2, and Appendix. The Word, Inc., G.P.O. Box 450, Adelaide, South Australia.
Pamphlet	*Jehoshaphat: A Lesson for Our Times.*

Pamphlet	*The Resurrection of the Body.*
Pamphlet	*Sheol and Hades: Their Meaning and Usage in the Word of God* (see 1902, 1903 Articles).
Article	*God's Building.*
Article	*The Laws of Correspondence in Holy Scripture.*
Articles	*The Two Natures in the Child of God.* Truth For Today, Lafayette, Ind.
Articles	*The Zionist Movement in Its Relation to Prophecy.* Address at Prophecy Investigation Society, London, April 1904.

-1906-

Article	*The Knowledge of God.*
Article	*Leaven: Its Biblical Usage and Interpretation.*
Article	*The Sons of God.*
Article	*The Transfiguration.*
Article	*The Vail.*

-1907-

Book	*How to Enjoy the Bible.* American Christian Press, New Knoxville, Ohio.
Pamphlet	*The Lord's Prayer: Its Dispensational Place and Interpretation.*
Article	*The Good Deposit: or, Paratheke.*
Articles	*Hebrews XI.*
Articles	*The Lord's Day: Rev. 1:10.* Address at Prophecy Investigation Society, London, November 1906.
Articles	*The Pauline Epistles: The Dispensational Teaching of Their Chronological Order.*
Articles	*The Songs of Degrees.*

-1908-

Book	*The Chief Musician: or, Studies in the Psalms and Their Titles* (see 1904, and 1907, *The Songs of Degrees*). Truth For Today, Lafayette, Ind.
Article	*Canonical and Chronological Order of Scripture: Samuel and Jeremiah.*
Article	*Try the Spirits.*

-1909-

Book	*The Companion Bible. Part I. The Pentateuch.*
Article	*The Doxology of Romans (16:25–27).*
Article	*The Selah in Psalm XLIV* (see 1908, *The Chief Musician*).
Articles	*The Selahs of Psalms XLVI, XLVII, XLVIII* (see above).

-1910-

Book	*The Companion Bible. Part II. Joshua to Job.*
Book	*The Story of the Breton Mission.*
Article	*The Site of Zion.*
Review	*Trusting God in Sickness: A Review of Two Pamphlets,* by Philip Mauro.
Review	*When Did This Dispensation Begin,* by Ada B. Habershon.

-1911-

Book	*The Companion Bible. Part III. Psalms to Song of Solomon.*
Book	*Great Cloud of Witnesses in Hebrews Eleven* (see 1907, *Hebrews XI*). Kregel Publications, Grand Rapids, Mich.
Article	*Alnwick and Glanton.*
Article	*The Breaking of Bread.*
Article	*Difficulties in Dispensational Teaching.*
Articles	*The Lord Hath Spoken: The Foundations of Dispensational Truth.*

-1912-

Book	*The Companion Bible. Part IV. Isaiah to Malachi.*

Published Posthumously

-1914-

Book	*The Companion Bible. Part V. The Four Gospels.*
Article	*Abraham Believed God.*
Article	*The Accomplished Decease.*

Article	*The Christian's Standing, Object, and Hope.*
Article	*Crucified with Christ.*
Article	*The Cursing of Balak and the Blessing of God.*
Article	*The Dispensational Plan of the Bible.*
Article	*Following Hard.*
Article	*Glory of the Eternal Trinity.*
Article	*I Am Black. I Am Vile. I Am Undone.*
Article	*Mephibosheth: or, the Kindness of God.*
Article	*Nehemiah: or, The Opposition of the Enemy.*
Article	*Peter's Fall and Peter's Recovery.*
Article	*They Sang His Praise. They Soon Forgot His Works.*
Article	*Thou Remainest.*
Article	*Three Attitudes and Utterances of David.*
Article	*Truth for the Day of Trouble.*

-1915-

Article	*Athaliah and Jehosheba.*
Article	*The Days of the Upright.*
Article	*Divine Promotion and Preservation.*
Article	*Earth's Curse and Its Removal.*
Article	*Five Postulates for Interpretation.*
Article	*A New Creation.*
Article	*The One Sacrifice.*
Article	*The Pharisee and the Publican.*
Article	*Praise for Divine Goodness.*
Article	*Stablished–Strengthened–Settled.*
Article	*The Woman of Canaan.*

-1921-

Book	*The Companion Bible. Part VI. Acts to Revelation.*

-1922-

Book	*The Companion Bible.* Kregel Publications, Grand Rapids, Mich.

LATER PUBLICATIONS

Book	*The Foundations of Dispensational Truth* (see 1911,

	The Lord Hath Spoken) Truth For Today, Lafayette, Ind.
Book	*Selected Writings.*
Music	*A Prayer Hymn for Those in Active Service.* Arr. by George Arthur Clarke, Boston, Mass. Whittemore Associates, 1942. Words by Isabella Stephenson. Music by Ethelbert William Bullinger.

At various times, collections of the pamphlets were privately printed in book form.

Notes

THE DESIGNATION "DRF Collection" has been used for all material made available by Mrs. Dorothy Fielder. The abbreviation "TBS" means Trinitarian Bible Society.

Introduction

1. For readers who want to delve deeper into these subjects, a large body of more detailed literature is available. Many of these sources are listed in the bibliography.
2. Sir Charles Petrie, *The Victorians* (New York: Longmans, Green, 1961), 40.
3. Ibid., 23.
4. Walter E. Houghton, *The Victorian Frame of Mind 1830–1870* (New Haven: Yale University Press, 1957), 1–5 passim.
5. Petrie, *The Victorians*, 65.
6. Elizabeth Longford, *Victoria R.I.* (New York: Harper & Row, 1973), 37.
7. Asa Briggs, *Victorian People: A Re-assessment of Persons and Themes, 1851–1867* (Chicago: University of Chicago Press, 1955), 2–3.
8. Ibid., 2.
9. W. Baring Pemberton, *Lord Palmerston* (London: Batchworth, 1954), 180.
10. Petrie, *The Victorians*, 52.
11. Ibid., 52–53.
12. Houghton, *Victorian Frame of Mind*, 1.
13. Ibid., 3.
14. James Laver, *Victorian Vista* (London: Hulton, 1954), 206.
15. Houghton, *Victorian Frame of Mind*, 8.
16. Ibid., 11.

17. Petrie, *Victorians,* 228.
18. Laver, *Victorian Vista,* 202.
19. "Canterbury Wesleyans," *Canterbury Wesleyan Methodist Circuit Magazine,* July 1912.
20. Marvin R. O'Connell, *The Oxford Conspirators: A History of the Oxford Movement, 1833–1845* (London: Collier-Macmillan, 1969), 45.
21. Leslie Paul, *A Church by Daylight: A Reappraisement of the Church of England and Its Future* (London: Geoffrey Chapman, 1973), 50.
22. Roger Anstey, "John Wesley and Methodism," The Beaney Institute, Canterbury, n.d.
23. Owen Chadwick, *The Victorian Church: Part One 1829–1859* (London: SCM, 1987), 370.
24. George Reginald Balleine, *A History of the Evangelical Party in the Church of England* (London: Longmans, Green, 1908), 37.
25. Rupert Davies and Gordon Rupp, eds., *A History of the Methodist Church in Great Britain,* vol. 2 (London: Epworth, 1978), 174.
26. Kenneth Scott Latourette, *The Nineteenth Century in Europe: The Protestant and Eastern Churches,* vol. 2 of *Christianity in a Revolutionary Age* (London: Eyre & Spottiswoode, 1960), 264–270 passim.
27. Laver, *Victorian Vista,* 203.
28. John R. H. Moorman, *A History of the Church in England* (London: Adam & Charles Black, 1973), 376–377.
29. Ibid., 377.
30. Ken Petty, *Origins of Modern Spiritualism* (New Knoxville, Ohio: Way International, 1978), 22–23.
31. Ibid., 23.
32. Owen Chadwick, *The Victorian Church: Part Two 1860–1901* (London: SCM, 1987), 110, 112.
33. Alec Vidler, *The Church in an Age of Revolution: 1789 to the Present Day* (London: Hodder & Stoughton, 1961), 112.
34. T. H. Hilken, *St. Stephen's, Walthamstow 1875–1928* (London: Church Book Room, 1928), 9, 10.
35. Moorman, *Church in England,* 2d ed., 395.
36. Ethelbert William Bullinger, *A Month's Musings: A Daily Portion from the Writings of Dr. Bullinger,* no. 112, DRF Collection.

Chapter One: Childhood

1. John Boyle, *Portrait of Canterbury* (London: Robert Hall, 1980), 110–11.

2. "The Cradle of Our Race," *The Methodist Recorder,* 7 December 1911.
3. Frank W. Jessup, *History of Kent* (London: Phillimore & Co., 1974), 22–23.
4. "Canterbury Tales," *The Methodist Recorder,* 12 July 1906.
5. Jessup, *History of Kent,* 31.
6. Richard Church, *Portrait of Canterbury* (London: Hutchinson & Co., 1968), 42–43.
7. Stapleton and Company, *Topographical History and Directory of Canterbury* (London, 1838), 4.
8. Boyle, *Portrait of Canterbury,* 84.
9. St. Peter's Street Chapel, Canterbury, *Parish Record Book.*
10. Public Census Records for Canterbury, England, 1871, The Beaney Institute, Canterbury.
11. John A. Vickers, *The Story of Canterbury Methodism 1750–1961* (Bognor Regis West, Sussex: WHMS), 16.
12. "Ethelbert William Bullinger," birth and baptismal announcement, DRF Collection.
13. Rupert Davies and Gordon Rupp, eds., *A History of the Methodist Church in Great Britain,* vol. 2 (London: Epworth, 1978), 110–11.
14. Ibid., 98.
15. Ibid.
16. Owen Chadwick, *The Victorian Church: Part One 1829–1859* (London: SCM, 1987), 372.
17. Wallace Harvey, interview with author, Whitstable, England, 14 January 1985.
18. Letter, Ethelbert W. Bullinger to W. H. Longhurst, 17 September 1881, Canterbury Cathedral Old Choristers' Association Archives, Canterbury.
19. "Where Boys Sing to the Worship and Glory of God," *Kent Messenger,* 26 July 1957.
20. "Account of the Choral School of Canterbury Cathedral," *The Gentleman's Magazine,* May 1817.
21. Ethelbert had actually just turned ten when he joined the choir in 1848.
22. Letter, Joshua Stratton to Rev. F. S. Nash, 21 January 1858, DRF Collection.
23. Letter, W. H. Longhurst to Ethelbert W. Bullinger, 20 June n.d. DRF Collection.

24. Letter, Ethelbert W. Bullinger to W. H. Longhurst, 17 September 1881, Canterbury Cathedral Old Choristers' Association Archives, Canterbury.

Chapter Two: King's College

1. Letter, John White to the Warden, New College, Oxford, 24 May 1859, DRF Collection.
2. Letter, Frederick G. Nash to New College, Oxford, 19 May 1859, DRF Collection.
3. Letter, Doris Blair to Dorothy Fielder, n.d., DRF Collection.
4. John Buxton and Penry Williams, *New College, Oxford, 1379–1979* (Oxford: The Warden and Fellows of New College, 1979), 72.
5. Ibid., 77. Part of the rigid division between the upper class and those below them had always been the unwritten law that only the sons of "gentlemen" could attend university. See the introduction.
6. Ibid., 280.
7. Raymond Needham and Alexander Webster, *Somerset House: Past and Present* (London: T. Fisher Unwin, 1905), 267.
8. Gordon Huelin, *King's College, London,1828–1978* (London: University of London, 1978), 19.
9. *King's College Calendar 1860–61* (London: King's College, 1861), 61.
10. Ibid., 62–63.
11. "Ethelbert William Bullinger," King's College, London, Student Records, 1859–60.
12. *King's College Calendar 1860–61,* 60–61.
13. Ibid., 63–64, 70–71.
14. Testimonial, Rev. Alexander J. McCaul for E. W. Bullinger, 24 November 1865, DRF Collection.
15. Sidney Lee, ed., *Dictionary of National Biography,* vol. 12 (London: Smith, Elder & Co., 1909), 445–46.
16. Harold P. Morgan, "Seven Questions in Dispute," *Questions and Answers* 3 (April–May 1945): 11.
17. Sidney Lee, ed., *Dictionary of National Biography,* 2d Supp. (London: Smith, Elder & Co., 1912), 1:618–19.
18. Ibid., 3:108–9.
19. Sidney Lee, ed., *Dictionary of National Biography,* 15:1323.
20. Testimonial, Rev. E. H. Plumptre for E. W. Bullinger, 28 November 1865, DRF Collection.

21. Testimonial, Rev. J. J. Stewart Perowne for E. W. Bullinger, 11 January 1865, DRF Collection.

22. *King's College Calendar 1861–62*, 73.

23. J.S.C., *An Appreciation of Dr. E. W. Bullinger* (England: Printed by the Author, n.d.), 6.

24. Certificate of Deaconate, Ethelbert William Bullinger, 7 July 1861, DRF Collection.

25. Letter, Joshua Stratton to E. W. Bullinger, 8 July 1861, DRF Collection.

Chapter Three: The Early Parishes

1. Public Census Records, London, England, 1861, Victoria Library, London.

2. V. Leff and C. H. Blunden, *Riverside Story: The Story of Bermondsey and Its People* (London: Civic Publicity Services, 1963), 1.

3. Charles H. Welch, *Charles H. Welch: An Autobiography* (Banstead, Surrey: Berean Publishing Trust, 1960), 10.

4. Mervyn Wilson, *Bermondsey: A Brief History and Description of Bermondsey Parish Church, St. Mary Magdalen, with St. Olav, St. John and St. Luke* (Southwark: Dramrite Printers, 1976), 7.

5. Leff and Blunden, *Riverside Story*, 11.

6. Bermondsey United Charity Schools, *Committee Notes*, 27 November 1862, Harvard Library, Borough of Southwark, Southwark, London.

7. Ordination Certificate, Ethelbert William Bullinger, 6 July 1862, DRF Collection.

8. J.S.C., *An Appreciation of Dr. E. W. Bullinger* (England: Printed by the Author, n.d.), 6–7.

9. "Ethelbert Augustine Bullinger," Birth Announcement in Bullinger Family Bible, DRF Collection.

10. A. Tindal Hart, *The Curate's Lot: The Story of the Unbeneficed English Clergy* (London: John Baker, 1970), 130–31.

11. Testimonial, Dr. Alexander McCaul for E. W. Bullinger, 25 May 1863, DRF Collection.

12. Letter, Dr. J. J. Stewart Perowne to E. W. Bullinger, 24 August 1863, DRF Collection.

13. T. Hugh Bryant, *Norfolk Churches* (Norwich: Norwich Mercury, 1903), 215.

14. J. Charles Cox, *County Churches of Norfolk* (London: George Allen & Sons, 1910), 67.

15. Testimonial, Rev. Kenelm H. Digby for Rev. E. W. Bullinger, 27 November 1865, DRF Collection.

16. John 16:21: "A woman when she is in travail hath sorrow, because her hour is come: but as soon as she is delivered of the child, she remembereth no more the anguish, for joy that a man is born into the world."

17. Letter, Rev. Kenelm H. Digby to Rev. E. W. Bullinger, 26 July 1866, DRF Collection.

18. Letter, J. Lark, Esq., to Rev. E. W. Bullinger, 27 July 1866, DRF Collection.

19. Letter, J. Lark, Esq., to Rev. E. W. Bullinger, 23 August 1866, DRF Collection.

20. F. H. W. Sheppard, ed., *Northern Kensington,* vol. 37 of *Survey of London* (London: Athlone, 1973), 200–1.

21. "Bernard Stratton Bullinger," Birth Announcement in Bullinger Family Bible, DRF Collection.

22. E. W. Bullinger, *A Critical Lexicon and Concordance to the English and Greek New Testament* (Grand Rapids: Zondervan, 1975), 7.

23. Letter, Rev. John Philip Gell to Rev. E. W. Bullinger, 13 August 1868, DRF Collection.

24. D. G. Mumby, "Pages from the Past," *St. Augustine's Leytonstone Parish News,* December 1949.

25. Gold coins valued at approximately one English pound each.

26. St. John's, Leytonstone, Presentation to Rev. E. W. Bullinger, 10 December 1870, DRF Collection.

Chapter Four: The Bethnal Green Workhouse School

1. Mary Sturt, *The Education of the People: A History of Primary Education in England and Wales in the Nineteenth Century* (London: Routledge and Kegan Paul, 1967), 85–86.

2. Ibid., 86.

3. Roger Steer, *George Müller: Delighted in God* (London: Hodder & Stoughton, 1975), 72–73.

4. Ibid., 61.

5. Walter Monnington and Frederick J. Lampard, *Our London Poor Law Schools* (London: Eyre & Spottiswoode, 1898), 75.

6. Parish of St. Matthew, Bethnal Green, *Minute Book of Board of Governors of the School: 1870* (London: Eyre & Spottiswoode, 1870).

7. "People of Leyton," *Leyton Ratebooks, 1870 July to 1871 July,* Vestry Museum Library, Walthamstow, London.

8. Parish of St. Matthew, Bethnal Green, *Minute Book,* 24 October 1871.

9. George Macaulay Trevelyan, *The Nineteenth Century,* vol. 4 of *Illustrated English Social History* (London: Longmans, Green & Co., 1957), 119–20.

10. Parish of St. Matthew, Bethnal Green, "Duties of the Chaplain," Article 64, *The Government of the School* (London: Eyre & Spottiswoode, 1872).

11. Parish of St. Matthew, Bethnal Green, *Minute Book,* 20 January 1874.

12. Ibid., 21 October 1873.

13. Ibid., 30 December 1873.

14. Ibid., 8 January 1874.

15. Ibid., 17 March 1874.

16. Ibid., 14 April 1874.

17. Ibid., 9 May 1874.

18. Ibid., 26 May 1874.

Chapter Five: The Walthamstow Years

1. W. G. S. Tonkin, *The Anglican Church in Walthamstow* (London: Walthamstow Antiquarian Society, 1963), 58.

2. Ibid., 58–59.

3. Ibid.

4. George Edward Roebuck, *The Story of Walthamstow* (London: Walthamstow Corp., 1952), 5.

5. T. H. Hilken, *St. Stephen's, Walthamstow, 1875–1928* (London: Church Book Room, 1928), 6.

6. George F. Bosworth, *More Walthamstow Houses, and Their Interesting Associations* (London: Walthamstow Antiquarian Society, 1928), 13.

7. Hilken, *St. Stephen's,* 10.

8. Ibid., 6.

9. Ibid., 8.

10. Ibid., 8–9.

11. Ibid., 10.

12. Ibid., 11.

13. J. S. C., *An Appreciation of Dr. E. W. Bullinger* (England: Printed by the Author, n.d.), 8–9.

14. Hilken, *St. Stephen's,* 15–16.

15. Ibid., 9–10.

16. E. W. Bullinger, *A Critical Lexicon and Concordance to the English and Greek New Testament* (London: Longmans, Green & Co., 1877), dedication.

17. Ibid., preface.

18. The Seventeenth Annual Meeting of the Church Congress, Croydon, *The Official Report,* 12 October 1877.

19. Review of *A Critical Lexicon and Concordance to the English and Greek New Testament,* in *The British Quarterly Review,* October 1877.

20. Review of *A Critical Lexicon and Concordance to the English and Greek New Testament,* in *The Record,* October 1877.

21. Letter, Lord Beaconsfield to Rev. E. W. Bullinger, 20 September 1877, DRF Collection.

22. Letter, C. Payne Smith to Rev. E. W. Bullinger, 3 October 1877, DRF Collection.

23. Letter, Archibald Campbell Tait to E. W. Bullinger, 20 September 1877, DRF Collection.

24. Executive Order, Archibald Campbell Tait to Sir James Plaisted Baron Penzance, 17 August 1881, Lambeth Palace Archives, London.

25. "The Lambeth Degrees," Lambeth Palace Archives, London.

26. "Form of Conferring Degrees by the Archbishop of Canterbury," Lambeth Palace Archives (London: Abbey, n.d.).

27. Royal Proclamation of the United Kingdom, 9 September 1881, DRF Collection.

28. Letter, Dr. Edward Hayes Plumtre to E. W. Bullinger, 8 August 1881, DRF Collection.

29. "St. Stephen's," *The Walthamstow and Leyton Guardian,* 24 September 1881.

30. Letter, Elizabeth Dodson to E. W. Bullinger, 8 August 1881, DRF Collection.

31. Letter, William Exton to E. W. Bullinger, 9 August 1881, DRF Collection.

32. Mrs. Dorothy Fielder, interview with author, 14 April 1987.

33. Letter, E. W. Bullinger to the Congregation of St. Stephen's, Walthamstow, 19 October 1888, DRF Collection.

34. Letter, T. L. St. Albans to E. W. Bullinger, 26 October 1888, DRF Collection.

35. Letter, H. W. Carter and Edward Tomlinson to E. W. Bullinger, December 1888, DRF Collection.

36. Hilken, *St. Stephen's, Walthamstow,* 42.

Chapter Six: The Trinitarian Bible Society

1. Andrew J. Brown, *The Word of God Among All Nations* (London: Trinitarian Bible Society, 1981), 7.
2. Ibid., 7–8.
3. Ibid., 8.
4. Ibid., 12.
5. Ibid., 13.
6. Ibid., 14–16.
7. Ibid., 19.
8. Ibid., 22.
9. Ibid., 23.
10. Ibid., 23–24
11. Ibid., 38–41, 70.
12. Brown, *The Word of God Among All Nations*, 44.
13. Ibid., 47–48.
14. Letter, Rev. John Robbins to The Committee, Trinitarian Bible Society, 20 March 1867, DRF Collection.
15. C. T. Lipshytz, "The Late Rev. Dr. Bullinger, A Man of One Book," *Immanuel's Witness*, September 1913, 192.
16. "The Two Bible Societies," reprinted from *The Portsmouth Times* (Portsmouth: J. Stephens, 1872), 8–9.
17. Ibid., 10.
18. *The Holy Bible, Translated from the Latin Vulgate* (London: George Henry & Co., 1850), Exodus 20:5.
19. Ibid., Matthew 3:2.
20. Ibid., Genesis 3:15.
21. Ibid., 9.
22. Brown, *The Word of God Among All Nations*, 64.
23. Ibid., 64–65.
24. Ibid., 57–58.
25. Ibid., 66–70.
26. E. W. Bullinger, *The Story of the Breton Mission* (London: By the Author, 1910), 11.
27. Ibid., 13–15.
28. Brown, *The Word of God Among All Nations*, 76–77.
29. Bullinger, *Breton Mission*, 71.
30. Ibid., 27.
31. Ibid., 22–24.
32. Ibid., 71–74.

33. G. LeCoat, "Breton Tunes," preface to *Chants Chrétiens edités et composés par G. LeCoat de Tremel* (London: 7 St. Paul's Church-yard, 1889).

34. Brown, *The Word of God Among All Nations,* 79.

35. Samuel Hinds Wilkinson, *The Life of John Wilkinson* (London: Morgan & Scott, 1908), 232.

36. Brown, *The Word of God Among All Nations,* 79–80.

37. Wilkinson, *The Life of John Wilkinson,* 235–36.

38. "Twenty-Four Sacred Books," *The Quarterly Record of the Work and Witness of the Trinitarian Bible Society,* December 1952, DRF Collection.

39. E. W. Bullinger, *The Massorah,* 2d ed. (London: Eyre & Spottiswoode, 1897), 30.

40. Christian D. Ginsburg, preface to *Introduction to the Massoretico-Critical Edition of the Hebrew Bible* (New York: KTAV, 1966).

41. "The Late Dr. E. W. Bullinger," *Things to Come* 19 (July 1913): 73.

Chapter Seven: The Last Parishes

1. Alan Crosby, *A History of Woking* (London: Phillimore, 1982), 74.

2. Ibid.

3. Mary Anne Lloyd, *Susanna Meredith: A Record of a Vigorous Life* (London: Hodder & Stoughton, 1903), 11.

4. Ibid., 26.

5. Ibid., 31–33.

6. Ibid., 44–46.

7. Ibid., 57–58.

8. Ibid., 60.

9. "The Princess Mary Village Homes," Addlestone, Surrey Registry Office, Kingston-on-Thames, 1890.

10. *Kelly's Surrey Directory, 1890, Addlestone,* Surrey Registry Office, Kingston-on-Thames, 1890, 1144.

11. *Twentieth Annual Report of the Princess Mary Village Homes, 1889–90,* Surrey Registry Office, Kingston-on-Thames, 1890.

12. Ibid., "Concerning Religious Instruction."

13. Letter, Elsie Kitching to Elizabeth Dodson, 25 June 1913, DRF Collection.

14. Letter, E. W. Bullinger to The Congregation of St. Stephen's, Walthamstow, 19 October 1888, DRF Collection.

15. Robert Braithwaite, ed., *The Life and Letters of Rev. William Pennefather* (London: John F. Shaw, 1878), 531.

16. Ibid., 535.
17. E. W. Bullinger, "The Importance of Prophetic Study," in *Ten Sermons on the Second Advent*, 4th ed. rev. (London: Eyre & Spottiswoode, 1901), 1–2, 4, 6–7.
18. E. W. Bullinger, preface to *The Apocalypse: or, The Day of the Lord* (London: Samuel Bagster, 1972).
19. Letter fragment, unsigned, 17 May 1888, DRF Collection.
20. E. W. Bullinger, *The Inspiration and Authority of Holy Scripture* (London: Eyre & Spottiswoode, 1906), 1, 7, 14.
21. Census for Woking, 1891, Public Records Office, Kingston, Surrey.
22. Basil F. L. Clarke, *The Building of the Eighteenth Century Church* (London: SPCK, 1963), 189.
23. Ibid., 187–88.
24. "Brunswick Chapel 1891–1894" Papers of the Bishop of London, Guildhall Library, London.
25. E. W. Bullinger, *The Witness of the Stars* (Grand Rapids: Kregel, 1976).
26. Ibid., 1, preface.
27. Robert Brown, *A Reply to Dr. Bullinger's So-Called "Witness of the Stars"* (London: William Wileman, 1894), 69.
28. Letter, E. W. Bullinger to Mr. Roth, 11 November 1892, DRF Collection.
29. Brown, *Reply to Dr. Bullinger*, 1–3.
30. Ibid., 72.
31. E. W. Bullinger, *Number in Scripture: Its Supernatural Design and Spiritual Significance* (Grand Rapids: Kregel, 1978), 45.
32. Ibid., 21.
33. Ibid., 88.
34. Robert Anderson, *Spirit Manifestations and "The Gift of Tongues"* (Edinburgh: Loizeaux Brothers, 1979), 4.
35. R. Herbert Story, "Edward Irving," *Scottish Divines, 1505–1872, Lecture VII*, in *St. Giles' Lectures* (Edinburgh: Macniven and Wallace, 1883), 236.
36. Edward Irving, *Farewell Discourse to the Congregation and Parish of St. John's, Glasgow* (Glasgow: Waugh and Innes, 1822), 18–20.
37. Andrew J. Brown, *The Word of God Among All Nations* (London: Trinitarian Bible Society, 1981), 9.
38. Ibid., 26–27.

39. Edward Irving, "The Second Advent of Our Lord, and His Ever-lasting Kingdom," Lecture 5, *Five Lectures* (London: John Bennett, 1835), 52–60 passim.

40. E. W. Bullinger, *Christ's Prophetic Teaching in Relation to the Divine Order of His Words and Works,* in *Selected Works* (London: Lamp, 1960), 104–5.

41. Harold H. Rowdon, *The Origins of the Brethren 1825–1850* (London: Pickering & Inglis, 1967), 1–2.

42. J. S. Teulon, *The History and Teaching of the Plymouth Brethren* (London: Christian Knowledge Society, 1883), 9–10.

43. Ibid., 171–75.

44. Kenneth Scott Latourette, *The Nineteenth Century in Europe: The Protestant and Eastern Churches,* vol. 2 of *Christianity in a Revolutionary Age* (London: Eyre & Spottiswoode, 1960), 345.

45. Thomas Croskery, *Plymouth-Brethrenism: A Refutation of its Principles and Doctrines* (London: William Mullon, 1879), 108, 123.

46. E. W. Bullinger, *"The Kingdom" and "The Church"* (London: Eyre & Spottiswoode, 1892), 1–3.

47. Roger Steer, *George Müller: Delighted in God* (London: Hodder & Stoughton, 1975), 158–59.

Chapter Eight: *Things to Come*

Unless otherwise noted, all references in this chapter are from *Things to Come*.

1. Vol. 1 (December 1894): 101.

2. Vol. 1 (July 1894): 1.

3. Ibid.

4. Vol. 19 (July 1913): 73.

5. Vol. 4 (March 1898): 108.

6. Vol. 4 (June 1898): 144.

7. Vol. 12 (November 1906): 132.

8. Vol. 15 (October 1909): 109.

9. Vol. 10 (November 1904): 203.

10. Vol. 2 (April 1896): 191.

11. Vol. 10 (November 1904): 203.

12. Vol. 4 (August 1897): 23.

13. Vol. 3 (December 1896): 71.

14. Vol. 16 (November 1910): 123–24.

15. Vol. 12 (January 1906): 10.

16. Vol. 11 (October 1905): 120.
17. Vol. 5 (September 1898): 32.
18. Vol. 11 (October 1905): 120.
19. Vol. 14 (July 1908): 84.
20. Vol. 12 (August 1906): 96.
21. Vol. 1 (July 1894): 17.
22. C. T. Lipshytz, "The Late Rev. Dr. Bullinger: A Man of One Book," *Immanuel's Witness,* September 1913, 192.
23. Vol. 2 (February 1896): 150.
24. "Theodore Herzl" *New Encyclopedia Britannica,* 15th ed. (Chicago: Encyclopedia Britannica, 1986), 5:896.
25. E. W. Bullinger, *The Apocalypse* (London: Samuel Bagster, 1972), 348.
26. Vol. 10 (October 1904): 191.
27. Bullinger, *Apocalypse,* 3.
28. Ibid., 8.
29. See the introduction, p. 29
30. Vol. 12 (April 1906): 45.
31. Vol. 12 (August 1906): 95.
32. See the introduction, p. 32.
33. Vol. 6 (April 1900): 116.
34. Vol. 10 (August 1903): 19.
35. Ibid.
36. Ibid., 19–20.
37. Vol. 10 (February 1904): 93.
38. Vol. 5 (March 1899): 108.
39. Vol. 12 (February 1906): 23.

Chapter Nine: The Later Years
1. TBS, *Committee Minute Book, 5 October 1891 to 7 January 1901,* 30 September 1895, TBS Archives.
2. Public Census Records, General Register Office, London, 1896.
3. Ibid., 1902.
4. Mrs. Dorothy Fielder, interview with author, 26 March 1984.
5. Letter, Secretary of State, Department of the Interior for the Independent State of the Congo, to Bernard S. Bullinger, 25 May 1900, DRF Collection.
6. E. W. Bullinger, *Figures of Speech Used in the Bible* (Grand Rapids: Baker, 1981), xii.

7. E. W. Bullinger, *"Also"* (New Knoxville, Ohio: American Christian Press, 1981), 1.

8. Bullinger, *Figures of Speech,* vii.

9. Ibid., ix.

10. Ibid., xv.

11. Ibid., ix.

12. Ibid., x–xi.

13. 18 shillings.

14. "Figures of Speech," *Things to Come* 6 (November 1899): 60.

15. Letter fragment, writer unknown, TBS Archives.

16. TBS, *The Quarterly Record of the Trinitarian Bible Society,* January 1899 (London: Eyre & Spottiswoode), 32.

17. Barbara W. Tuchman, *The Proud Tower: A Portrait of the World Before the War 1890–1914* (New York: Macmillan, 1966), chap. 2, pp. 63–113 passim.

18. C. T. Lipshytz, "The Late Rev. Dr. Bullinger: A Man of One Book," *Immanuel's Witness,* September 1913, 190. The Anarchist movement, which sought to overturn existing governments, espoused violence as a method of achieving its goals. During the last decade of the nineteenth century and the early years of the twentieth many acts of terrorism were committed, particularly in the countries of continental Europe.

19. Samuel Burch, Esq., *Inaugural Address,* International Congress of Orientalists, London, 14 September 1874, 3–4.

20. TBS, "The Twelfth Congress of Orientalists," *The Quarterly Record,* January 1900, 29–31.

21. Ibid.

22. See the introduction, p. 22.

23. TBS, "Romanism in Spain," reprint, *The Quarterly Record,* January 1904, 1–5.

24. Ibid., 6–8.

25. Arthur P. M. Anderson, *Sir Robert Anderson, KCB LLD: A Tribute and Memoir* (London: Morgan & Scott, 1919), 21–32 passim.

26. TBS, "Seventy-Ninth Annual Meeting Report," *The Quarterly Record,* July 1910, 3.

27. Ralph Nevill, *London Clubs and Their History and Treasures* (London: Chatto & Windus, 1911), 237.

28. Anderson, *Sir Robert Anderson,* 46.

29. Ibid., 40.

30. Robert Anderson, C.B., *The Buddha of Christendom* (London: Hodder and Stoughton, 1899), vii.

31. Letter, Robert Anderson to E. W. Bullinger, 2 June 1913, DRF Collection.

32. Obituary, "Death of Lord Blythswood," *The London Times*, 2 October 1916, 10.

33. "Barbican Mission to the Jews—Board of Governors," *Immanuel's Witness*, September 1913.

34. Anderson, *Sir Robert Anderson*, 85.

35. A. P. Moore-Anderson, *Sir Robert Anderson and Lady Agnes Anderson* (London: Marshall, Morgan & Scott, 1947), 83.

36. Ibid.

37. TBS, "Rev. James C. Smith," *The Quarterly Record*, October 1904, 3.

38. E. W. Bullinger, *Four Prophetic Periods*, 10th ed. (London: Eyre & Spottiswoode, 1915), 6.

39. Letter, E. W. Bullinger to A. E. Knoch, 2 May 1908.

40. E. W. Bullinger, *The Rich Man and Lazarus*, in *Selected Writings* (London: Lamp, 1960), 107.

41. Ibid.

42. Ibid., 109.

43. Ibid.

44. William Hoste, *The Intermediate State: A Reply to Dr. Bullinger* (London: Alfred Holness, 1911), 7.

45. E. W. Bullinger, *The Church Epistles (Romans to Thessalonians)*, 2d ed. (London: Eyre & Spottiswoode, 1905), 5.

46. Ibid., 8.

47. Ibid., 11–13.

48. E. W. Bullinger, *The Mystery*, in *Selected Writings* (London: Lamp, 1960), 256.

49. Ibid., 266–67.

50. Ibid., 270.

51. Ibid., 286.

52. E. W. Bullinger, "The Pauline Epistles: The Dispensational Teaching of Their Chronological Order," *Things to Come* 13 (April 1907): 38.

53. Harold P. Morgan, "Dr. E. W. Bullinger: The Man and His Work," *Questions and Answers*, January 1943, 7.

54. E. W. Bullinger, "Strife About Words," *Things to Come* 9 (July 1902): 10.

55. TBS, *Committee Minute Book, 4 February 1901 to 8 March 1909,* 4 March 1907.

56. Letter, E. W. Bullinger to A. E. Knoch, 11 April 1907.

57. TBS, *The Quarterly Record,* July 1907.

58. TBS, *Committee Minute Book,* 7 October 1907.

59. Anna Cameron, interview with author, London, June 1984.

60. *Things to Come* 13 (December 1907): 144.

61. Ibid., preface.

Chapter Ten: Life at Bremgarten

1. E. W. Bullinger, *How to Enjoy the Bible* (London: Samuel Bagster, 1980),v–xi.

2. Ibid., xiii–xiv.

3. Ibid., xvii.

4. Ibid., xi.

5. E. W. Bullinger, "Five Postulates for Interpretation," *Things to Come* 21 (October 1915): 118.

6. "Enjoying the Bible?" *Things to Come* 19 (November 1913): 132.

7. E. W. Bullinger, preface to *Things to Come* 13 (November 1907).

8. C. T. Lipshytz, "Our Great Loss," *Immanuel's Witness,* September 1913, 129.

9. TBS, "The Late Secretary, The Rev. E. W. Bullinger, D.D." *The Quarterly Record of the Trinitarian Bible Society,* July 1913, 8.

10. Ibid.

11. Letter, E. W. Bullinger to Elizabeth Dodson, n.d., DRF Collection.

12. Letter, M. Lomax to Elizabeth Dodson, 8 June 1913, DRF Collection.

13. Letter, Maggie to Elizabeth Dodson, 7 June 1913, DRF Collection.

14. Mrs. Dorothy Fielder, interview with author, 10 December 1983.

15. Mrs. Dorothy Fielder, interview with author, 26 March 1984.

16. "Some Tributes to the Late Dr. Bullinger," *Things to Come* 19 (August 1913): 89.

17. J. J. Beddow, "The Late Rev. Dr. Bullinger: An Appreciation," *The English Churchman,* 26 June 1913.

18. "Death of Dr. Bullinger," *Walthamstow Guardian,* 14 June 1913.

19. E. W. Bullinger, *Fifty Original Hymn-Tunes* (Woking, Surrey: Published by the Author, 1889), 26–27.

20. Mrs. Dorothy Fielder, interview with author, 3 April 1984.

21. E. W. Bullinger, Personal Notebooks, DRF Collection.

22. Ibid.

23. Ibid.
24. E. W. Bullinger, "He Gives in Sleep," *Things to Come* 2 (October 1895): 88.
25. Hereward Senior, *Orangeism in Ireland and Britain, 1795–1836* (London: Routledge & Kegan Paul, 1966), 298.
26. Ibid., 282.
27. Letter, Arthur Woodhurst to Elizabeth Dodson, 5 July 1913, DRF Collection.
28. E. W. Bullinger, preface to *The Chief Musician: or, Studies in the Psalms and Their Titles* (London: Eyre & Spottiswoode, 1908).
29. Ibid., v.
30. TBS, "The Hebrew Bible of the Trinitarian Bible Society," *The Quarterly Record,* October 1909, 32–39.
31. Ibid., 39–40.
32. Ibid., 40–46.
33. TBS, *Committee Minute Book, 3 May 1909 to 27 July 1917,* 6 December 1909, TBS Archives.

Chapter Eleven: *The Companion Bible*

1. E. W. Bullinger, preface to *Things to Come* 16 (November 1910).
2. Letter, William Barron to Charles Welch, 10 June 1912, Papers of Mrs. Winifred Carpenter.
3. E. W. Bullinger, preface to *The Companion Bible* (Grand Rapids: Zondervan, 1974), vii–viii.
4. Ibid., v.
5. C. T. Lipshytz, "The Late Rev. Dr. Bullinger: A Man of One Book," *Immanuel's Witness,* September 1913, 190.
6. Letter, E. W. Bullinger to A. E. Knoch, 7 December 1909.
7. Letter, E. W. Bullinger to A. E. Knoch, 28 September 1912.
8. See p. 8.
9. J. J. Beddow, "The Late Rev. Dr. Bullinger," *The English Churchman,* 26 June 1913.
10. Letter, E. W. Bullinger to A. E. Knoch, 6 October 1909.
11. TBS, "Henry Charles Bowker," *The Quarterly Record of the Trinitarian Bible Society,* October 1920, 26.
12. Charles H. Welch, *Charles H. Welch: An Autobiography* (Banstead, Surrey: Berean Publishing Trust, 1960), 41.
13. Ibid., 41.

14. Charles H. Welch, "Dispensational Expositions," *Things to Come* 15 (April 1909): 43–46.

15. W. St. Clair Tisdall, review of *The Companion Bible, Part I,* in *The Record,* 8 April 1910.

16. Review of *The Companion Bible, Part I,* in *Sword and Trowel,* March 1910.

17. See p. 17.

18. Review of *The Companion Bible, Part I,* in *The Daily News,* 25 February 1910.

19. Review of *The Companion Bible, Part I,* in *The Inquirer,* 26 March 1910.

20. Review of *The Companion Bible, Part I,* in *New York Observer,* 12 May 1910.

21. Review of *The Companion Bible, Part II,* in *The Christian's Pathway,* February 1911, 59.

22. Review of *The Companion Bible, Part II,* in *The Expository Times,* February 1911.

Chapter Twelve: The Last Years

1. Deo Volente, "God Willing."

2. E. W. Bullinger, "Editor's Table," *Things to Come* 16 (December 1910): 143.

3. TBS, *The Quarterly Record of the Trinitarian Bible Society,* July 1911, 1.

4. TBS, "William Tyndale," *The Quarterly Record,* October 1925, 5–7.

5. Ibid., 7.

6. F. G. Llewellin, *Brave William Tyndale* (London: Protestant Truth Society, 1936).

7. TBS, *The Quarterly Record,* January 1914, 8.

8. Review of *The Companion Bible, Part III,* in *The Christian,* 12 October 1911, 28.

9. E. W. Bullinger, "Editor's Table," *Things to Come* 17 (November 1911): 132.

10. "The Great *Cloud of Witnesses," Things to Come* 17 (December 1911): 144.

11. E. W. Bullinger, *Great Cloud of Witnesses in Hebrews Eleven* (Grand Rapids: Kregel, 1979), 1.

12. Ibid., 7.

13. Lamp Press, Publication Announcement, n.d., Papers of Mrs. Winifred Carpenter.

14. E. W. Bullinger, "Difficulties in Dispensational Teaching," *Things to Come* 17 (October 1911): 111.

15. E. W. Bullinger, *The Foundations of Dispensational Truth* (London: Samuel Bagster, 1972), 81.

16. Ibid., 276.

17. Ibid., 82.

18. Ibid., 279–80.

19. TBS, *The Quarterly Record,* October 1910, 27.

20. "The Late Dr. Bullinger," *Things to Come* 19 (November 1913): 132.

21. E. W. Bullinger, preface to *Things to Come* 12 (1906).

22. E. W. Bullinger, "The Serpent of Genesis 3," Appendix Nineteen of *The Companion Bible* (Grand Rapids: Zondervan, 1974), 25.

23. Owen Chadwick, *The Victorian Church, Part Two* (London: SCM, 1987), 82–83.

24. Ibid.

25. Bullinger, *The Great Cloud of Witnesses,* 412–413.

26. Review of *The Companion Bible, Part IV,* in *The Record,* 7 February 1913.

27. E. W. Bullinger, preface to *Things to Come* 18 (November 1912).

28. E. W. Bullinger, "Last Will and Testament," 9 January 1913, Somerset House, London.

29. Ibid.

30. TBS, *Committee Minute Book,* 6 March 1913.

31. TBS, *The Quarterly Record,* July 1913, 4.

32. Letter, T. A. Howard to Elizabeth Dodson, 30 May 1913, DRF Collection.

33. Elizabeth Dodson, *Ethelbert William Bullinger, D.D.* (London: Wilkinson Bros., 1913), 2–7.

Chapter Thirteen: Afterward

1. Letter, G. LeCoat to Elizabeth Dodson, 6 June 1913, DRF Collection.

2. Letter, Maggie to Elizabeth Dodson, 7 June 1913, DRF Collection.

3. TBS, *Committee Minute Book, 3 May 1909–27 July 1917.*

4. Ibid.

5. Letter, G. W. Taylor to Elizabeth Dodson, 8 June 1913, DRF Collection.

6. Letter, George Crichton to Elizabeth Dodson, 9 June 1913, DRF Collection.

7. Letter, J. Scott Challice to Elizabeth Dodson, 9 June 1913, DRF Collection.

8. TBS, Funeral Announcement, 11 June 1913, DRF Collection.

9. TBS, *The Quarterly Record of the Trinitarian Bible Society,* July 1913, 4.

10. Letter, Mabel L. Carter to Elizabeth Dodson, 6 June 1913, DRF Collection.

11. Letter, James B. Delap to Dr. McKilliam, reprinted in *Things to Come* 19 (August 1913): 90.

12. Telegram, William Barron to E. W. Bullinger, 29 July 1913, DRF Collection.

13. Charles H. Welch, *Charles H. Welch: An Autobiography* (Banstead, Surrey: Berean Publishing Trust, 1960), 112.

14. Letter, Ellen F. Griffith to Elizabeth Dodson, 5 August 1913, DRF Collection.

15. Letter, C. Swann to Elizabeth Dodson, 8 June 1913, DRF Collection.

16. Welch, *An Autobiography,* 112.

17. Letter, Russell Schaefer to the author, 8 January 1989.

18. Letter, W. T. Broad to Elizabeth Dodson, 12 October 1913, DRF Collection.

19. E. W. Bullinger, Personal Papers, DRF Collection.

20. C. T. Lipshytz, review of *The Companion Bible, Part V,* in *Immanuel's Witness,* December 1914, 435.

21. "The Tyndale Memorial," *The Record,* 7 November 1913, TBS Papers.

22. TBS, "Obituary—Pasteur G. LeCoat," *The Quarterly Record,* April 1914, 30.

23. TBS, "Pasteur LeCoat's Tomb in Tremel," *The Quarterly Record,* October 1914, 19–20.

24. TBS, "Dr. C. D. Ginsburg," *The Quarterly Record,* April 1914, 30.

25. Obituary, "Dr. Ginsburg," *The London Times,* 9 March 1914.

26. "Signs of the Times: War!" *Things to Come* 20 (September 1914): 106.

27. "The Companion Bible: Vol. V. The Four Gospels," *Things to Come* 20 (December 1914): 143.

28. Review of *The Companion Bible, Part V,* in *Watchword and Truth,* March 1915.

29. "Editor's Table," *Things to Come* 21 (October 1915): 119.

30. H. C. Bowker, *Things to Come* 21 (November 1915), preface.

31. Elizabeth Dodson and F. W. Carter, *An Assignment,* 7 December 1934, Barron & Morton, Solicitors, London.

32. Welch, *An Autobiography,* 112.

33. TBS, "H. C. Bowker" *The Quarterly Record,* October 1920, 26.

34. James Moffatt, review of *The Companion Bible,* in *The British Weekly,* 14 December 1922, 260.

35. Review of *The Companion Bible,* in *The Witness Watchtower,* February 1923, 14.

36. Review of *The Companion Bible,* in *The Christian,* 14 December 1922, 48.

37. TBS, *Committee Minute Book, 1932–1944,* 6 January 1933.

38. Ibid.

39. Andrew Brown, *The Word of God Among All Nations* (London: TBS, 1981), 137.

40. Elizabeth Dodson and F. W. Carter, *An Assignment,* 7 December 1934, Barron & Morton, Solicitors, London.

41. Letter, J. W. Thirtle to Elizabeth Dodson, 23 April 1931, DRF Collection.

42. Algernon J. Pollock, *An Examination of Dr. E. W. Bullinger's Bible Teaching* (New York: Loizeaux Bros., 1940), 65.

43. Letter, Harold P. Morgan to Elizabeth Dodson, 16 April 1936, DRF Collection.

44. Harold P. Morgan, "Dr. E. W. Bullinger: The Man and His Work," *Questions and Answers,* January 1943, 3.

Epilogue

1. Henry Grube, "Some Present-Day Errors . . . Bullinger's Blunders," *Sermons and Subjects,* 1978, 44–345.

2. E. W. Bullinger, *The Apocalypse* (London: Samuel Bagster, 1972), i.

3. Warren W. Wiersbe, foreword to *The Giver and His Gifts,* by E. W. Bullinger (Grand Rapids: Kregel, 1979), vii–viii.

4. Letter, Dr. Elizabeth Johnson and Dawn Slife Clark to the author, 19 December 1998. As of this writing the following works by E. W. Bullinger are in print: *The Companion Bible* (Grand Rapids: Kregel, 1990); *The Witness of the Stars* (Grand Rapids: Kregel, 1979); *The Book of Job* (Grand Rapids: Kregel, 1990); *Commentary on Revelation [The Apocalypse]* (Grand Rapids: Kregel, 1984); *Great Cloud of Witnesses in Hebrews Eleven* (Grand Rapids: Kregel, 1979); *Number in Scripture* (Grand Rapids: Kregel, 1978); *Ten Sermons on the Second*

Advent, (Grand Rapids: 1996); *Word Studies on the Holy Spirit [The Giver and His Gifts]* (Grand Rapids: Kregel, 1979); *Figures of Speech Used in the Bible* (Grand Rapids: Baker, 1981); and *A Critical Lexicon and Concordance to the English and Greek New Testament* (Grand Rapids: Kregel, 1999).

5. Bullinger, *The Apocalypse,* xii.

Bibliography

"Account of the Choral School at Canterbury Cathedral." *The Gentleman's Magazine*. May 1817.

Adams, Carol. *Ordinary Lives: A Hundred Years Ago*. London: Virago, 1982.

Aldrich, Roy L. "An Outline Study on Dispensationalism," *Bibliotheca Sacra* 118, no. 470 (April 1961).

Anderson, Arthur P. M. *Sir Robert Anderson, KCB LLD: A Tribute and Memoir*. London: Morgan & Scott, 1919.

Anderson, Robert, C.B. *The Buddha of Christendom*. London: Hodder and Stoughton, 1899.

——. *Spirit Manifestations and "The Gift of Tongues."* London: Evangelical Alliance, 1909.

Anstey, Roger. *John Wesley and Methodism*. Canterbury: The Beaney Institute, n.d.

Balleine, George Reginald. *A History of the Evangelical Party in the Church of England*. London: Longmans, Green & Co., 1908.

Bardsley, Charles Waring. *English Surnames: Their Sources and Significance*. Devon: David and Charles Publishing, 1969.

Bass, Clarence. "Backgrounds to Dispensationalism." *Encounter* 23 (winter 1962):124–125.

Bell, W. Lees. *The History of Bermondsey*. London: Shaw & Sparks, 1883.

Bermant, Chaim. *London's East End*. New York: Macmillan, 1975.

Bignell, Alan. *Kent Lore*. London: Robert Hall, 1983.

Bosworth, George F. *More Walthamstow Houses, and Their Interesting Associations*. London: Walthamstow Antiquarian Society, 1928.

Bowker, H. C. *The Gospel of the Glory of Christ*. Edinburgh: Darien, 1912.

Bowen, Desmond. *The Idea of the Victorian Church: A Study of the Church of England.* Montreal: McGill University Press, 1968.

Boyle, John. *Portrait of Canterbury.* London: Robert Hall, 1980.

———. *Rural Kent.* London: Robert Hall, 1976.

Braithwaite, Robert, ed. *The Life and Letters of Rev. William Pennefather.* London: John F. Shaw & Co., 1878.

Briggs, Asa. *Victorian People: A Re-assessment of Persons and Themes, 1851–1867.* Chicago: University of Chicago Press, 1955.

Brown, Andrew J. *The Word of God Among All Nations: A Brief History of the Trinitarian Bible Society 1831–1981.* London: Trinitarian Bible Society, 1981.

Brown, Ivor. *Dickens and His World.* New York: Henry Z. Walck, 1970.

Brown, Robert. *A Reply to Dr. Bullinger's So-Called Witness of the Stars.* London: William Wileman, 1894.

Bryant, T. Hugh. *Norfolk Churches.* Norwich: Norwich Mercury Office, 1903.

Bullinger, E. W. *"Also."* New Knoxville, Ohio: American Christian Press, 1981.

———. *The Apocalypse: or, "The Day of the Lord."* London: Samuel Bagster, 1972.

———. *The Church Epistles.* London: Eyre & Spottiswoode, 1905.

———. *The Companion Bible.* Grand Rapids: Kregel, 1990.

———. *A Critical Lexicon and Concordance to the English and Greek New Testament.* Grand Rapids: Kregel, 1999.

———. *Figures of Speech Used in the Bible.* Grand Rapids: Baker, 1981.

———. *The Foundations of Dispensational Truth.* London: Samuel Bagster, 1972.

———. *Four Prophetic Periods.* London: Eyre & Spottiswoode, 1915.

———. *The Giver and His Gifts: or, The Holy Spirit and His Work.* Grand Rapids: Kregel, 1979.

———. *Great Cloud of Witnesses in Hebrews Eleven.* Grand Rapids: Kregel, 1979.

———. *How to Enjoy the Bible.* Grand Rapids: Kregel, 1990.

———. *The Kingdom and the Church.* London: Eyre & Spottiswoode, 1892.

———. *Number in Scripture: Its Supernatural Design and Spiritual Significance.* Grand Rapids: Kregel, 1978.

———. *Selected Writings.* London: Lamp, 1960.

———. *The Story of the Breton Mission.* London: By the Author, 1910.

———. *Things to Come: A Journal of Biblical Literature, with Special Refer-

ence to Prophetic Truth. 21 vols. London: "Things to Come" Publishing Co., 1895–1915.

———. *The Witness of the Stars.* Grand Rapids: Kregel, 1979.

———. Pamphlets listed in "Chronological List of Works."

Buxton, John, and Penry Williams. *New College, Oxford, 1379–1979.* Oxford: The Warden and Fellows of New College, 1979.

Cairns, Earle E. *Christianity Through the Centuries.* Grand Rapids: Zondervan, 1977.

"Canterbury Wesleyans." *Canterbury Wesleyan Methodist Circuit Magazine* (July 1912).

Carter, J. S. *An Appreciation of Dr. E. W. Bullinger.* England: By the Author, n.d.

Chadwick, Owen. *The Victorian Church.* 2 vols. 3d ed. London: SCM, 1987.

Chancellor, E. Beresford. *The Annals of the Strand.* London: Chapman & Hall, 1912.

Chapman, Rev. W. Hay, and Rev. Sholto D. C. Douglas. *Hymns for Special Services and Prayer Meetings.* London: Bemrose & Sons, 1885.

Church, Richard. *Portrait of Canterbury.* London: Hutchinson & Co., 1968.

Clark, Andrew, ed. *The Colleges of Oxford: Their History and Tradition.* London: Methuen & Co., 1891.

Clarke, Basil F. L. *The Building of the Eighteenth Century Church.* London: SPCK, 1963.

Clarke, Edward T. *Bermondsey: Its Historic Memories and Associations.* London: Elliot Stock, 1901.

Coad, F. Roy. *A History of the Brethren Movement.* Exeter: Paternoster Press, 1976.

Comber, Rev. Thomas. *A Sermon Preached at the Church of the United Parishes of St. Mary Somerset and St. Mary Mounthaw Before the Orange Institution of Great Britain.* London: J. Eedes, 1824.

Costigan, Giovanni. *Makers of Modern England: The Force of Individual Genius in History.* London: Macmillan, 1967.

Cox, J. Charles. *County Churches of Norfolk.* London: George Allen & Sons, 1910.

Cox, Montagu, and Philip Norman, eds. *London County Council Survey of London.* London: B. T. Batsford, 1930.

"Cradle of Our Race, The." *The Methodist Recorder* (7 December 1911).

Croskery, Rev. Thomas. *Plymouth Brethrenism: A Refutation of Its Principles and Doctrines.* London: William Mullon, 1879.

Crosby, Alan. *A History of Woking*. London: Phillimore, 1982.

Curtis, Stanley James. *History of Education in Great Britain*. London: University Tutorial Press, 1948.

D. D. *The Errors of the Plymouth Brethren*. Dublin: George Drought, 1876.

Davies, Rupert, and Gordon Rupp, eds. *A History of the Methodist Church in Great Britain*. Vol. 1. London: Epworth, 1965.

Davies, Rupert, A. Raymond George, and Gordon Rupp, eds. *A History of the Methodist Church in Great Britain*. Vol. 2. London: Epworth, 1978.

Dent, Caroline. *The Testimony of the Stars to Truths Revealed in the Bible*. Abridged from *Mazzaroth: or, The Constellations*, by Miss Frances Rolleston. London: Rivingtons, 1879.

Dewar, M. W. *Orangeism: A New Historical Appreciation*. Belfast: The Grand Lodge of Ireland, 1967.

Duff, David. *Victoria Travels*. London: Frederick Muller, 1970.

Essex County Council. *Georgian Essex*. Essex Record Office Publication No. 38. Chelmsford: J. H. Clarke & Co., 1963.

Forbes, P. W. *Spiritualism Exposed*. Birmingham, ca. 1875.

"Form of Conferring Degrees by the Archbishop of Canterbury." London: Abbey, n.d.

Fraser, Antonia, ed. *The Lives of the Kings and Queens of England*. New York: Knopf, 1975.

Fry, Herbert. *London in 1880*. London: David Bogne, 1880.

Ginsburg, Christian D. *Introduction to the Massoretico-Critical Edition of the Hebrew Bible*. London: Trinitarian Bible Society, 1897.

Gitney, W. T. *The History of the London Society for Promoting Christianity Among the Jews from 1809–1908*. London: London Society for Promoting Christianity Among the Jews, 1908.

Gladstone, Florence M. *Notting Hill in Bygone Days*. London: T. Fisher Unwin, 1924.

Gray, Tony. *The Orange Order*. London: The Bodley Head, 1972.

Grube, Henry. "Some Present-Day Errors: Bullinger's Blunders." *Sermons and Subjects*. Lynchburg, Va.: Milestone, 1978.

Hall, S. C. *The Use of Spiritualism*. London: E. W. Allen, 1884.

Hammock, W. G. *Leytonstone and Its History*. London: Batten & Davies, 1904.

Hart, Andrew Tindall. *The Curate's Lot: The Story of the Unbeneficed English Clergy*. London: John Baker, 1970.

Hearnshaw, F. J. *The Centenary History of King's College, London 1828–1928*. London: George Harrap & Co., 1929.

Hibbert, Christopher. *Daily Life in Victorian England*. New York: American Heritage, 1975.

——. *The Royal Victorians*. New York: Lippincott, 1976.

Hilken, T. H. *St. Stephen's, Walthamstow 1875–1928*. London: Church Book Room, 1928.

Hoste, William. *The Intermediate State: A Reply to Dr. Bullinger*. London: Alfred Holness, 1911.

——. *Pentecost–and After*. London: Alfred Holness, 1909.

Houghton, Walter E. *The Victorian Frame of Mind 1830–1870*. New Haven: Yale University Press, 1957.

Huelin, Gordon. *King's College, London, 1828–1978*. London: University of London, 1978.

Irving, Edward. *Farewell Discourse to the Congregation and Parish of St. John's, Glasgow*. Glasgow: Waugh & Innes, 1822.

Jessup, Frank W. *A History of Kent*. London: Phillimore & Co., 1974.

John, Malcolm. *Around Historic Kent*. Kent: Tunbridge Wells, 1978.

Kaplan, Irving, ed. *Zaire: A Country Study*. Washington, D.C.: American University, 1979.

Kenyon, Sir Frederic. *The Bible and Modern Scholarship*. London: John Murray, 1948.

Keswick Convention. *The Story of the Convention's Fifty Years' Ministry and Influence*. London: Marshall Bros., 1925.

King's College Calendar, 1861–62. London: King's College, 1862.

Latourette, Kenneth Scott. *The Nineteenth Century in Europe: The Protestant and Eastern Churches*. Vol. 2 of *Christianity in a Revolutionary Age: A History of Christianity in the Nineteenth and Twentieth Centuries*. London: Eyre & Spottiswoode, 1960.

Laver, James. *Victorian Vista*. London: Hulton, 1954.

Leary, William. *My Ancestor Was a Methodist*. Manchester, n.d.

LeCoat, G. "Breton Tunes." Preface in *Chants Chrétiens edités et composés par G. LeCoat de Tremel*. London: 7 St. Paul's Churchyard, 1889.

Leff, V., and C. H. Blunden. *Riverside Story: The Story of Bermondsey and Its People*. London: Civic Publicity Services, 1963.

Leigh, E. C. Austen. *List of English Clubs in All Parts of the World for 1893*. London: Spottiswoode & Co., 1893.

Llewellin, F. G. *Brave William Tyndale*. London: Protestant Truth Society, 1936.

Lloyd, Mary Anne. *Susanna Meredith: A Record of a Vigorous Life*. London: Hodder & Stoughton, 1903.

Longford, Elizabeth. *Victoria R.I.* New York: Harper & Row, 1973.

Madsen, A. *The Loyal Orange Institution: Facts v. Fables.* Melbourne: C. W. Burford, 1898.

Malden, H. E., ed. *The Victoria History of the Counties of England: Surrey.* London: Constable & Co., 1911.

Marsh, Peter Timothy. *The Victorian Church in Decline: Archbishop Tait and the Church of England.* London: Routledge & Kegan Paul, 1969.

Mauro, Philip. *Trusting God in Sickness.* London: Samuel E. Roberts, 1910.

Mee, Arthur. *The King's England: Kent.* London: Hodder & Stoughton, 1969.

———. *The King's England: Norfolk: Green Pastures and Still Waters.* London: Hodder & Stoughton, 1949.

Melton, J. Gordon, ed. "The Independent Fundamentalist Family." *The Encyclopedia of American Religions.* Vol 1. Wilmington, N.C.: McGrath, 1978.

Message of Keswick and Its Meaning, The. London: Marshall, Morgan & Scott, 1939.

Mildmay Mission. *Trusting and Toiling on Israel's Behalf.* 1896.

Miller, Andrew. *The Brethren: A Brief Sketch.* London: G. Morrish, 1879.

———. *Short Papers on Church History from the Apostolic Age to the Twentieth Century.* London: Pickering & Inglis, 1929.

Monnington, Walter, and Frederick J. Lampard. *Our London Poor Law Schools.* London: Eyre & Spottiswoode, 1898.

Moore-Anderson, A. P. *Sir Robert Anderson and Lady Agnes Anderson.* London: Marshall, Morgan & Scott, 1947.

Moorman, John R. H. *A History of the Church in England.* 2d ed. New York: Morehouse-Barlow Co., 1967.

———. *A History of the Church in England.* London: Adam & Charles Black, 1973.

Morgan, Harold P. *The Revolt Against the Distinctive Ministry of the Apostle Paul.* Buffalo, New York: Morgan & Wallace, 1936.

Morgan, Kenneth O., ed. *The Oxford Illustrated History of Britain.* Oxford: Oxford University Press, 1981.

Mumby, D. G. "Pages from the Past." *St. Augustine's Leytonstone Parish News,* December 1949.

Murray, John. *A Handbook for Travellers in Surrey, Hampshire and the Isle of Wight.* London: John Murray, 1888.

Neatby, William Blair. *A History of the Plymouth Brethren.* London: Hodder & Stoughton, 1902.

Needham, Raymond, and Alexander Webster. *Somerset House: Past and Present*. London: T. Fisher Unwin, 1905.

Nevill, Ralph. *London Clubs and Their History and Treasures*. London: Chatto & Windus, 1911.

Noel, Napoleon. *The History of the Brethren*. 2 vols. Denver, Colo.: W. F. Knapp, 1936.

Norman, E. R. *Anti-Catholicism in Victorian England*. New York: Barnes & Noble, 1968.

O'Connell, Marvin R. *The Oxford Conspirators: A History of the Oxford Movement, 1833–1845*. London: Collier-Macmillan, 1969.

Ogilvy, James S. *A Pilgrimage in Surrey*. London: George Routledge & Sons, 1914.

Parish of St. Matthew, Bethnal Green, London. "Article 64, Duties of the Chaplain," *The Government of the School*. London: Eyre & Spottiswoode, 1872.

———. *Minute Book of the Board of Governors*, 1870–1874.

Paul, Leslie. *A Church by Daylight: A Reappraisement of the Church of England and Its Future*. London: Geoffrey Chapman, 1973.

Petrie, Charles. *The Victorians*. New York: Longmans, Green & Co., 1961.

Pemberton, W. Baring. *Lord Palmerston*. London: Batchworth, 1954.

Petty, Ken. "Origins of Modern Spiritualism." New Knoxville, Ohio: Way International, 1978.

Phillips, G. W. *The History and Antiquities of the Parish of Bermondsey*. London: J. Unwin, 1841.

Pickering, Hy. *Chief Men Among the Brethren*. London: Pickering & Inglis, 1932.

———. *100 World-Known Witnesses to the Second Coming*. London: Pickering & Inglis, 1935.

Pollock, Algernon J. *An Examination of Dr. E. W. Bullinger's Bible Teaching*. New York: Loizeaux Bros., 1940.

Princess Mary Village Homes, Addlestone. *Records, 1870–1981*. Kingston-on-Thames: Surrey Registry Office.

Pugh, R. B., ed. *A History of the County of Essex*. Vol. 5 of *The Victoria History of the Counties of England*. London: Oxford University Press, 1966.

Quennell, Marjorie, and C. H. B. *A History of Everyday Things in England, Vol. IV: 1815–1914*. London: B. T. Batsford, 1958.

Roebuck, George Edward. *The Story of Walthamstow*. London: The Walthamstow Corp., 1952.

Rowdon, Harold H. *The Origins of the Brethren,s 1825–1850*. London: Pickering & Inglis, 1967.

S. M. *What Is Spiritualism? The Answer to the Great Question of the Day*. London: E. W. Allen, 1884.

Sellers, Ian. *Nineteenth-Century Nonconformity*. London: Edward Arnold, 1977.

Senior, Hereward. *Orangeism in Ireland and Britain, 1795–1836*. London: Routledge & Kegan Paul, 1966.

Sheppard, F. H. W., ed. *Northern Kensington*. Vol. 37 of *Survey of London*. London: Athlone, 1973.

Spiritualism in 1866. London: Job Caudwell, 1866.

Stapleton and Company. *Topographical History and Directory of Canterbury*. London, 1838.

Steer, Roger. *George Müller: Delighted in God*. London: Hodder & Stoughton, 1975.

Stock, Eugene. *The English Church in the Nineteenth Century*. London: Longmans, Green & Co., 1910.

Story, R. Herbert. "Edward Irving"—Lecture VII in *Scottish Divines 1505–1872*. Edinburgh: Macniven and Wallace, 1883.

Strachan, Gordon. *The Pentecostal Theology of Edward Irving*. London: Darton, Longman and Todd, 1973.

Stratton, H. J. M. *Chertsy and Addlestone in the Past*. Surrey: H. J. M. Stratton, Langtons, 1980.

Sturt, Mary. *The Education of the People: A History of Primary Education in England and Wales in the Nineteenth Century*. London: Routledge and Kegan Paul, 1967.

Tait, Arthur J. *Charles Simeon and His Trust*. London: Society for Promoting Christian Knowledge, 1936.

Teulon, Josiah Sanders. *The History and Teaching of the Plymouth Brethren*. London: Christian Knowledge Society, 1883.

Thirtle, James William. *The Lord's Prayer*. London: Morgan & Scott, 1915.

———. *Old Testament Problems*. London: Henry Frowde, 1907.

———. *The Titles of the Psalms*. London: Henry Frowde, 1904.

Tonkin, W. G. S. *The Anglican Church in Walthamstow*. London: Walthamstow Antiquarian Society, 1963.

Trevelyan, George Macaulay. *British History in the Nineteenth Century (1782–1901)*. London: Longmans, Green & Co., 1933.

———. *English Social History: A Survey of Six Centuries, Chaucer to Queen Victoria*. London: Longmans, Green & Co., 1942.

———. *The Nineteenth Century.* Vol. 4 of *Illustrated English Social History.* London: Longmans, Green & Co., 1957.

Trinitarian Bible Society. *The Old Paths, Why Forsake Them?* London: W. MacIntosh, 1874.

Tuchman, Barbara W. *Bible and Sword: How the British Came to Palestine.* New York: Macmillan, 1956.

———. *The Proud Tower: A Portrait of the World Before the War 1890–1914.* New York: Macmillan, 1966.

Vickers, John A. *The Story of Canterbury Methodism (1750–1961).* Bognor Regis West, Sussex: WHMS, n.d.

Vidler, Alec R. *The Church in an Age of Revolution: 1789 to the Present Day.* London: Hodder & Stoughton, 1961.

Wall, Cecil. "The Lambeth Degrees." *British Medical Journal,* 2 November 1935.

Welch, Charles H. *Charles H. Welch: An Autobiography.* Banstead, Surrey: The Berean Publishing Trust, 1960.

What Is the Trinitarian Bible Society? By a Former Subscriber to the British & Foreign Bible Society. London: E. Marlborough & Co., 1874.

Wiersbe, Warren W. Foreword to *The Giver and His Gifts.* Grand Rapids: Kregel, 1979.

Wilkinson, Samuel Hinds. *The Life of John Wilkinson: The Jewish Missionary.* London: Morgan & Scott, 1908.

Wilson, Mervyn. *A Brief History and Description of Bermondsey Parish Church, St. Mary Magdalen, with St. Olav, St. John and St. Luke.* Southwark: Dramrite Printers, 1976.

Wright, Christopher. *Kent Through the Years.* London: B. T. Batsford, 1975.

Index

The Companion Bible
This classic study Bible in the King James version has almost two hundred appendices, including explanations of Hebrew words and their uses, charts, parallel passages, maps, lists of proper names, calendars, and timelines. Notes and appendices written by E. W. Bullinger.

0-8254-2203-5, burgundy hardcover
0-8254-2288-4, burgundy bonded leather
0-8254-2177-2, black bonded leather
0-8254-2237-x, black genuine leather
0-8254-2099-7, enlarged type, burgundy hardcover

Also from Kregel Publications

The Book of Job

An exposition of the earliest written book of the Bible with a new translation by Bullinger. In addition, figures of speech and divine names and titles are given special attention. Every Bible student will find much practical help in this unique approach to the book of Job.

0-8254-2291-4   200 pages   paperback

Commentary on Revelation

The pastor, teacher, and serious Bible student will find a wealth of interpretive insights in this verse-by-verse commentary. Also discusses key interpretive problems in Revelation.

0-8254-2289-2   738 pages   paperback

A Critical Lexicon and Concordance to the English and Greek New Testament

English words appear in alphabetical order along with equivalent Greek words, their literal and derivative meaning, and a list of passages in which each word appears. Includes a comprehensive Greek-English index, vocabulary of New Testament Greek, concordance of proper names, and appendix of biblical references to common pronouns, participles, and conjunctions.

0-8254-2096-2   1,056 pages   hardcover

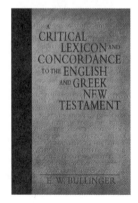

Great Cloud of Witnesses in Hebrews Eleven

A devotional and expositional study of Hebrews 11 discusses faith's worship, faith's walk, faith's witness, faith's obedience, and faith's suffering.

"No other book on Hebrews 11 . . . contains more solid spiritual teaching and practical truth than this one."

—Warren W. Wiersbe

0-8254-2247-7   472 pages   paperback

How to Enjoy the Bible: A Guide to Better Understanding and Enjoyment of God's Word

A basic introduction to the study of the Bible. Bullinger brings to the reader insights on the Bible and its background. Chapter subjects include: the object and subject of the Word of God, rightly dividing the Word of God, first occurrences of select words in the Scriptures, figures of speech in the Bible, and interpretation and application.

0-8254-2213-2   466 pages   paperback

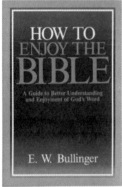

Number in Scripture: Its Supernatural Design and Spiritual Significance

An invaluable guide to the study of biblical numerology. The first section reveals the amazing designs involved in the numbers and numerical features of the Word of God which give evidence to the Designer. The second part covers the spiritual significance and symbolic connotations of those numbers which repeatedly appear in the same or similar contexts throughout the Bible.

0-8254-2238-8   312 pages   paperback

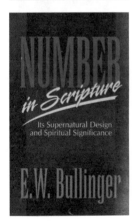

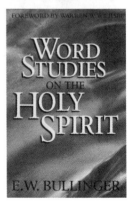

Also from Kregel Publications

George Müller of Bristol: His Life of Prayer and Faith
by A. T. Pierson

This classic biography tells of George Müller's dependence on prayer and how his compassionate concern for the orphans in his hometown of Bristol, England, shaped decades of missionary and social endeavors throughout the world.

"Not only does one grow to love George Muller through this work, one grows in knowledge of and love for, his faithful, powerful, and incomprehensible God."

—Rosemary Jensen, Executive Director
Bible Study Fellowship (BSF) International

0-8254-3464-5   384 pages   paperback

Spurgeon: Prince of Preachers
by Lewis Drummond

The definitive biography of the "prince of preachers," Charles Haddon Spurgeon, shares never-before-told stories and little-known facts about the legendary preacher who dominated his own day and whose influence still permeates the Christian landscape today.

"Dr. Drummond's book is itself remarkable and will surely become the most definitive biography of Spurgeon."

—*Faith & Mission*

0-8254-2472-0   896 pages   hardcover

Spurgeon & Son
by Craig Skinner

Charles Haddon Spurgeon is well remembered as the greatest preacher of the nineteenth century, but what is not so well known is the story of the other Spurgeon—Thomas, one of Charles's twin sons—who succeeded his father as pastor of Metropolitan Tabernacle in London. The drama of Thomas Spurgeon's life will inspire and challenge readers to a greater trust in God.

0-8254-3699-0   276 pages   paperback

The Sir Robert Anderson Library Series

The Coming Prince

0-8254-2115-2   384 pages   paperback

Daniel in the Critics' Den

0-8254-2133-0   200 pages   paperback

Forgotten Truths

0-8254-2130-6   168 pages   paperback

The Gospel and Its Ministry

0-8254-2126-8   224 pages   paperback

Redemption Truths

0-8254-2131-4   192 pages   paperback

The Silence of God

0-8254-2128-4   232 pages   paperback

Types in Hebrews

0-8254-2129-2   192 pages   paperback

"Sir Robert Anderson is a giant among giants
and anything he wrote is worth having on one's
library shelf."

–Baptist Testimony

"Anderson was a gifted layman who stood tall for
Bible truth in his day.

–Biblical Evangelist

"To sit at the feet of a man with such knowledge,
mental power, and courage and native wit, who is
at the same time Spirit taught, is for the true
Christian one of the greatest privileges."

–James M. Gray